Paul,
the Passionate Scholar

A Verse-by-Verse Analysis of the Complete Writings of the
Apostle Paul Presented in Approximate Chronological Order

PART 1
Galatians, I & II Thessalonians, I Corinthians (7 Chapters)

JOHN D. ROUSE, MA

Olympus Story House
www.olympusstoryhouse.com

Contents

List Of Illustrations

I. Galatians:

    1. Map of the Galatian district in Asia Minor.

II. I Thessalonians:

    2. Inscription of Thessaloniki, King Philip's wife: (Statue base, circa BC 175)

III. Corinth:

    3. The Emperor Nero coin, drawing AD 67 or 68

    4. The Bema.

    5. The west Bema waiting Area.

    6. Peirene water fountain.

    7. Dining Sanctuary above the City

    8. Erastus inscription.

    9. Corinth main theater.

    10. Synagogue sign in stone.

    11. The Lechaion Road.

    12. Kenchreai: the eastern port of Corinth.

    13. The Corinth amphitheater.

    14. Amphitheater comparison.

Preface: *Paul the Passionate Scholar*

This is an unusual book for a number of reasons. First, this is one of the first attempts to assemble the entire corpus of Paul into one book. The thirteen letters of Paul, with the typical length of the commentaries, would normally run over 6,000 pages in length with the massive amount of information that has been discovered in the past 2,000 years of research, expressed in hundreds of publications. Second, the technical advances in the grammar and the structure of Koine Greek has also added many volumes of research data that must be mastered by authors attempting to start such a project. Third, could such a project be assembled that would contain enough background and textual information that would be useful, especially to lay people, to teachers in churches, and to students of the Word in Bible colleges and universities, and also would have practical value within a one-volume text? That was the challenging scope of the design of *Paul: the Passionate Scholar*: a scholarly presentation for lay people, and with a focus primarily on the understanding of the text.

It was our opinion that the language of the NT Greek held many keys for unlocking the riches of God's 'palace,' in a special tour of each room, marveling over the magnificent stories of valor and tender moments of selfless love, lavishly displayed in rich colors and stirring narratives that invigorate the soul. Appreciation is enhanced when one ponders the rich variety of those colors, carefully collected on the palette of the original artist many centuries ago. Reflecting on the substance requires analyzing the vocabulary expressed within those paintings. The vocabulary was the color that the artist selected and used to create those masterful word pictures. The grammar slowly reveals the substance behind the scenes. The magnificent story begins to stir the soul and quicken the imagination. The various artists commissioned for such a task expressed themselves using very different brushes, with varied approaches, but they always had a dramatic flair for words, the 'paint' they used within such a noble artistic endeavor. If this 'tour' of the 'palace' could open the mind-windows of the reader, and reflect the magnificent beauty of this 'palace,' then the years of labor in its construction would not have been in vain.

To explore and understand the 'tools of the trade' of heavenly communication, studying the Greek of Paul seems mandatory, and that study opens the windows to splendor and beauty never seen in human literature. What is the result of meandering along the way, examining one room after another of Paul's writings? First, the language of the artist begins to delineate his style of expression from other writers. His emotion can occasionally even reveal his strong passion, sometimes expressed in sentence fragments, called by grammarians, 'anacolutha,' or 'broken sentences.' In addition, students who take the time to reflect with a lingering and thoughtful examination, discover subtle ramifications of expression, as well as the differences that Paul exhibited in his overall style of writing. Therefore, this study will take readers on a tour of Paul's magnificent literary expressions.

Therefore, this volume could be considered a 'mini-commentary' of all thirteen letters of the Apostle Paul. It is also unique because it is one of the first commentaries to utilize extensively the newest Bauer lexicon (basically a Greek dictionary, identified as BDAG in this book), released in 2000, after 45 years of earlier editions. It is, by our estimation, one of the richest sources of lexigraphical data ever published.

But reasons for reader involvement transcend these considerations, because this volume represents God's Word to mankind. There is power behind these expressions; power to change lives, power to invigorate the soul; power to develop maturity in the lives of Christians; and power to convict the sinner by offering a far more satisfying lifestyle for the here and now, as well as the future, instilling joy and peace that can never be found in a life without God.

The background of this approach was developed over an eight year period of teaching a rather new course in the NT, supplemented by more than twelve years spent in specialized courses in Greek, wandering through various research libraries worldwide, and photographically exploring some of the archaeological sites where Paul actually walked and taught.

The class was initiated when I was asked to teach a Greek class in our church's weekly Training Hour, a new course of Greek for students whose future plans included attending seminary. However, the class also was open to people in the church who expressed their desire to learn the NT and gain insight into the language expressed by Paul and other writers of the NT. A new class in Greek slowly began to emerge, and gradually was tailored, not only for future seminary students, but mainly for eager students of the NT: lay people, rather than potential scholars.

With a lifelong background in education, especially in curriculum development, and a major in Greek at Bob Jones University and some Classical Greek and Classical Archaeology at UCLA, as well as several photographic survey trips to Italy and Greece, and extensive research at the British Museum while writing a scientific book on mineralogy, I saw an opportunity to develop a radically different kind of NT Greek class, one that would appeal to lay people who were intellectually curious, and Bible teachers who wanted useful background information and penetrating textual data that the original Greek could bring to light. The uniqueness of those students was that few, if any, had any background in the language of Koine Greek, nor were most of them planning to take such courses in the future.

I modeled the class roughly on several graduate level Greek courses I had taken at Bob Jones University, where the students would investigate one of Paul's books in a semester with a verse by verse analytical study. The focus of this new class was to study the books in an expositional, verse by verse manner, exploring idiosyncrasies of vocabulary and grammar, but also to share the historical and archaeological backgrounds of the epistles as we advanced through the text. Vocabulary and complex grammatical structures were carefully introduced, and repetition reinforced the learning. I developed handouts to cover the contents of each class, in case students had to miss a session. We would evaluate complex grammatical structures and vocabulary for in-depth meanings of the verses. The choice of complex and advanced Greek grammatical highlights was prioritized to include only such original Greek grammatical examples that would enhance the comprehension of the text under study and avoid pedantic grammar points that didn't have a direct bearing on the text under study. The background for the NT books studied would include, not only commentaries and linguistic specialty texts, but also secular history, and pertinent archaeological and geographical information, either at the beginning of the book studied, or, when appropriate, within the text.

The new class started with the writings of John, and much time was utilized over the next two years refining the strategies and developing techniques by gradually conveying Greek grammar to non-Greek students. We used a white board to illustrate the Greek text, with frequent illustrations of vocabulary and grammatical structure. The next major project of the class was to study all the epistles of Paul, one by one, presented to the students in approximate chronological order. The coverage of the books of Paul took just over five years to complete. The weekly class handouts provided the skeletal structure of each section of the epistle under study.

In Paul: the Passionate Scholar, the translation of the Biblical text is mine, and the translation approach of the text was intended to be in close alignment with the words and grammatical structure of the Greek text, but not always in perfect accord with smooth English stylistic expression. If a word was thought necessary to be added to the text, either by an implied meaning, or added for clarification, that word was presented in parentheses. The Greek NT text that was used throughout was Aland, et al., The Greek New Testament, Fourth Revised Edition, Ninth Printing, 2005.

The content of this book of Paul will certainly lack a major amount of commentary information. However, I attempted to include what I could in order to complement the epistles with most of the major issues. Primarily, it was my intention to include as a priority the kind of commentary information that would aid in the interpretation of the textual passages, but also enclosing some important background information to assist the student or teacher, in developing a comprehensive understanding of each book, and the times during which it was written. It was often a fine line to decide which illustrative material to include which would supplement the text with enough details to aid in the overall comprehension of Paul's writings, particularly since I had collected hundreds of photos in black and white and color when I visited both Rome and Corinth.

In the presentation of this book, I am indebted to the faithfulness of my students, who kept attending the class year after year, while I refined the curriculum to the current level. This book is dedicated to my students who often asked penetrating questions and guided my thinking on how the class would best serve their needs. I want to especially recognize Mary Farr who attended the class from the very beginning, eight years ago. Also, I am indebted to other students, Dr. Greg Philson and his son, Dr. Matt Philson, both of whom have provided much personal encouragement along the way, and some needed technical assistance from time to time. In addition, I have shared for editing some of my manuscript material with our pastor, Rev. John Snyder, who has also been very encouraging and supportive. But I take the final responsibility for any errors that may be discovered after publication.

About the Author

The origin of this volume can be found over 50 years ago when the author attended Bob Jones University, majoring in history and Greek, graduating there in 1964. Further study supplemented his undergraduate work by taking further graduate and post-graduate courses at California State University at Los Angeles, earning an M.A. in 1971. More courses were taken at UCLA in Latin, Classical Greek, archaeology, and art history, with enough work in the latter area to earn a major in that field. In addition, for preparation for several photographic research trips to Greece and Rome in 1968 and 1971, Mr. Rouse conducted independent research at the UCLA research library that extended over three years on topics regarding NT archaeology and research. The two six week research trips to Rome and Greece concentrated on the ruins of ancient Rome, and in Greece, on Athens and Corinth. In 1970, Mr. Rouse was asked to edit an 800 page manuscript of a Cal. State Univ. professor specializing in Byzantine archaeology, which he finished in one year.

From 1975 to 1985 Mr. Rouse became a gem cutter and a research gemologist and was the founding president from 1981 to 1983 of Jewelry Tech Institute, Inc. in Garden Grove, California, a jewelry arts trade school. In 1983 he was asked to come to Bangkok, Thailand, to become the managing director of the Asian Institute of Gemological Sciences, Inc. In his first year, he led a curriculum revision and added tours throughout Thailand for visiting gemologists and gem buyers, both endeavors providing needed income for the institute. While there, Mr. Rouse was asked to write a scientific book on garnet by an agent of a distinguished publishing house on scientific books located in London. With much of his initial work finished at the institute, Mr. Rouse asked his employers in Bangkok to send him to London for several months to continue his research at the British Museum and put him in contact with the major gemological scholars in London. While there, he continued his research in various museums in London and was accepted as a visiting scholar at the British Museum, where he was allowed a research room and was able to order various pieces of Greek and Roman jewelry from the museum exhibits for specialized photography. Two months were utilized in the summer of 1984, mainly at the British Museum library. In 1985, he was in London again in the summer, for another two months of research, this time exclusively at the British Museum back rooms. His book was published in 1986 and it was highly recommended by several international scholars. Graeco-Roman research in the British Museum re-energized his love of the Scriptures and the Pauline world of the first century A.D.

On his return to the U.S. he re-entered his teaching career in the Los Angeles Unified Schools, where he taught numerous high school subjects, including gem-cutting, to high-risk students for the next 11 years. In 1994 he was one of several gemological scholars asked to revise several chapters of the major gemological text, *Gems*, released in 1995. Moving to Colorado in 1997, Mr. Rouse was associated first as an instructor in adult education, then for three more years as an administrator for the adult education department of Pueblo Community College. In 2005, he designed a Greek NT class for his church, and that class formed the basis of this book. Five years were utilized in teaching all the writings of Paul, and another year for editing. From 2005 to 2014, he has continuously taught the NT in Greek for students who love the Scripture.

Note to the Reader

This study of Paul's letters has been prepared with care and reverence, exploring each verse in depth and offering insights into translation and meaning.

Because of the richness of the material and the length of the work, the study has been divided into two parts.

- **Part One** will carry us through Galatians, I Thessalonians, II Thessalonians, and the first seven chapters of I Corinthians.
- **Part Two** will continue with the remaining chapters of I Corinthians and the rest of Paul's letters.

We invite you to begin this journey here in Part One, knowing that the exploration will continue seamlessly in Part Two.

Select Bibliography: General

LEXICONS:

Abbreviations:

BAGD   *A Greek-English Lexicon of the New Testament and Other Early Christian Literature.* By W. Bauer. Trans. and rev. by W.F. Arndt, F.W. Gingrich, and F.W. Danker. Chicago: University of Chicago Press, 1979.

BDAG   *A Greek-English Lexicon of the New Testament and Other Early Christian Literature.* Based on Walter Bauer's Griechisch-deutsches Wörterbuch zu den Schriften des Neuen Testaments und der frühchristlichen Literatur, sixth edition, eds. Kurt Aland and Barbara Aland, with Viktor Reichmann and on previous English editions by W.F. Arndt, F.W. Gingrich, and F. W. Danker. The University of Chicago Press, Chicago and London, 2000. This work was used extensively.

DANKER   *The Concise Greek-English Lexicon of the New Testament of the New Testament.* By Frederick William Danker, Chicago and London, University of Chicago Press, 2009.

THAYER   *A Greek-English Lexicon of the New Testament Being Grimm's Wilke's Clavis Novi Testamenti* translated, revised and enlarged by Joseph Henry Thayer, First Edition, Harper and Brothers, Franklin Square, New York, 1887, copyright, 1986.

GREEK GRAMMAR:

DANA AND MANTEY   *A Manual Grammar of the Greek New Testament.* By H.E. Dana and Julius R. Mantey, The Macmillan Company, new edition, 1957, Twenty-sixth Printing, New York, 1962.

MOUNCE   *Basics of Biblical Greek Grammar.* By William D. Mounce, Zondervan, Second Edition, Grand Rapids, Michigan, 49530, 2003.

ROBERTSON	*A Grammar of the Greek New Testament in the Light of Historical Research*. By A. T. Robertson, Broadman Press, Nashville, Tennessee, 1934.
WALLACE	*Greek Grammar Beyond the Basics, An Exegetical Syntax of the New Testament*. By Daniel B Wallace, Zondervan, Grand Rapids, Michigan, 49530, USA, 1996.
SMYTH	*Greek Grammar*. By Herbert Weir Smyth, Harvard University Press, Cambridge, Massachusetts, 1956, Fifth Printing, 1968.

GENERAL RESEARCH:

ARCHAEOLOGY	*Hesperia*. A scientific archaeological journal published for Greek archaeological research since 1932 by the American School of Classical Studies at Athens. It does not cover western Asia Minor, since most of that area currently belongs to Turkey.
BROWN	*Roman Architecture*. By Frank E. Brown, George Braziller, Inc., New York, 1967.
CARY	*The Oxford Classical Dictionary*. Eds., M. Cary, J.D. Denniston, J. Wight Duff, A.D. Nock, W.D. Ross, and H.H. Scullard, with the assistance of H.J. Rose, H. P. Harvey, and A. Souter, Oxford at the Clarendon Press, Oxford University Press, London, Reprinted, 1968.
CASTAGNOLI	*Orthogonal Town Planning in Antiquity*. By Ferdinando Castagnoli, The MIT Press, Cambridge, Massachusetts and London, England, 1971.
DAVIS	*A Dictionary of the Bible*. By John D. Davis, Baker Book House, Grand Rapids, Michigan, 1956.
KOHLENBERGER	*The Exhaustive Concordance to the Greek New Testament*. By John R. Kohlenberger, Edward W. Goodrick, and James A. Swanson, Zondervan, Grand Rapids, Michigan, 1995.
JOSEPHUS	*The New Complete Works of Josephus*. Translated by William Whiston and Commentary by Paul L. Maier, Kregel Publications, Grand Rapids, Michigan, 1999.

LIGHTFOOT — *The Apostolic Fathers*. Translated and edited by J. B. Lightfoot, Baker Book House, Grand Rapids, Michigan, 1962

O'CONNOR — *St. Paul's Corinth, Texts and Archaeology*. By Jerome Murphy-O'Connor, A Michael Glazier Book published by The Liturgical Press, Collegeville, Minnesota, 1983 and 2002.

PHILO — *Philo and Paul among the Sophists*. By Bruce W. Winter, second edition, William B. Eerdman's Publishing Company, Grand Rapids Michigan and Cambridge, U.K., 2002.

RAMSAY — *St. Paul the Traveller and the Roman Citizen*. By W. M. Ramsay, Baker Book House, Grand Rapids, Michigan, 1966.

RE — *Realencyclopädie der classischen Alterumswissenschaft*, By A. Pauly et al., (in German), from 1893.

ROLLER — *In Search of God the Mother, the Cult of the Anatolian Cybele*. By Lynn E. Roller, the University of California Press, Berkeley, Los Angeles, and London, 1999.

SCRANTON — *Greek Architecture*. By Robert L. Scranton, George Braziller, Inc., New York, 1967.

SMITH — *Smith's Bible Dictionary*. By William Smith, revised and enlarged by F.N. and M.A. Peloubet, Thomas Nelson Publishers, third printing, 1962.

STEGENA — *The Greek-English Analytical Concordance of the Greek-English New Testament*. By J. Stegenga, Hellenes-English Biblical Foundation, Jackson, Mississippi, 1963.

STRONG — *The New Strong's Concise Concordance of the Bible*. By James Strong, Thomas Nelson Publishers, Nashville, Tennessee, 1985.

WINTER — *After Paul Left Corinth, The Influence of Secular Ethics and Social Change*. By Bruce W. Winter, William B. Eerdmans Publishing Company, Grand Rapids, Michigan and Cambridge, U.K., 2001.

WITHERINGTON — *Conflict & Community in Corinth, a Socio-Rhetorical Commentary on 1 and 2 Corinthians*. By Ben Witherington, III, William B. Eerdmans Publishing Company, Grand Rapids, Michigan and Carlisle, Cumbria, U.K., 1995.

CHAPTER 1
GALATIANS

Illustration 1:
Map of the Roman Province of Galatia, from BC 25 to AD 137
The North and South Galatian Theories

Map used by permission, © James A. Fowler

THE SOUTH GALATIAN THEORY

One of the better descriptions of this theory can be found in F.F. Bruce's excellent work on the Epistle to the Galatians, a Commentary on the Greek Text, 1982, pp. 5-18. He reviewed the literature on the subject and summarized the findings of W. M. Ramsay's foundational publications on the subject in the late 1800's, who wanted to prove the validity of the North Galatian theory. But after visiting the area in modern Turkey and studying the geography and road systems in the region came to the conclusion that the South Galatian theory was actually correct. This theory basically held that the route of Paul was through the 'South Galatian' area, including the towns and cities of Iconium, Antioch of Pisidia, Lystra, and Derbe. Galatians, holding this theory, was therefore the first letter Paul wrote, written perhaps as early as late AD 48, or mid-49, following the trip which occurred in mid-48 to early AD 49. As Bruce remarked, most scholars since then have accepted the South Galatian theory, in spite of some vigorous, but unsatisfactory arguments to the contrary (Bruce, pp. 14-18).

The North Galatian Theory

The North Galatian Theory was in vogue during most of the 1800's, until Ramsay's publications came out in 1893 and 1899, thoroughly challenging this theory. The North Galatian theory held that Paul travelled to the north part of Galatia, concentrating on the large capital of Roman Galatia, Ancyra, and ancillary towns in the north. The dates for each theory were very divergent; The North Galatian trip must have occurred at the beginning of the third missionary journey of Paul, and not before the mid-fifties, or later.

CHAPTER 1
Galatians, circa AD 49

Anticipate the Message of Galatians:
"Beware of the wolf at the door of the chicken house."

Background Information
Who were the Galatians?

Celts: The term was used interchangeably with Galli or Celtae. Hence they were the Gauls (or Celts) from Europe, some of whom were invited as mercenaries in BC 278 by the king of Bithynia in Asia Minor who wanted to use them as a standing army. A large migration ensued and they populated a large area south of Bithynia, nearly stretching to the Mediterranean Sea. They brought with them much of their own culture and language, but over the subsequent few centuries they learned Greek. Clusters of immigrants settled either in southern Galatia or northern Galatia.

Location of the Galatian region in the first century AD: The area of the Galatians was taken over by Rome in BC 189. The Romans gradually added new territory to the Roman province of Galatia until about BC 25. A Roman road was constructed through southern Galatia in BC 6 (Via Sebaste), but it did not include northern Galatia. This road led from Ephesus through southern Galatia to Tarsus and Antioch. Another road led from Lystra into northern Galatia to the capital, Ancyra, a large Romanized city, which Paul apparently did not visit on his first missionary journey.

Date of Galatians: The latest scholarly view is that the letter was written to the southern Galatians (not the northern) in AD 49, in areas visited by Paul during his first Missionary Journey in AD 48. Therefore, it was Paul's first published letter in the NT, written even before the Thessalonian epistles. Galatians 1:6, **"...so quickly deserting....**" suggested that the letter followed *very soon* after Paul's First Missionary Journey to them. Witherington proposed, after some detailed study (pp. 13-20), that the date of the First Missionary Journey was approximately AD 48. He dated the writing of Galatians then, to approximately AD 49, (Witherington, 9, 20), just before Paul's trip to the Jerusalem Council recorded in Acts 15: 2b-29.

Where was Paul when he wrote Galatians? It was probably written from Antioch on the Orontes River, where Paul stayed with a large concentration of Gentile and some Jewish believers. The postscript ("written from Rome") added to the conclusion of the King James Version, was likely a late addition based on incorrect data at the time.

Why did Paul write the letter? Judaizers came to Galatia and insisted that the Christians had to be circumcised and follow the Jewish ceremonial laws in order to be saved. Paul must have received the word in Antioch.

Who was the emperor at the time? Claudius Caesar (AD 41-54) In this period Christians would be allowed to have their own religion, and, with Jews, provided with kosher foods at markets in the major Roman imperial cities, and freedom from military service, which originated during the reign of Augustus Caesar.

Legal Status of the Christians: Until AD 64, when Nero blamed the burning of Rome on the Christians, the legal status of Christians was one that corresponded to the privileges given to the Jews, which were established by Augustus in exchange for Jewish help given to him during the civil wars. When Paul was brought before Gallio in Corinth by the Jews in AD 51, his legal status (and that of the Christians) remained the same. The case against Paul was dropped. As long as Christians were identified as part of a Jewish sect, their legal status was assured. But that became strained when the Jews started riots because of the Christians. Emperors wanted to know what was at the root of these riots, and Emperor Claudius first punished Jews by exiling them from Rome. When Christians were separating themselves from the synagogues and the Jewish religion, Christians became vulnerable to future imperial legal problems.

The controversy of the letter: Paul and Barnabas had just completed their first missionary journey, and settled in at their home base of Syrian Antioch. They had not been there very long, perhaps within weeks of their arrival, when news came from a concerned believer in one of the Galatians churches. He brought news that visitors had come from Jerusalem with identity papers signed by James, the head of the Jerusalem church. They were apparently official representatives from the Christian churches of Judea. Members of the Galatian churches welcomed them into their homes and churches. They were received as legitimate Christian dignitaries from Judea, and were treated with honor. However, this visitor to Paul at Antioch also brought troubling news. The substance of their teaching bothered some of the Christians of Galatia, and they likely sent this emissary to Paul for clarification. These people were probably Jewish Christians from Judea, who mixed elements of the Gospel with Jewish traditional 'law,' including adherence to the Mosaic law and circumcision, as requirements for salvation. Some of the Galatian church leaders must have been thoroughly confused.

Their teaching involved making their Gentile church members into an inferior class of believers. They also talked about circumcision as a requirement for salvation. But it was more than that. They were also taught that they had to observe the Jewish calendar and all of its festival days and many other rituals of Judaism. These were considered by the Judean visitors as major elements of Christianity. It seemed to the Galatians that they had to earn the right to stay saved by following all these rituals.

Many believers in the Galatian churches were very receptive to these teachings, and even a number of the men were lining up in the various cities and towns of Galatia to become circumcised. Other believers in the vicinity were thoroughly confused by these requirements. Furthermore, they were very articulate and forceful in presenting these requirements, declaring that becoming a Christian was only the first step in the road to salvation, and they needed much more instruction regarding the requirements of the Mosaic law, which required time for their 'good' works to be properly effective in establishing their status in the Christian world.

Since they were apparently authorized by the Jerusalem church leadership, one must wonder about the churches of Jerusalem and the major doctrines of the faith held by the apostles. Paul had visited with James some years after his conversion, and he seemed to be in agreement with Paul on the basics. However, these issues were at the very core of Christianity. What happened to James?

James could have known these Judean church leaders, but he wasn't in close contact with their teachings, and how they might have changed over time. Furthermore, James may have turned a blind eye to what was developing in those churches some distance away from the capital, because the consequences might have developed into a major split within the churches of Judea and the churches of Jerusalem. Perhaps James wanted to keep the peace as much as possible, because the emotions of the Judean leaders could deepen a rift in whatever agreement they had developed over the years after Pentecost.

Paul, however, hearing this news was infuriated. He saw instantly the implications of their teaching. It was old Judaism dressed in the robe of Christianity: 'faith comes by works,' and that had to develop over time to sort out the 'faith pretenders' from the genuine believer. 'Works' was the major ingredient of this movement in order to gain salvation. Paul could not start writing his letter soon enough. He knew that this would be a major issue that could destroy whatever work he had begun under the strong influence and power of the Holy Spirit. Paul got it right; there was some evidence that many others failed to get it right. But what happened to James? Paul could not deal with that problem now. He had to put this issue to rest immediately. Eventually, it seems that James finally did get it right. His letter to the Judean churches was written approximately four years later in AD 52 (we believe) and was aflame with passion addressed to these 'argumentative and hateful teachers' within the Judean churches.

THE GALATIANS TEXT
Paul's Initial Response: *Beware of False Prophets*
Galatians Chapter 1: 1-10

'Salutation' Galatians 1:1-5

1:1: "Paul, an apostle, not of men, neither through mankind, but through Jesus Christ and God (the) Father, who has raised Him from the dead,"

In his letter to the Galatians in which he concentrated on the heretical positions of the Judaizers, Paul had to establish his credentials, and the source of his apostleship, which the Judaizers would have questioned. His apostleship was not made by a vote of the Judean leaders, nor their church members. It was given by Christ Himself and God the Father.

1:2: "and all the brothers with me, to the churches of Galatia…"

Paul always had a group of fellow-workers at his side, which would assure the Galatians that Paul was not alone in his ministry. Many other leaders, sympathetic with Paul's theological positions, were with him as he wrote.

1:3: "Grace to you and peace from God our Father and (the) Lord Jesus Christ…."

Paul frequently commended the ideas of God's grace (χάρις) and peace (εἰρήνη) to his churches. After all, God's grace created salvation and blesses believers. His peace was also a precious possession of every believer. Both grace and peace are also objects of growth within the lifelong sanctification process of Christians.

1:4: "…who gave Himself on behalf of our sins, in order that He may deliver us from the present evil age according to the will of God and our Father,"

'Gave Himself' was **δόντος ἑαυτόν**. The 'gave' was an aorist active participle indicating a point-of-time action at the crucifixion, rather than underscoring the painful and lengthy process that was involved. Paul saw the crucifixion as a single transaction. 'On behalf of' was **ὑπὲρ**, 'in order to atone for a person's sins' or 'remove them' (BDAG).

'Deliver' was **ἐξέληται** from **ἐξαίρω**, 'to deliver out of.' The middle voice of the verb suggested that a beneficial consequence would follow for the person who was delivered from this evil age. The subjunctive tense indicated that the act of 'delivering' was the intention of God, but it also opened the possibility that not everyone will accept the deliverance. The subjunctive mode was the mode of possibility for human beings, but not a certainty for some (i.e., those who rejected the Messiah).

"...according to the will of God and our Father," God's will was the driving force behind His salvation. It was accomplished through His will, and Christ's submission to that will. God was also Paul's Father, as well as all believers, since believers were now children of God the Father.

1:5: "To whom (is) the glory into the ages of (the) ages, amen."

Paul virtually always concluded his salutations with a doxology to God for what He gave to mankind.

'There is only One Gospel' Galatians 1:6-10

1:6: "I am amazed how soon that you turned away from the One who called you by the grace (of Christ) to another Gospel,"

'Amazed' was θαυμάζω, 'to be astonished' or 'disturbed' about something (BDAG). 'Turned away' was μετατίθεσθε from μετατίθημι, literally 'to change one's mind,' or 'to have a change of allegiance,' or 'be a deserter.' (BDAG). The middle voice described the activity as willful and consequences would follow.

"...from the One who called you by the grace (of Christ) to another Gospel," They were deserting from God the Father, who was the one having called them by the Lord's grace. 'To *another*' gospel was ἕτερον, 'another of a different kind,' as opposed to ἄλλο, 'another object of the same kind' as in verse 7.

1:7: "which is not another, except that certain ones are throwing you into confusion and wanting to alter the gospel of Christ."

'Another' here was ἄλλο, 'another of the same kind' reinforcing the idea that there could not be another kind of gospel. It must be another of a different kind, hence, not the same. If certain elements were added to the genuine gospel, then it became a false gospel. The Judaizers were insisting that circumcision was necessary for salvation. Paul was saying that the addition of circumcision would invalidate the true gospel. 'Faith' plus nothing was the correct prescription. Change that, and everything would fall apart.

1:8: "But even if we, or an angel from heaven may preach [to you] other than the one we preached to you, let him be accursed."

Paul was assuring the Galatians that there was only one gospel: the one they preached originally to them. Even if Paul changed his mind and added something else to the requirements, the Galatians should not listen to him, and cling to the original message. The first 'preach' was εὐαγγελίζηται, a present subjunctive middle verb meaning to 'continually preach' with a consequence to the preacher if he preached the wrong message. The second 'preach' was εὐηγγελισάμεθα, an aorist indicative middle, indicating a positive consequence to the preacher if he preached this message ('faith + nothing = salvation'). 'Cursed' was 'anathema,' (ἀνάθεμα), indicating a curse of God, common in the OT.

1:9: "As we said before (verse 8), and I say again, if anyone evangelizes you (with something) other than that which you received, let him be accursed."

Paul here repeated the injunction for serious emphasis. This was a vital issue, and the stakes could not have been higher. Add any 'work' to faith, then a person did not have salvation.

1:10: "For now, am I persuading men or God? Or am I seeking to please men? If I were still pleasing men, I would no longer be the slave of Christ."

"For now, am I persuading men or God?" Paul was not trying to persuade God at all, ever. He was in the business of persuading men and women. 'Persuading' was πείθω, meaning to 'persuade through the presentation of the gospel of Christ.' He wanted to see all men and women submit to the gospel of Christ in order to be saved.

"…Or am I seeking to flatter men?" Pagan priests may have encouraged men and women to give gifts to false gods by whatever deceptive means they could use. Paul could not do that. He was not a charlatan, confusing people with magic tricks. This was God's message he was proclaiming to mankind. He was not trying to please people: he was trying to bring them to Christ for salvation. Actually Paul sought to please God, not men. 'Please' was ἀρέσκειν, a present progressive tense infinitive, meaning, in the negative sense, 'to continually flatter, or to continually win favor among people' (BDAG) to gain their loyalty, their support, and their money for their nefarious ideas, philosophy, or to gain fame.

'How Paul Became an Apostle' Galatians 1:11-24:

1:11: "For I make known to you brothers, the gospel which was preached by me that it was not according to a human (source):"

'I make known' was γνωρίζω, related to the deep knowledge of γινώσκω. Paul was revealing here a point of deep knowledge that he wanted them to understand, because it would clarify his apostleship that was being questioned. 'According to a human source' was κατὰ ἄνθρωπον, literally, 'according to mankind.'

9

1:12: "For neither did I receive it from a human source, nor was I taught (by others), (it came) by a revelation of Jesus Christ."

Paul needed to explain where his knowledge of the gospel originated. His accusers were trying to tell the Galatians that Paul was a late-comer who had no credentials. 'By a revelation' was δι᾽ ἀποκαλύψεως, literally, 'through a revelation.'

1:13: "For you heard (about) my conduct formerly (while) in Judaism, that I persecuted the church of God to an extraordinary degree, I made havoc of it."

In telling his story, he pointed out that he was a persecutor of the church. 'Persecuted' was ἐδίωκεν, 'one who harasses another based on his or her religious beliefs' (BDAG). Paul was in a position of influence within Judaism, and he excelled in carrying out that persecution. He even admitted that he made havoc of the churches in Judea, and he was about to do the same in Damascus when the Lord stopped him. 'Made havoc' was ἐπόρθουν, from πορθέω, 'to pillage, or annihilate' (BDAG).

1:14: "And I advanced in Judaism beyond many of my contemporaries among my people, being more exceedingly zealous of my patriarchal traditions."

Paul was clearly establishing himself as an extremist leader of Judaism before his conversion. 'Advanced' was προέκοπτον, from προκόπτω, meaning 'to advance in status or rank' (BDAG).

1:15: "But when [God] was pleased, who set me apart from my mother's womb and having called (me) through His grace..."

This sentence continued to verse 17. Here Paul acknowledged that God the Father was instrumental in his conversion even before he was born. By stating God's choice in his conversion, Paul was clearly indicating that he was commissioned by God Himself, not by man. Paul also acknowledged that his calling originated by His grace, a concept that Paul recognized throughout his writings and teaching. Paul was always grateful for that grace. 'Set me apart' was ἀφορίσας, from ἀφορίζω, meaning 'to set apart' or 'appoint' (BDAG). 'Called' was καλέσας, an aorist participle from καλέω, indicating a formal commissioning at a single point of time: either at or before his birth, or at his conversion.

1:16: "...to reveal His Son in me, in order that I may preach Him among the Gentiles, immediately I did not confer with flesh and blood..."

Paul's commission involved preaching Christ among the Gentiles. Note that he acted immediately without having formal discussions with Christians in Damascus about what the gospel included. 'Reveal' was ἀποκαλύψαι, the aorist infinitive, meaning, 'to fully reveal something.'

1:17: "nor did I come up to Jerusalem toward those who were apostles before me, but I left for Arabia and I came back to Damascus."

Paul did not indicate what he did in Arabia. It is possible that he found a synagogue somewhere there and went into a secluded study of the OT, in order to fully grasp the Messianic coming of Christ. His whole world had fallen around him and he would have needed to clarify for himself the OT record, in order to explain Christ as the Messiah to Gentiles as well as Jews.

1:18: "Next after three years I came up into Jerusalem to visit Peter and I remained with him for fifteen days,"

Paul carefully worded this verse to explain that he only spent about two weeks with Peter, and probably not much discussion, if any, on doctrine.

1:19: "and other apostles I did not see except James, the brother of the Lord."

He also saw James, but apparently had no long discussions with him about the doctrines of the faith. The three may have had discussions about future missions beyond Jerusalem, and probably agreed that it would be preferable for Paul's obvious safety, not to minister in Judea, while on his way to Antioch. One reason behind this verse was to convince readers that the source of Paul's gospel was to be found in the direct revelation of the Lord Jesus and the Holy Spirit, thereby qualifying him to speak firsthand as an apostle of Christ.

1:20: "And the things I am writing to you, behold, in the presence of God, I am not lying."

Here Paul affirmed that he was speaking the truth. He may have been accused of lying by the Judean heretics.

1:21: "Then I came into the regions of Syria and (the regions of) Cilicia."

Paul may have gone through Judea to get to Syria, where he likely lodged with Christians in Antioch, an important merchant city on the caravan road going east. Many Gentiles would congregate here, before proceeding east, or even to the south. Here was probably where his Gentile ministry was seriously started.

He and Barnabas would eventually start the first missionary journey from Antioch. By mentioning Cilicia, he was probably referring to his hometown of Tarsus, mentioned in Acts 9:30.

1:22: "But I was continually unknown by face among the churches of Judea which are in Christ."

Paul here made it very clear that he avoided the churches in Judea. He was not recognized when he passed through the area, and he made no acquaintances. 'Unknown by face' was ἀγνοούμενος τῷ προσώπῳ, literally, 'continually unknown by face.' This procedure was likely discussed by Peter and James and they suggested to Paul that he avoid the Judean churches. The reason seemed clear: such a controversial figure as Paul coming to the churches in this region may have stirred up controversy, which may have alerted Paul haters of his presence. It was also possible that the churches in Judea had already strayed from faith by grace alone, by adding certain ceremonies of traditional Jewish culture as prerequisites for salvation. They certainly were still tradition-conscious when Paul came to Jerusalem years later to deliver the offering of the Gentile churches. Paul's presence even among the churches of Jerusalem was always taken with suspicion.

1:23: "But they were only continually hearing that the one formerly persecuting us is now preaching the faith which he formerly ravaged,"

Here Paul acknowledged that the people of the churches in Judea had heard the story of Paul's conversion, but he had no personal contact with them. 'They were continually hearing' was a periphrastic construction (ἦσαν ἀκούοντες), emphasizing the 'continual action of hearing.' His fame had reached them, but they had never heard him speak.

1:24: "And they were glorifying God for me."

However, they did show gratitude to God for saving such a troublesome persecutor. 'For me' was ἐν ἐμοὶ, often translated 'in me.' However, in this construction it is implied that the people of the Judean churches were glorifying God for what God had achieved in converting Paul to the faith. 'Glorifying' God was ἐδόξαζον, an imperfect tense verb indicating a past action that continued over time in the past.

"The Private Meeting between Equals"
Galatians Chapter 2:1-10:

'The Private Conference at Jerusalem' **Galatians 2:1-3:**
Background correlations between Galatians and Acts:
Was this conference in Galatians 2, the same as the one in Acts: Acts 11, 12, or 15?

Other Possibilities for this meeting:

1. This meeting in Galatians 2:1-10 was earlier that the Jerusalem conference of Acts 15:1-2. This was the view of F.F. Bruce, p. 128, and Witherington, although Witherington identified the Galatian meeting here in 2:1-10 as identical to the meeting of Acts 11 and 12, pp. 16-19.

2. This Galatian meeting was not reported in Acts.

The Public Purpose of the Trip (from Antioch to Jerusalem): It was possibly a relief mission to help the suffering Judean Christians during a famine.

The Unstated Purpose of the Trip: The purpose was likely to meet with the Jerusalem leaders privately to talk about Paul's Gospel to the Gentiles, and get theological agreement from the leaders there, especially on the issue of circumcision.

The Problem: Judean 'Christians,' or Judaizers became suspicious of the meeting, and convinced one or more of the Jerusalem leaders to allow one or more of these 'Christians' to sit in during the conference, and 'spy' on the content.

2:1: "Then, after fourteen years, again I went up to Jerusalem taking along Barnabas and Titus."

Paul here stated that the very next time he visited Jerusalem was fourteen years later. He also brought Barnabas and the Gentile, Titus, with him.

2:2: "I went up according to revelation: and I set before them the gospel which I preach among the Gentiles, and privately, before the men of reputation, lest, somehow, I am running in vain or I ran (in the past in vain)."

Paul claimed here that he went up to Jerusalem 'by revelation,' indicating that it was the Lord's will to attend this conference, not Paul's will.

2:3: "But not even Titus, who was with me, being a Greek, was required to be circumcised."

Titus was allowed to attend the meeting, even though he was not circumcised.

2:4-6: The spies who sneaked in: Paul considered them to be 'false brethren,' probably Judean 'Christians.'

2:4: "But (it was) on account of the false brothers who were smuggled in (that this question later arose), such ones who slipped in to spy out our freedom which we have in Christ Jesus, in order that they may enslave us."

"...Smuggled in...." was παρεισάκτους, pertaining 'to a group being smuggled, or secretly brought into a meeting,' which left some doubt whether they were allowed in by one or more of the leaders, or whether they sneaked in unawares. Their purpose for 'coming in' was clear: to spy on the group:

παρεισῆλθον κατασκοπῆσαι, 'they slipped in to spy out the meeting,' or 'lie in wait' showed their nefarious motives (BDAG). This was supposed to be a private meeting. If they had wormed their way into the meeting, someone should have asked them to leave. The fact that no one did, suggested that the Jerusalem leaders were at fault. If the meeting was held at Antioch, where Paul had some control, things might have been different.

2:5: "But to them we did not yield for an hour in submission, in order that the truth of the gospel may remain unimpaired toward you."

"…Yield…." was εἴξαμεν from εἴκω, meaning 'to give in to someone's demand, yield' (BDAG).

"…Unimpaired…." was διαμείνῃ, meaning that the gospel may continue to have a relationship with individual believers in Galatia. The subjunctive mode was the mode of possibility. The outcome of this meeting was very critical for the gospel advancing, in Paul's view.

2:6: "But as for the men who are thinking to be something— it does not matter to me what sort of people they once were, for God does not have favorites, for they who think themselves to be something are not coming to me for advice,"

[This verse was an anacoluthon, a sentence fragment.] Here, in addition to a sentence fragment, Paul seemed to be talking about these men who came to the meeting uninvited. They were once perhaps very influential spiritual leaders, but chose the heretical path. Even though they were famous and well-known to some of the Jerusalem leaders, Paul made note of a very important truth. A believer should not be influenced by such men, once they turned their back on Christ.

"…Not coming to me for advice…." was προσανέθεντο, from προσανατίθημι, 'to consult with.' These VIP's from another place made the discussions difficult, though Paul made it clear (verse 5) that their influence was not allowed to hamper the business at hand.

'Result of the Meeting' Galatians 2:7-10:

2:7: "But on the contrary, having seen that I have been entrusted with the gospel of the uncircumcision even as Peter (has been entrusted with) the gospel of the circumcision."

[This verse was another anacoluthon, a 'broken' sentence]. Here Paul noted a major result of the meeting. Paul was entrusted, πεπίστευμαι, 'to believe in someone to the degree that the person believing has complete confidence in that person,' BDAG). The verb was a present perfect indicative passive voice, likely intensive: 'having a strong continuation of that trust.' God had every reason to continually trust Paul. By implication God had that same continual trust in Peter also.

2:8: "For the One who was at work in Peter for (the) apostleship of the circumcision worked also in me for the Gentiles."

"...At work...for...." was ἐνεργῆσας, from ἐνεργέω, 'to work at,' for the benefit of another (middle voice). Paul praised Peter in this situation that the two were equals with respect to their work as apostles.

2:9: "And having known the grace that has been given to me, James and Peter and John, who seem to be pillars, they gave a handshake to me and Barnabas, in order that we are for the Gentiles, and they for the circumcision:"

"...Handshake...." was two words, δεξιάς and ἔδωκαν, literally, 'they gave right hands.' This meeting, in spite of the intrusion by uninvited heretics, went very well.

2:10: "only that we may remember the poor, which also I was zealous to do the same thing."

"...Zealous...." was ἐσπούδασα, 'eager to perform a needed task,' (BDAG), an aorist indicative active verb.

The Final Results of the Meeting:

First, the Jerusalem leaders did not demand that the Gentile Christians be circumcised (2:3). Second, Paul and company would focus largely on the mission to the Gentiles. Third, Peter and company would focus on the mission to the Jews. Fourth, Paul would remain willing to sponsor future relief missions to the Judean Christians in case of a famine.

"Rocky Equals and Salvation by Faith Alone"
Galatians 2:11-21

'Rocky Equals: Trouble in Antioch' **Galatians 2:11-14:**
2:11: "But when Peter came to Antioch, I stood against him to his face, because he stood condemned."

2:12: "For before certain ones came from James, he ate together with the Gentiles, but when they came, he withdrew and he separated himself, fearing those from the circumcision."

Paul here revealed Peter's double standard, and confronted him to his face. Apparently the Judaizers had left Antioch before Paul came back from his travels. But he found out, probably from some Gentile Christians who were offended by Peter's action. The 'circumcision' likely identified the Judaizers who were traveling to Paul's churches, persuading people that they couldn't be saved without being circumcised. Peter exhibited the same kind of fear here that he did when Christ was arrested, denying allegations that he was acquainted with Jesus to the crowds. But as he matured spiritually, these events evaporated with time and experience.

2:13: "Also, the rest of the Jews were joined together with this hypocritical judging, where even Barnabas was carried away with their hypocrisy."

'Joined together' was συνυπεκρίθησαν, a compound verb, συν + υπο + κρινομαι, which meant, literally, 'to judge over together' or a 'joining of a hypocritical judging of others.' To add insult to injury, all the Christian Jews, including Barnabas, participated with Peter in this degrading act. The passive verb indicated that they were under someone's influence, not the influence of the Holy Spirit.

2:14: "But when I saw that they did not act rightly toward the truth of the gospel I said to Peter in front of everyone, if you (being) a Jew are being like a Gentile and not living like a Jew, how can you require the Gentiles (to live) like a Jew?"

"…Act rightly…." was ὀρθωποδοῦσιν, meaning literally, 'walking in a straight course,' It was a progressive present tense, indicating that the 'walking straight' was expected to be consistent and continual.

'Salvation by Faith Alone for Jew and Gentile' Galatians 2:15-21:

2:15: "We ourselves (are) Jews by birth and not sinners from (the) Gentiles:"

This was a statement expressing the old order of things, which Peter and the other Jews were resuscitating, in order to separate Jewish Christians from Gentile Christians. The effect of imposition of this old order on Gentile Christians renewed the wall that separated Jews from Gentiles before Christ took down that wall. The old order magnified one group of people over another, when in actual fact, Christ merged the two groups into one social

16

category. Notice the language of racial domination: 'We ourselves' (ἡμεῖς) elevated the subject of the understood verb ('are') with an emphasis that elevated Jews over Gentile believers. 'Jews by birth' (φύσει Ἰουδαῖοι) placed physical birth over spiritual birth. Immediately the Jew felt elevated to an artificially high level of spirituality than the Gentile convert. 'Sinners from the Gentiles' rebuilt the wall all over again. Christ brought equality between the races, because the Holy Spirit worked His miracles of transformation among both groups equally. This was a dangerous manifestation of old world prejudices that should have brought the two groups together.

But Peter, to his credit, recognized the danger of allowing these radical Judaizers to see the Gentiles and Jews mixing together, even in Antioch. There were radical Jews roaming around, looking for examples of this kind of equality. Some of them would resort to murder if they witnessed it. The Judaizers may have been aware of these strict Jewish radicals, and these radical groups did represent a danger to the church at Antioch. Just because they were north of the Jewish state did not exempt the Christian community of their influence. Perhaps Peter was fearful, not just for himself, but also for the whole Jewish Christian community. If the word of this equality ever circulated to these radical groups, there could be trouble. Yet, Peter was 'spiritually speaking,' wrong in what he did, for it threatened to break apart the Christian community from the inside.

2:16: "[and] having known that a human being is not being justified by works of (the) Law except through faith of Jesus Christ, and we ourselves did believe in Christ Jesus in order that we may be justified out of (the) faith of Christ and not from works of the Law, because from works of the Law shall no flesh be justified."

Paul here developed the basis for his theological discussion about the current ineffectiveness of works as a means of salvation. Christ tore down the wall that separated Jews from Gentiles. Peter and the Jewish Christians were trying to build it up again. A new attitude was required that should have governed Christian conduct. 'Justification' was the key word here that should have brought the group together as equals. It was used three times in this verse and all three were used as passive verbs, indicating that God was performing the task of justification equally on Jew and Gentile alike.

The first example was 'having known (εἰδότες from οἶδα, a perfect tense participle) that a man is not justified (δικαιοῦται) by works of the law....'

The second example was '...**we did believe in Christ Jesus in order that we may be justified (δικαιωθῶμεν) from the faith of Christ** (faith *of Christ*, an objective genitive, in spite of grammatical scholars who are now claiming that this was a subjective genitive, 'Christ's faith,' see the NET Bible notes on this passage).' Here the example was in the subjunctive mode, the mode of possibility. 'From' was a preposition of source, ἐκ, indicating that the individual's justification' originated from the 'faith of Christ,' not His faith, but the believer's faith in Christ.

The third example revealed a future justification: 'from the works of the law shall no flesh be 'justified,' **δικαιωθήσεται**.' Justification was God's work in humans (Jews and Gentiles) that was based on Christ's sacrifice, and activated by a sinner's belief in Him as the saving Messiah, to Jew and Gentile alike. The wall was broken. 'Don't try and rebuild it.' This was God's work. Man should not be allowed to rebuild the walls of pride and prejudice by trying to earn salvation.

2:17: "But if (we) seeking to be justified by Christ, and we ourselves are found as sinners, (is) therefore Christ a minister of sin? God forbid!"

Here Paul answered the argument that without the regulations of the law, then Christians could keep on sinning. But as Paul emphatically declared here, that was a lie of the Devil. Justification was by faith alone, and works were involved as a response to the Christian's transforming grace of the Holy Spirit. The motive was accompanied by the power not to sin.

2:18: "For if what things I destroy, again I rebuild, I make myself a transgressor"

'If I destroy a justified life by grace and I try to rebuild it by works, I make myself a transgressor.' Works were futile to use as a tool for justification.

2:19: "For I myself died to the law through the law, in order that I might live to God:"

Paul's identity in his justified life was Christ crucified. He paid the price for Paul's (and every believer's) sin. The law was the old order that never saved anyone. The law brought only an awareness of sin, not the removal of it nor its effects. Paul died to the law metaphorically in order to live under a new relationship with Christ resulting in life.

2:20: "I have been crucified together with Christ; I myself am no longer living, but Christ is living in me: and the life that I now live in the flesh, I live by faith in the Son of God who loved me and gave Himself for me."

"**I have been crucified together with Christ….**" The main verb here was συνεσταύρωμαι, a perfect extensive indicative passive; Paul here likely was referring to his conversion experience on the Damascus Road over a decade earlier. When he was converted he viewed himself as participating together with Christ's crucifixion. The preposition σύν added the meaning 'together' with the core verb. In that moment of time, Paul recognized that he died to his old nature. The perfect tense was likely extensive, indicating that Paul intended to emphasize the consummation of crucifixion at his conversion. The passive voice indicated that the act of crucifixion was an act brought about, in Paul's case, by the Holy Spirit, as Paul advanced in his sanctified life as a believer.

"**…I myself am no longer living, but Christ is living in me and the life that I now live in the flesh, I live by faith in the Son of God ….**" Paul here stated several facts about his new life. First, he admitted that he himself, 'the old man,' was no longer alive. Second, he recognized that since his conversion, Christ Himself was living in him through the Holy Spirit. Both verbs expressing 'living' were present progressive tenses indicating a continual experience of living, whether in the state of the 'old man,' or in the state of the 'new man.' The 'former life,' although a continual living experience, was now replaced by the new man, which continued his life to the present day of writing this letter. So it was with all believers. The 'new man or new woman' represented the transformed life of the believer. Paul could now say, 'Christ lives in me and has transformed me.'

"**…who loved me and gave Himself for me.**" This phrase was the driving force of Paul's new life. He recognized, at his conversion that Christ, by personally intervening in his life, changed Paul's direction. Christ did this because of His love for Paul, the wayward sinner. From this point of conversion, Paul was dedicated and invigorated to spread this gospel of God's grace to all mankind. That same experience should be true for every believer in Christ.

2:21: "I am not declaring invalid the grace of God: for if righteousness (is) through the law, then Christ died without purpose."

"**…Righteousness….**" was δικαιοσύνη. It might have come through the law. If it did there would have been no reason for Christ to have died on the cross. The term was a legal one that described God's declaration of 'acquittal' for each believer. It does not mean 'make one righteous,' unless the a person examines carefully the whole process of being 'declared righteousness,' including, first of all, conversion, then the process of making one holy during the period of sanctification by means of the Holy Spirit's interaction within the believer. The final act of making one 'righteous' will be made complete at the Parousia (the Rapture), when every believer will be changed (I Cor. 15:51, 52). At that moment, every believer will finally be '*made* righteous.'

Chapter 3: *"Saved by Faith Alone"*
Galatians 3:1-14

Background:

The Pharisaic Rabbinical Schools of the first century A.D. (Data from F.F. Bruce, Galatians, p. 159, ff.; also a general Google search):

The strict Shammai Rabbinical School: They believed that a Jew must keep the Law at least 99% of the time. If a person missed even 1.1%, he was guilty of violating the Law. The evidence is unclear whether Paul was a member of either school, but his strictness and his radical views before conversion seem more related to this school than the Hillel school. Certainly the denunciations of the Pharisees by Jesus were related to members of this school, since they were always blaming Jesus for breaking the Sabbath after his healings on that day.

The more liberal and humanistic Hillel Rabbinical School: If a Jew lived up to 51% of the Law, then he was living an acceptable life according to the Law. Gamaliel, who taught Paul, was possibly from the school of Hillel, especially since he was in line to lead the group, and his relationship with the Hillel family, where he was likely a possible son or grandson to the original Hillel. It would be expected that Nicodemos was related to this school, partly because of his more liberal, and more intellectually and reasonable conduct than other Pharisees.

Paul in his former life as a Rabbi, claimed to live blameless before the Law, 100% of the time (Phil. 3:6). Even that was not good enough, as he discovered at his conversion. The Law was then deemed by Paul to be <u>totally</u> inadequate, even the sections of the Law dealing with repentance. The provisions for repentance under the Law were replaced by Christ's sacrifice; consequently those provisions were now invalid and meaningless.

"Correcting the False Notions of the Judaizers" Galatians 3:1-14:

3:1: "O mindless Galatians, who hypnotized you, for whom Jesus Christ crucified was advertised before your very eyes?"

Paul was very blunt here, because the issue was extremely serious. "Mindless" was the literal translation of ἀνόητοι, an alpha privative (ἀ + νόητοι, from νοῦν, 'thinking with a disengaged mind.') 'Hypnotized' was ἐβάσκανεν, from βασκαίνω, a NT hapax ('used only here' in the NT), meaning originally to give someone the 'evil eye.' Here, it more likely meant 'to hypnotize' or 'bewitch' someone. The Galatian believers seemed to be tricked into believing a serious lie. "Advertised" was προεγράφη, literally 'written down beforehand,' as in an advertising sign or poster.

3:2: "This only I want to learn from you: from the works of the law did you receive the Spirit, or from the hearing of faith?"

Paul here presented them with a question: "What was the source of receiving the Holy Spirit? Did you receive it by any good works you did, or simply by believing with faith the message of salvation?" They were to fill in the answer, which was obvious: faith came through believing, not through any good work.

3:3: "So, are you mindless ones, beginning in the Spirit, are you ending now in (the) flesh?"

Paul here returned to his energetic and accusatory tone in order to emphatically make his point. **"Mindless ones"** was the same word in verse 1: ἀνόητοι, the repetition used here for a strong emphasis. The beginning of the faith was by means of the Holy Spirit; the position they were taking now invalidated the work of the Spirit, by putting in place a fleshly trust in works to complete the salvation process.

3:4: "Such things (that) you suffered (were) in vain? If indeed they are power in you, (was it) from works of the law or from (the) hearing of faith?"

Now Paul turned to the source of their faith. "Who supplied the Holy Spirit to them? Who worked in them with power?" The source of their conversion and the source of their power obtained afterward was by the unmerited grace of God, not their works. It was a gift that they could not possibly earn.

3:6: "Even as Abraham believed God, it was counted to him for righteousness."

The same faith that Abraham demonstrated carried down the centuries and applied to all believers in OT times and even now, through Christ. It was the Abrahamic Covenant that predated the law.

3:7: "Know therefore, that those who are from faith, these are the sons of Abraham."

Therefore, the sons of God were those who, like Abraham, believed God, and it was counted to them for righteousness. They were the true sons of Abraham. 'Know' was the **γινώσκω** kind of knowing, in contrast with the **οἶδα** know that came to man through tradition or culture. It was the intellectual and spiritual knowledge in the present progressive tense command form (**γινώσκετε**), emphasizing the continual action of knowing which was required of them.

3:8: "And the Scripture, foreseeing that out of faith God (produced justified Gentiles, preaching the gospel in advance to Abraham that all the Gentiles will be fully blessed in Thee."

God, who authored the Holy Scriptures, foresaw that this symbol to Abraham would be carried down the centuries, emphasizing that justification did not come by works, but by faith alone. Paul quoted here from Genesis 12:3 in the last phrase. 'Foreseeing,' which was **προιδοῦσα**, a compound verb, **προ** 'before' + **ιδοῦσα**, 'having seen', literally meant, 'having seen in advance.' 'Justified ones,' was **δικαιοι**, indicating that God looked at the converts to faith in Christ as if they had never sinned. He saw each believer through the lens of Christ, and saw only pure individuals. Thus they were blessed by God the Father through faith alone. The gospel was preached to Abraham just as it was preached to the Gentiles two thousand years later: the good news was salvation by faith alone.

3:9: "So, those of faith are blessed with the faith of Abraham."

In Paul's conclusion about Abraham, he emphasized again that the results of faith brought the same blessing that God brought to Abraham: life rather that death.

3:10: "For as many as are (seeking justification) by works of the law, they are under a curse, for it has been written that, 'Cursed (is) everyone who does not persevere in the Scriptures in the book of the law to do them.'"

The curse of the law was associated with God's judgment of mankind. Paul quoted Deut. 27:26 to make his point. This reference to the Dodecalogue strongly emphasized that the source of avoiding the curse was to be found in the Scriptures, which would lead Jews and Gentiles to the same salvation provided by the coming Messiah. Many Jews overlooked God's provision of faith without works through His Messiah. They chose to die a second death by trusting in works, and ignoring God's message and messengers.

3:11: "And clearly no one is justified in the sight of God, because the righteous will live from faith:"

The law and faith are two separate entities according to Paul. No one was able to live by means of the Law; they could only find life by the faith that enabled them to perform good works. No one who claimed to keep the law could make them part of their heart. It was an impossibility trying to use good works as stepping stones to God the Father's favor. But it was possible to obtaion God's favor through faith in Christ with the assistance of the Holy Spirit.

3:13: "Christ redeemed us from the curse of the law by becoming a curse on our behalf, because it has been written, 'Cursed is everyone who hangs on a tree,"

Christ took on the curse of the law instead of mankind. He paid that penalty by dying a cruel death on the 'cursed tree.' The phrase, "...on our behalf...." was a critical limiting factor here: the death of Christ was designed for all humanity as a general principle. But, as a matter of a specific principle, it was designed only for those individuals who were exercising faith in Christ. The "our" in this phrase limited the application of Christ's death only to believers like Paul, believing Galatians, and others like them, down through the centuries.

3:14: "In order that the blessing of Abraham may occur to the Gentiles by Christ Jesus, in order that we might receive the promise of the Spirit through faith."

There were two result clauses here: First, that the blessings of Abraham ('life') that would occur to the Gentiles by means of Christ (the instrumental use of the preposition ἐν), and, second, for all believers to receive the promise of the Holy Spirit by faith.

The Argument from Scripture
Galatians 3:15-29

'The Promise of God' Galatians 3:15-20

3:15: "(Even though) I speak on a human level, (involving a person's last will and testament), likewise, no one annuls or adds (a codicil) upon a covenant having been put into effect beforehand."

In other words, once a will has been put into effect by the testator while he lives, it cannot be changed after his or her death. The promise of God was therefore a valid guarantee of fulfilment.

3:16: "The promises to Abraham were told also to his seed. He did not say 'and to his seeds,' as many, but as to one, 'And to your seed,' which is Christ."

Interestingly, Paul explained that the details of his will were told to his seed, singular, and referring to Christ Jesus. In verse 29, he said, "I am the Lord." There was no mention of faith here: The Abrahamic Covenant established that issue. They did not have the power to practice these statutes because they did not have the faith to internalize them. 'and to his seeds,' referred to the descendants as plural, meaning all those in Christ. Here, Christ was the seed of Abraham in the sense that He was the heir apparent of God's promises to Abraham, which He later conferred on all His believing children, identified as those who were justified by faith alone. 'Were told' was ἐρρέθησαν, the aorist indicative passive tense of λέγω, 'I say.' The passive voice indicated that the telling was made by another person, likely God the Father to Christ.

3:17: "And I say this: (the) covenant, having been validated in advance by God, is not annulled (by the) law, which came into being four hundred and thirty years after, as though the law makes the effectual promise null and void."

Here Paul used idiomatic legal language to say that because the Covenant of Abraham predated the law by over four centuries, there was no reason to suggest that the covenant was no longer in effect. The law did not replace or invalidate the existence of this promise and its effectiveness even after the law was given by Moses. The whole foundation of the Christian conversion by faith alone was based on this promise by God some four thousand years ago, and is still valid today. 'Validated in advance' was προκεκυρωμένην, a compound verb (προ + κυρόω) expressed in the passive present perfect participle. Paul used the perfect intensive present tense to explain that the Covenant of Abraham was a timeless process where the beginning and conclusion falls into the background to express the continual activity of justification by faith alone. The meaning of this verb was 'to validate beforehand,' that is, before the law was given and before Christ came. The second word for 'not invalidated' was the same root word, ἄκυροῖ, with an alpha privative which negated the root meaning, without the prefix, προ, 'before.' Here the meaning was 'annul,' and the tense was a present tense active, indicating a continual action that cannot be altered. The 430 years listed here by Paul was a quotation from Abraham and Moses as 645 years according to Bruce, p. 173. It probably was closer to about 550 years (circa BC 2000 to BC 1450). The 430 years listed here by Paul was a quotation from the LXX (the Septuagint, the Greek translation of the OT in the third century BC), used widely by Jesus and the writers of the NT. The MT (Jewish Masoretic Text) gave the years between

Abraham and Moses as 645 years according to Bruce, p. 173. It probably was closer to about 550 years (ca. BC 2000 to BC 1450).

3:18: "For if the inheritance (is) from the law, (it is) no longer from the promise: but (it is) by a promise that God granted it to Abraham."

A person cannot have it both ways: either justification came by faith alone based on the promise to Abraham; or, it came by means of works of the law which was man-centered, generating arrogance and haughtiness, and not given by God and His grace.

'Inheritance' was **κληρονομία**, 'lottery winners,' from **κλῆρος**, meaning 'an object used for casting lots' + **νεμομαι** 'to possess,' (Thayer). The promise (**ἐπαγγελίαν**) was to Abraham from God. If that promise was based upon works, then, using Paul's logic, it could not be a promise. But the OT text expressly stated that the inheritance was a promise, not yet fulfilled.

3:19: "Therefore why the law? It was put in place for the sake of the transgressors until the seed may come, to whom the promise had been made, having been administered through angels, by the agency of a mediator."

'For the sake of' was **χάριν**, meaning either, 'for the sake of' or indicating a reason for something. The law was put into place 'for the sake of the transgressors' would suggest that they would be affected in some way, possibly even encouraged to sin further. But later, in verse 24, Paul explained that the law's purpose had been a strict 'schoolmaster' to point believers to Christ (see verse 24, below). The 'mediator' here was likely Moses, who was the mediator of the law between God and the sinful Israelites. The mention of 'angels' as administrators was puzzling, since the OT had no record of angels as administrators of the law (Bruce, p. 176), and the idea is best left open for now.

3:20: "But a mediator is not for one party only, but God is one."

In this verse about a mediator, it is, first, obvious that there are always two or more parties represented by a mediator.

Broad Focus: The Argument from Scripture
Galatians 3:10-14

'The Curse of the Law' Galatians 3:10: Deut. 27:26:

The Shechemite Dodecalogue: 12 curses were delivered by the Levites standing on Mt. Ebal. The blessings were also mentioned in chapter 28: verses 1 through 6. This was a ceremony emphasizing the curses established by God for, generally, certain 'secret crimes.' The people would respond with an 'Amen' after each curse was read by the Levites.

Paul was quoting the 12th curse: the more comprehensive act. Paul was generalizing the 'Law' here to mean the whole written Torah. Those Jews who chose to live 'under the Law' were living under this particular curse.

The reason they were cursed: they were not 'confirming the words of the Law by doing them.' In other words, the curse came because they were not <u>practicing</u> the Law.

NOTE: There was no place in this 'Dodecalogue' for earning merit by keeping them. Also, no one was capable of keeping the <u>whole Law</u>: therefore, **EVERYONE** came under this curse.

Verse 11: Paul's new life regarding justification (Hab. 2:4b) and summary of his views on justification:

The Law was inadequate for justification purposes, but universal in its application to all Jews or Gentiles. All humankind was under the curse (**Deut. 27:26**), and was publicly displayed (**Deut. 21:23**). Thus, the Law's purpose was to put Jews under the curse, not bring justification (**Lev. 18:5**).

1. Justification is based only on Christ's death on the cross: He was our "scapegoat." (Bruce)
2. The cross experience by Christ is capable of freeing us from the curse. He took the curse for us.
3. But **faith in Christ** was mandatory to make the application effective. Faith counterbalanced the curse of the Law and produced life (**Hab. 2:4b**).
4. Justification before God was the result of accepting Christ as the perfect sacrifice for the individual's sin, whether Jew or Gentile. The reception of the Holy Spirit was the validation given by God to the Christian: whether Jew or Gentile.

SUMMARY VIEW

Paul's View of Justification
Justification by works of the Law: ROAD CLOSED!
BUT: This road is open: *Justification by Faith alone!*

3:12: Refer to Lev. 18:5 "You shall therefore keep my statutes and my rules; if a person does them, he shall live by them:

3:13: Refer to Deut. 21:23: This passage referred to a stoned man who was hung on a tree to show others that person was cursed. Christ took the curse upon Himself. He was the substitute, providing the basis of justification.

Verse 14: *The finale: Two Purpose Clauses:*

1. He took the curse upon Himself in order that the Gentiles may receive the blessings of Abraham.
2. He also did it in order that 'we' (Jews and Gentiles: <u>both groups</u>) might receive the promise of the Spirit through faith.

BROAD VIEW
Outline of Galatians 3:21-29: *"The Old and the New"*

"The Covenant from God Revived"

I. Topic 1, the Abrahamic Covenant: "The Law vs. The Abrahamic Covenant"

"Is the Law contrary to the Promises made By God to Abraham?" 3:21-22.

  A. 3:21: This was a possible inference that some people, reading the earlier section about the Law, might have supposed that Paul was making. But Paul answered that question by affirming very strongly: "No Way!!!" Both the promises made to Abraham and the Law transmitted to Moses were from God. Both had their validity by God.

  B. A hypothetical condition introduced by "if" indicated that they had different functions:

    1. The Promises produce life and righteousness through faith (inferred).
    2. The Law cannot produce righteousness, otherwise righteousness would come by the Law.
    3. The Law imprisons the whole human race under sin for a single purpose: that the Promise of faith in Jesus Christ may be given to those who will believe. 3:22.

II. Topic 2, The Law: "The message of the Law" 3:23-25.

  A. Prior to the coming of Faith, Jewish Christians were under a guardian, being confined and restricted in their freedom until the promised Faith in Christ would be revealed, 3:23.

B. The metaphor from life: the "pedagogue" refers to the Law as a "baby sitter" for young children (7 to 19 or sometimes 20). The "baby-sitter" was:
   1. Restrictive: the child was under the control of the pedagogue.
   2. Temporary: once the child reached the age of adulthood, then the 'pedagogue' was no longer needed. When Christ came, the Law was no longer necessary (3:24-25).

III. Topic 3, the "Message to Gentile Christians" 3:26-29.
   A. Gentile Christians had a new status: "You are all sons of God through faith in Christ Jesus," 3:26.
   B. As many of 'you' who were baptized in Christ, 'you' were clothed by Christ: 'you' took on His robe that produced righteousness, 3:27.
   C. The revolutionary result of the passing of the pedagogue (the Law):
      1. The old class distinctions of "Jew" and "Gentile" were gone.
      2. The old distinctions of "slave" and "free" were no longer in force.
      3. Even the class distinctions between male and female were erased.
      4. "You yourselves (all) were one in Christ."
      5. "You have become Abraham's seed, grafted into the family line: you were now heirs right along with the Jewish Christians." 3:29

The Text: '*The Purpose and Freedom from the Law*' Galatians 3:21-25:

3:21: "Therefore, (is) the law contrary to the promises [of God]? Certainly not! For if the law which has the power to produce life, in the same way, righteousness would be from the law:"

The law could not produce life; only the promise of life by faith alone was capable of producing life. The law and the promises did not conflict; but they were different. One convicted the sinner of sin and death; the other provided life through acquittal and eternal life.

3:22: "But the Scripture has included all under (the power of) sin, in order that the promise of faith may be given to those who are believing."

Although the law did produce more sin, it was also the means by which men were convicted of sin, and therefore, the need for a Savior was also established.

3:23: "Before faith came we were guarded and being confined under law, until the revelation of the faith that was to come."

'Before justification by faith came by Christ, Jews and Gentiles were under guard, having been confined in the prison-house of the law.

3:24: "So the law has been our schoolmaster until (the coming of) Christ, in order that we might be justified by faith:"

The law was school-master (παιδαγωγός) until Christ came and provided an alternative legal situation for men and women.

3:25: "But (now) that faith has come, we are no longer under a custodian."

The person who applied justification by faith was then free.

***The Resulting Effect: Jews and Gentiles are united in Christ*: Galatians 3:26-29:**

3:26: "For you all are sons of God through faith in Christ Jesus:"

The effect of faith in Christ was a family unity defined as sons of God.

3:27: "For everyone of you were baptized into Christ, you put on Christ."

'Put on Christ' was ενδύσασθε, was 'to put on,' as a robe.

3:28: "(In Him) not one is a Jew nor a Gentile, not one is a slave nor a free person, not one is a man, nor a woman, for all of you are one in Christ Jesus."

All categories of people who were formerly very divisive were now unified as one in Christ Jesus.

3:29: "And if you (are) of Christ, therefore you are the seed of Abraham, heirs according to the promise."

These same individuals were now the (plural) seeds of Abraham, now heirs (κληρονόμοι, 'lottery winners') of the promise made to Abraham 4,000 years ago.

GALATIANS CHAPTER 4

'Heirs and slaves: Differences and Similarities' Galatians 4:1-2:

4:1: "But I say, as long as the heir is a child, he does not differ at all from a slave, although being the master of all."

"**But I say, as long as the heir is a child he does not differ at all from a slave….**" Paul here drew a distinction between the child- heir of a household and a common slave of that house. There was a limitation upon the heir-apparent. In real life, Paul explained by using a metaphor of a large property holder, that the son was under the direction of a guardian and even teachers for a time that was appointed by the father of the house. The power of the son was strictly limited. In Jewish tradition, the son was under a steward; there were managers appointed for the son in the Mosaic Law. In Greek or Roman families, the same controls were placed over sons. Even though the son would inherit all the holdings of his father, the son could not be distinguished from the household slaves: they played together and often formed close relationships.

"...although being the master of all." The son, however, would remain subservient only while he grew into maturity. Although he was the future master of the household, he had no special 'rights' until that time came.

4:2: "But he is under guardians and stewards until the appointed day of the father."

But a day would come, decided by the father, when the son would be declared 'heir,' typically at maturity.

4:3: "So also we, when we were children, we were enslaved under the rudimentary elements of the world:"

The point of the 'children/heirs' related to the early lives of Christians. They were enslaved by the cultural mores of the world order until the proper time came. 'Children,' **νήπιοι**, were young people who had not reached legal age, and were considered minors (BDAG). The 'rudimentary elements' **στοιχεία**, possibly referred to the 'foundational principles' of religion, education, and cultural traditions of their culture, whether they were Greek, Roman, Jewish, or other Gentile races. The identification with the 'world' would seem to indicate this conclusion, all of which was overturned when Christ and His unifying salvation leveled all human cultures into one people, with one religion, one set of moral standards, and one supernatural future destiny, all initiated by a truly 'free' people, bound together by a new kind of love.

4:4: "But when the fullness of time came, God sent out His Son, being born of a woman, being made under the law,"

Christ came at the appropriate time and ordained by God the father. The 'how' and the timing were also under God's control. Christ came as any other human being would come into this world. He was born of a woman, although from a supernatural cause. He was also born as a Jew, under rudimentary elements of a Jewish culture and law. Christ was sent on a mission: **ἐκ + ἀποστέλλω**, 'to send someone out on an official mission for a specific objective' (BDAG). The timing of His arrival; the arrangements of how; the nation of His origin; and the specific nature of the mission were all originated by God the Father. Christ was also separated from His home: the **ἐκ** indicated a separation from one place to another.

4:5: "in order that He may ransom those under the law, in order that we may receive our son-ship."

"...Ransom...." was ἐξαγοράσῃ, 'to liberate a person out of' a difficult situation. It was often used this way to 'buy a slave out of the slave market,' and so rescue him (or her) from a cruel taskmaster. It could also have been used to buy off the claims of an injured man by interceding with a payment of money. Both of these meanings (from BDAG) could have been applicable here to indicate the ransom that was required to be paid with a third party intervention. Christ was that intervening party between a righteous God the Father and a sinful mankind. The 'son- ship' was υἱοθεςὶαν, 'a legal adoption,' between man and God. The verb **"we may receive"** was in the subjunctive mode, indicating that the possibility for the adoption exists for all those under the law. To activate that 'adoption' would have been initiated when an individual accepted the adoption made possible by the One who intervened on Mankind's behalf. God did not, nor would not, force people to be adopted against their will.

4:6: "And because you are sons, God sent out the Spirit of His Son into our hearts, crying out, Father, Father!"

"And because you are sons," Paul here explained that the gift of the Holy Spirit was given only to those individuals who were identified as sons (and daughters) within the realm of the adoption requirements.

"...God sent out the Spirit of His Son into our hearts, crying out, Father, Father!" The word, 'sent out' was the same word that Paul used in verse 4 when God 'sent out' His Son: ἐκ + ἀποστέλλω. Like Christ, the Holy Spirit was sent out from heaven on a special assignment. He was to populate the hearts of the adopted children. What the Spirit of God was crying out was 'Father! Father!' the Αββα was 'Father!' in Aramaic, one of the native languages of Palestine. The Ὁ πατήρ was 'Father!' in Greek, the universal language known throughout the Roman world at the time. The language was therefore no barrier for the adopted children to communicate with their Father, God. The phrase, 'Abba, Father' originated by Christ when He addressed God the Father in prayer at Gethsemane. It was repeated by Paul in Romans 8:15 and in this passage in Galatians, it indicated that believers had the same way of communication with God the Father as Christ did. 'Our hearts' made this a universal statement of Christian fact. Paul included himself as an equal partner with all believers in that process.

31

4:7: "Thus you are no longer a slave, but a son: and if a son, (you are) an heir through God."

"**Thus you are no longer a slave….**" Believers are thus (because of being adopted into the family of God) no longer a slave. Believers were no longer slaves to sin, but now they were slaves to Christ, because He paid the ransom for their freedom.

"**…but a son….**" The transaction that was accomplished by Christ included a freedom from sin's consequences, but also a new status of 'Son-ship' was conferred on every believer. These sons and daughters were the privileged few who were adopted by God the Father into His family.

"**…and if a son, (you are) an heir through God.**" 'If' set up a conditional statement (a protasis). Not all who recognized God or Christ would have been so honored. They had to come to God through Christ, humbly submitting to Him for adoption, occurring in a two-step process: conversion first, which immediately activated justification by God the Father and a communication link with Christ as Savior and Lord. The second process occurred over time: 'sanctification,' ἁγιάζω, not cited here, but was a major part of the Christian's walk. It meant, 'to make holy,' (Christ-like), and when applied to believers, completed the idea of Son-ship (see Acts 26:18 which revealed its source: 'faith in Christ' through the application of the Word of God, (John 17:19). The Holy Spirit was also involved in this process, as cited by Paul in I Cor. 6:11. 'Heir' was κληρονόμος, literally, a legal 'position' that was 'assigned' by an official.

'Christ needs to be formed in you' Galatians 4:8-20

4:8: "But formerly, not having known God, you were enslaved by nature to those beings which are not gods."

Paul here reminded them of their past, when they were enslaved by their own depraved nature to things that were not gods. They were now facing a major heresy that would drag them back into slavery. 'Not having known (an intensive perfect participle which emphasized, 'continually')' was εἰδότες, from οἶδα, 'not having known from your cultural traditions,' a knowledge that had been passed down from one generation to another.' This knowledge differed from the γινώσκω kind of 'knowing' in both the depth and the quality of knowing. Paul recognized here that they did not even have the cultural knowledge in their heritage to help them 'know' God. Consequently, they were enslaved by their own nature to those 'non-gods.' The 'intensive' perfect tense here stressed the 'continual nature' of their ignorance.

4:9: "But now (you), having come to know God, but rather, having been known by God, how is it that you turn again to the weak and beggarly elements, to which you desire again to be enslaved?"

"But now (you), having come to know God, but rather, having been known by God…." In their new life in Christ, the Galatians now 'have come to know God.' The aorist participle was ingressive, stressing the beginning of the action of 'knowing.' Here, and in the passive voice ('having been known'), Paul used the γινώσκω kind of 'knowing.' They had advanced beyond 'knowing' through a cultural tradition; they now 'knew God deeply, experientially and personally.' Furthermore, God also knew them in the same way.

"…how is it that you turn again to the weak and beggarly elements, to which you desire again to be enslaved?" 'Having known freedom, and being enslaved again?' Paul used confrontational language here to make a serious point. In their practices by Judean zealots, God was deep and remote. 'How could you return to the old religion which was so powerless? And why would you want to assist other believers to where they were before conversion? It was legalism with a new twist.

4:10: "You observe days and months and seasons and years."

Paul here pointed out one of their heretical practices. In order to gain favoritism with God, and gain a higher form of salvation, they were told they had to celebrate the Jewish calendar, and (according to Bruce, p. 205) were encouraged to accept circumcision. According to Paul, these rituals added 'works' to salvation for these Gentiles, which invalidated salvation by faith.

4:11: "I fear for you lest somehow in vain I labored for you."

Paul's expression of fear for them was deep and genuine. He labored for them and they responded well. Now they were about to be lost in a religious world of works, pride, and excessive accomplishment that was not real. They were being tempted to give up salvation by faith alone for a Judaic system of salvation by works alone.

4:12: "Brethren, I beg you, become as I myself (am), even as I (became) like you. You did me no wrong."

'Become as I am,' in other words, 'imitate me.' 'I (became) like you,' or 'I became your parent.' Paul was thus identifying with the Galatians.

33

4:13: "And you know that, at first, I preached to you on account of the physical infirmity,"

Paul did not give enough details to identify the infirmity, and various, but highly speculative, suggestions have been put forward. But, in spite of his malady, he was driven to finish his missionary trip with them.

4:14: "And your trial (I caused) by my physical infirmity you did not despise nor reject, but, as an angel of God you received me, as Christ Jesus (Himself)."

'Your trial' was the accepted reading by Aland (et al.), *The Greek New Testament,' the fourth revised edition*, although a variant reading was 'my trial,' found in some translations. 'Your trial' suggested that Paul's physical appearance caused the Galatians to undergo a test of how to accept him with this physical malady. They passed the test, and accepted Paul as they would have accepted an angel, or even Christ Himself.

4:15: "Therefore, where (is) your blessing (now)? For I testify to you, that if (it were) possible, having plucked out your eyes, you (would) have given (them) to me."

Back to the issue at hand: 'What happened to your happiness now that some of you have accepted the claims of the Judaizers?' 'Blessing' was μακαρισμός, 'being favored,' or, from its related noun, μακάριος, 'feeling privileged' (BDAG). The 'eye' issue could have related to the kind of malady that Paul was experiencing at the time, perhaps an infection that was swollen and weepy.

4:16: "Therefore, have I become your enemy by speaking the truth to you?"

The seriousness of following the Judaizers would also result in the Galatians treating Paul as an enemy, if they followed them. Paul tried to bring them back by saying, "If you follow them, you are choosing to become my enemy. Do you realize the seriousness of your actions?" 'Speaking the truth' or 'telling the truth' (BDAG) was ἀληθεύων, in a present progressive participle, emphasizing the continual action of 'speaking the truth.' The verb form was rare in the NT, used only twice: here, and in Ephesians 4:15.

4:17: "They are courting you for no good purpose, but they want to shut you off (from Christ) in order that you may show great interest in them."

"They are courting you for no good purpose...." 'Courting' was ζηλούσιν, from ζηλόω, usually meaning 'to be zealous about something.' But here, the word carried the meaning of 'being zealous over you,' to the point that they were putting pressure on the Galatians to change their theological position.

BDAG explained the idea well with the comment, 'to court someone's favor with the implication of desiring the other to be on one's own side.' The Judaizers were cleverly complimenting them in various ways in order to gain their support. But, as Paul said here, for no good purpose, **οὐ καλῶς**, literally, 'not beautifully,' or here, 'not in a manner free from objection' BDAG). They had ulterior motives for their manipulative actions.

"**...but they want to shut you off (from Christ) in order that you may show great interest in them.**" The purpose of their catering to the Galatians was made clear by Paul. 'Shut you off' was **ἐκκλεῖσαι**, from **ἐκκλείω**, 'to exclude' or 'withdraw from fellowship,' (BDAG). They willfully wanted 'to exclude the Galatians from Christ.' This was why they acted so graciously to the Galatians, hoping that they might show 'great interest' (again, **ζηλοῦτε**, from **ζηλόω**) in their message and cause.

4:18: "But it is well to express zeal in a good thing always, and not only in my presence with you."

Usually the verb **ζηλόω** is a positive virtue; Paul pointed that out here. It was especially good if they expressed zeal when Paul was absent, which would have been complimentary. But in this case, they revealed a gullibility that shocked Paul. They needed more maturity to resist the persuasive arguments of heresy.

4:19: "My children, whom I again experience birth pangs until Christ may be formed in you:"

Paul concluded this section by expressing his genuine concern for them and sharing with them the effect this news had on Paul himself. 'May be formed' was **μορφωθῇ**, referred to their lack of maturity and hope for future spiritual growth.

4:20: "And I would like to be present with you now and to change my tone, because I am disturbed by you."

Paul longed to be present with them. His 'tone' (**φωνήν**, 'voice sound') in this letter was harsh, because he was so disturbed (**ἀπορoῦμαι**, 'confused') by their tepid response.

'A Lesson from the Torah' Galatians 4:21-31:

4:21: "Tell me, those who want to be under the law, do you not hear the law?"

Paul here selected a lesson from the Torah to make a point about those who want to live under the restrictions and limitations of the law. He was addressing those Galatians who were inclined to believe the Judaizers, and were ready to live under the law. It was unknown how many of the Galatians were ready to follow those Judaizers, but it was possibly not a majority. Nevertheless, the threat was real, and would have caused a split in the church had Paul not intervened. Paul's tactic was to use the law to make his point that Christ represented the only legal way that believers could approach God without condemnation.

4:22: "For it has been written that Abraham had two sons, one by a slave-girl, and one by the freewoman."

Here Paul was referring to Ishmael and Isaac. But only one was legally the heir.

4:23: "But the one from the slave-girl had been born according to the flesh and one from the freewoman. But the one from the freewoman (was) through (the word) of promise.

According to Bruce (p. 216), the practice of having a child with a maid-servant was socially acceptable in that day, and rules in the Code of Hammurabi stated that the inheritance was to be split equally among the sons of each, although the son of the wife was to have the first pick of the proceeds. 'Promise' here was ἐπαγγελὶας, 'the word of God's promise' (BDAG) to Abraham and Sarah, representing the legality and full inheritance of the Isaac line.

4:24: "Such things are allegorical symbols: for there are two covenants, one from Mount Sinai which gives birth to bondage, which is Hagar."

"Such things are allegorical symbols...." 'Allegorical symbols' was ἀλληγορούμενα, a figure of speech indicating 'an analogy or likeness to express something,' BDAG. It was a verbal idea expressing something real, but using that image for 'another' purpose, ἄλλο 'other' + ἀγορεύω in Attic Classical Greek, meant 'to speak in the assembly,' (from Thayer and Liddell and Scott). The word was expressed here as a present participle, 'stated in allegorical symbols,' a form of a typological allegory, 'a narrative from OT history is interpreted in terms of the new covenant,' (Bruce, p. 217).

"There are two covenants...." 'Covenants' was διαθῆκαι, meaning a pact, or a binding statement by God alone, not requiring agreement between two parties (BDAG). It was often used as a last will and testament. One covenant was applied to Ishmael, the other to Isaac.

"from Mount Sinai which gives birth to bondage, which is Hagar...." Here Paul explained the first covenant, as applied Ishmael's mother, Hagar.

The Mount Sinai covenant connected Ishmael's inheritance with the giving of the law at Mt. Sinai, which also resulted in bondage.

4:25: "For this Hagar (represents) Mt. Sinai in Arabia: but it corresponds to (the) present Jerusalem, for it is enslaved with its children."

Geographically, the covenant of God assigned Ishmael's descendants to Mt. Sinai in Arabia. But just as there were two covenants of God, one for Isaac and one for Ishmael, there were two Jerusalem, the present, 'earthly Jerusalem' and the heavenly Jerusalem introduced in verse 26. The 'present Jerusalem' was infiltrated by 'Ishmaelites' who had enslaved the city by the law.

4:26: "But the Jerusalem above is free, which represents the mother of us (Sarah):"

The destiny of believers, however, was located in the 'free' city of Jerusalem, which was located in the spiritual realms of God's heaven. By implication, the 'now' city of Jerusalem was populated by slaves to sin, and headed for destruction, which actually occurred in 70 A.D. during the Jewish wars against Rome.

4:27: "For it has been written, *'Rejoice O barren,*
You who do not bear!
Break forth and shout,
You who are not in labor!
For the desolate has many more children
Than she who has a husband.'"

This quote was from Isaiah 54:1, a prophecy celebrating the barren Jerusalem after the Babylonian captivity (Bruce, p. 222). But like Sarah, in time, 'New Jerusalem' will flourish again. Paul saw in 'New Jerusalem' the vast influx of the Gentile church population as evidence of that growth and prosperity, and as a fulfillment of that prophecy. 'Old Jerusalem,' under God's judgment, was being destroyed, with the legalism that it fostered for generations. It was now the 'Jerusalem Now,' which was bereft of God's power and desolate. It was replaced by the 'Jerusalem Above,' populated by those who entered the door by faith alone through Christ.

4:28: "But you yourselves, brothers and sisters, according to Isaac, are the children of promise."

Now Paul identified the Gentile and Jewish believers as the children of promise. 'Promise' was ἐπαγγελίας, God's formal announcement concerning 'those born because of the promise' (BDAG) applied now to Christ's followers.

The emphatic 'you' was added by Paul to stress this very special status of the Galatian believers, especially in light of the seeming 'authority' that the Judaizers possibly used, by quoting the story of Abraham and Sarah, in order to try to convince them that they should be Jewish first, then Christian. But Paul affirmed here that they were already children of Abraham because of Christ.

4:29: "But even as it was then, the one born according to the flesh persecuted the one born according to the Spirit, even so (it is) now."

Just as Hagar persecuted Sarah before Isaac was born, and Ishmael persecuted Isaac, the Galatian believers should have expected persecution from the opposing forces of Judaism in Paul's day. The Galatians should have seen the Judaizers as enemies of Christ and the gospel.

4:30: "But what does the Scripture say? 'Cast out the slave woman and her son: the son of the slave woman shall not inherit with the son of the freewoman."

Hagar and Ishmael were sent away, as ordered by God. Ishmael would not share the inheritance with Isaac. The slave woman's son was cast out, without any rights whatever to the Promised Land. In the same way, the Galatian believers were to look upon the Judaizers as 'sons of the slave-woman.' Their flawed message should be rejected, and they should be sent away. This reference was from Genesis 21:10 and it was the order of Sarah to Abraham. Shortly thereafter, God ordered Abraham to do so.

4:31: "Therefore, brothers and sisters, we are not a child of the slave woman, but (we are) a child of the freewoman."

Paul now affirmed his conclusion on the identity of the children of Christ. The Galatians now had the OT story as evidence of that crucial fact.

'Freedom from Legalism' Galatians 5:1-15:

5:1: "Christ set us free us with liberty: therefore stand fast, and stop being entangled again by a yoke of slavery."

'Set us free' was ἠλευθέρωσεν, from ἐλευθερόω, meaning 'to set free' (BDAG), either from slavery or captivity. 'With liberty' was an instrumental dative with the definite article, revealing a specific kind of freedom that was instrumental in Christ freeing believers (Bruce, p. 226). 'Stand fast' was στήκετε from στήκω, a late form of ἵστημι, 'to stand fast' (BDAG), a present progressive verb, expressing a 'continual action'. 'Stop being entangled' was ἐνέχεσθε from ἐνέχω, literally, 'to hold in,' but here, 'be held by entangling' or 'to be constrained within by being trapped' (Thayer). The 'yoke' ζυγῷ, an instrumental dative used negatively here as a burden 'of slavery' that was placed on oxen, and in this case, metaphorically, referring to the Galatians who submitted themselves to this heresy.

5:2: "Behold, I myself Paul say to you that if you may be circumcised, Christ will profit you nothing."

The emphatic 'I' here ('I myself' in the Greek text) stressed that Paul was declaring that this practice of circumcision was not only unnecessary, but theologically detrimental to their entire belief system.

5:3: "And I declare again to every man being circumcised, that he is under the obligation (of the law) to do the whole law."

For a strong emphasis, Paul repeated his allegation that it was detrimental, and revealed just how it was devastating to them. Jewish circumcision was not a symbol of faith to the Jews, but a 'sign' that the person was 'righteous before God' on the basis of practicing the Mosaic Law. They differed on how much of the law was required by them, but it varied from about 50% for the more liberal Hillel Pharisees, to 99% in the more extreme Shammai Pharisees. Paul here shattered those notions by declaring that a person would have to follow the Law 100% of the time, not possible even for the most devout Jews. Thus it was impossible to rely on the Law for salvation.

5:4: "You are being released from Christ, those who are (trying to be) made righteous by the law, you fell away from grace."

The consequence of relying on the Law for salvation was 'to be released from Christ.' 'Released' was κατηργήθητε, from καταργέω, an aorist indicative passive, indicating that there was another force at work to separate them from Christ. The meaning of this verb was key: 'to cause the release of someone from an obligation (one has nothing more to do with it),' (BDAG). The Galatian believer who added circumcision to his theology has been fully released from his obligation to Christ for being saved by faith through God's grace. The result was catastrophic: 'you no longer have Christ as Savior.' 'You fell (ἐξεπέσατε, from: ἐκ 'out of' + πίπτω 'to fall') from grace.' The ἐκ in the compound verb intensified the lofty place from which the victim fell. The fall was fatal: the person had lost the grace of God.

5:5: "For we ourselves are waiting expectantly by the Spirit for (the) hope of righteousness by means of faith."

In contrast, Paul and all the other believers (note the emphatic 'we,') were anticipating the assurance of being declared righteous by God. The trigger for that event occurred at conversion, when the sinner accepted Christ as his or her own personal Savior, an act initiated by faith alone, not works. There were two instrumental datives in this verse: 'by the Spirit,' and 'by faith.' The Holy Spirit participated individually in conversion; the act of faith was the initiating force of salvation, and was rooted in Christ, who had earned the ability to declare righteous the repentant sinner.

5:6: "For in Christ Jesus neither circumcision nor uncircumcision is capable (of) anything, but faith being activated through love (is everything)."

Paul declared here that circumcision had no affect whatever on salvation. It was incapable of adding anything to the religious life of the Christian. Nor should it matter to Gentile Christians or Jewish Christians. They were now one people under God. The new order of the day was equality between the two groups, and was represented as a major cultural change that some, perhaps many Jewish Christians, could not fully grasp, nor accommodate into their thinking. Perhaps these Jewish Christians gave support to the Judaizers, placing additional internal pressure upon Gentile Christians to adopt at least some of the Jewish rituals, especially circumcision.

'Activated' was ἐνεργουμένη, from ἐνεργέω, meaning 'faith expressing itself through love,' (BDAG). The voice was taken here to be passive, not middle. There was the force of the Holy Spirit at work whose active participation created the conditions for faith to engage.

5:7: "You ran beautifully: who prevented you not to be persuaded by the truth?"

Paul was shocked that the Galatians relented so easily. 'Beautifully' was the adverb, καλῶς, sometimes, like its noun form, καλός, meant 'good.' However, it is the aesthetic term for something pleasing, or lovely, or stunningly beautiful. The Galatians ran exceptionally well; Paul wondered what had happened. Who were these heretics who were so persuasive that they caused the Galatians to veer so radically off course?

5:8: "This persuasion (is) not from the One who calls you."

This 'persuasion,' πεισμονή, also referred to in verse 7, indicated that there was some discussion about these new ideas, perhaps invoking debates. It was possible that some who disagreed with the ideas of the Judaizers were those who contacted Paul at Antioch on the Orontes River north of Palestine proper for his comments on the subject. Perhaps Paul, when he was with them, did not have the time to discuss the topic of circumcision. However, he now pointed out that this idea was not from Christ, who called them to His way of life. Since the origin was not from Christ, then they should know where it was from.

5:9: "A little leaven leavens the whole lump (of dough)."

A principle from bread-making could be used here that would bring clarity to the situation. Unleavened bread was used for all the Jewish rituals. The Jews considered the yeast that puffed the ritual bread up to add some foreign substance to the batter; therefore, it was a symbol of evil in the world. Paul used that same image here. A little evil affected the whole church in this way. The Judaizers were adding a little substance to Christian salvation in order to enhance it. But instead, it ruined it.

5:10: "I myself have confidence for you in the Lord that you will have no other mind: but the one troubling you will bear the judgment, whoever he may be."

Although confident in the Galatians, judgment was promised to those who troubled them. Did Paul know them? He may have thought it was one person, but not likely, although one person may have been more persuasive than the others with him.

5:11: "And if I myself, brothers, am still preaching circumcision, why am I still being persecuted (by the Jews)? Then the offense of the cross has ceased."

If Paul preached circumcision, then he would not be persecuted. Circumcision and the cross were incompatible.

5:12: "I would wish that even those who rise up against you would be mutilated."

Perhaps the circumcision knife would slip and cut them.

5:13: "For you yourselves were called in freedom, brothers: only do not use your freedom (as an opportunity) for the flesh, but through love serve one another."

Using the emphatic 'you,' Paul declared that 'you' were called to freedom. Using circumcision as an opportunity for boasting in the flesh was the key idea here. Paul had seen, as a believer, what circumcision had done to the Jews. He totally opposed it.

5:14: "For all the law has been fulfilled in one statement, by this: 'You shall love your neighbor as yourself.'"

The summary statement of the law was called for here. Love should silence boasting from circumcision. One who loved his neighbor fulfilled the whole law. It had nothing to do with circumcision.

"...**Has been fulfilled....**" was πεπλήρωται, a perfect intensive passive verb, emphasizing the *continual action* of fulfilling, irrespective of its past action of initiation, or the future action of consummation of that fulfilling. The overriding emphasis was intended to have been the fact that the law had been *continually* fulfilled, or satisfied, when the believer loved his neighbor as himself. That special love, the agape love, however, could only come from the Holy Spirit when He indwelled the believer and developed his or her character into Christ-likeness during the sanctification process of each believer. The law was continually fulfilled even in OT times through a personal and loving experience with God.

5:15: "But if you bite and devour one another, beware lest you may be consumed by one another."

'Bite' was δάκνετε, a NT hapax (used only here in the NT), 'to bite' as in a snake bite (BDAG). **"Devour"** was 'to chew each other up.' **'Consumed'** was ἀναλωθῆτε, 'destroy.' Biting, devouring and destroying were three verbs which gradually led to a sequential process of destruction. At the beginning of the confrontation, they were just biting each other with useless arguments. Then the fighting grew worse: they fought viciously with their opponents, until, finally, they were destroyed by the hate generated in the fighting. The Judaizers were capable of that kind of viciousness. The Galatian believers should just walk away from them. They should not try to engage them with arguments. They will lose, not by using the truth in an objective way, but by the subjective emotions stirred up by the arguments. These people were predators, and they must be viewed as violent and very dangerous.

'Good Fruit and Bad Fruit' Galatians 5: 16-26

5:16: "But I say, walk by the Spirit, and you may never fulfill the lust of the flesh."

Here, Paul countered any argument against Christians living a lawless kind of life, without any moral restrictions, much like the first century Jews accused Christians of living 'lawless' lives. Paul stated that the impulse for living morally was an inner drive that was produced by the Holy Spirit, rather than an external set of laws that no one had the power to live up to.

"…walk by the Spirit…." 'Walk' was περιπατεῖτε, a present progressive tense active imperative verb that stressed the idea of a continuous walk. It also implied *'walking hand in hand with Him,'* as a son might take the hand of his father while crossing a street. The son would rely on his father to determine whether it was safe to cross. The son would put his trust in the father. The act of holding hands would also involve closeness between the father and son. Walking hand in hand could also generate communication between the parent and the son. Since the father was holding his hand, the son would also be aware of the love that the father had for his son, to protect him in this way.

The meaning of the word was to physically walk, but here it was used metaphorically to indicate a life conduct over time. Since walking referred to taking one small step at a time, the pace was generally slow, but methodical, focused, and consistent, describing the way in which believers should walk by means of the Spirit. 'By the Spirit' was an instrumental dative, and was favored over 'in the Spirit,' a dative of sphere, since the Holy Spirit was providing the leadership and stimulus for the 'walk.' The believer accessed this walk by choosing to submit his or her will to the Lord. The power of the Spirit of Christ would then be engaged.

"…and you may never fulfill the lust of the flesh." 'Fulfill' was τελέσητε, from τελέω, in an aorist subjunctive form. The subjunctive mode suggested the possibility of something occurring, not a guarantee of it happening. But the promise to the believer, if it took place, was that the believer would never ('not ever,' οὐ μή) fulfill the lust of the flesh. The meaning of this verb was 'to carry out' or 'to perform' or 'keep' (BDAG). This represented the answer to the Jewish critics who said that Christians did not have a standardized moral law by which to live. It was the 'internalized law of the Spirit' or the 'inner law of love,' rather than an external demand without the power to perform it.

5:17: "For the flesh lusts against the Spirit, and the Spirit against the flesh, for these are contrary to one another, in order to stop you from doing the things you may want."

Paul here described the controls over which believers walked.

"For the flesh lusts against the Spirit, and the Spirit against the flesh…." This was the constant dilemma Christians faced. They still were hampered to some degree by the old nature within. There were two opposing forces: the 'old nature' driven by forces of evil, and the 'new nature' in the person of the Holy Spirit. Both sought predominance. The battle was won when the believer submitted his or her will to the leadership of the Holy Spirit. This descriptive struggle was also identified in Scripture as the 'sanctification process,' which worked internally in the believer to produce, over time, a 'Christ-like' life.

"…for these are contrary to one another, in order to stop you from doing the things you may want." The twin forces in the life of the believer did not work together. They were in conflict, 'contrary to one another.' 'Contrary,' was ἀντίκειται, in 'opposition' (to each other). The passive voice indicated that there was at least one person behind the scene trying to influence the outcome (the Holy Spirit or Satan). Those opposing forces were in place to accomplish a specific goal. That goal was **"in order to stop you from doing the things you may want."** That conflict within the believer was constant, but Satan's efforts were still under the control of God, who always acted for the betterment of the believer. As the believer grew more mature, the conflict lessened in intensity, and growth developed more rapidly.

5:18: "And if you are led by the Spirit, you are not under (the) law."

Paul here introduced a first class condition, where the protasis ('if clause') was an assumption of truth ('let's say you were led by the Spirit'). Then, if that was the case, then the apodosis (the second clause) was correct. 'Led' was ἄγεσθε, from ἄγω, meaning 'to lead/guide morally or spiritually; lead, encourage (in the direction of)' (BDAG). It had the passive voice, indicating that the Holy Spirit was doing the leading. It was also a present progressive tense verb revealing a continual action was occurring. The Holy Spirit 'was continually leading you.' When that condition was met, then the believer *was not under the law.* 'You are,' ἔστε, was also a present progressive tense, indicating a continual action: 'You are *continually* not under the law.'

5:19: "Now the works of the flesh are clear, such things as sexual immorality, impurity, wantonness…."

The list of eighteen vices was described in verses 19 through 21. The beginning of the list started here: 'sexual immorality' Πορνεία, referred to unlawful sexual immorality, 'prostitution or fornication, etc.,' (BDAG). 'Unlawful,' that was, according to Jewish law, not Roman or Greek law. 'Impurity' was ἀκαθαρσία, 'a state of moral corruption,' (BDAG).

'Wantonness' was ἀσέλγεια, originated by an alpha privative: ἀ ('not') + σελγεὶα, where this latter portion of the word possibly came from a city in Pisidia, (Σελγεὶα), whose citizens excelled in strictness with respect to morality, and, with the alpha privative (**"not"**), it meant,, literally, 'not moral,' or, according to Thayer, 'unbridled lust,' or 'wantonness.'

5:20: "...idolatry, sorcery, hostile people, strife, jealousy, rage, contentiousness, dissensions, heresies...."

'Idolatry' εἰδωλολατρὶα, was a major deviation according to Paul and Jewish law. 'Sorcery' was **φαρμακεὶα**, related also to drugs, sometimes combined with the magic arts and idolatry (Thayer). 'Hostilities' was **ἔχθραι,**(plural) people who hated or were hostile, (Thayer). 'Strife' was **ἔρις**, 'a contentious engagement in rivalry,' or 'quarrels about some issue' (BDAG). 'Jealousy' was **ζῆλος**, 'intense negative feelings over another's achievements or success,' or 'envy' (BDAG). 'Rage' was **θυμοὶ**, (plural) examples of 'a state of intense displeasure, indignation, or rage,' (BDAG).

'**Contentiousness**' was **ἐριθεὶα**, the debated meaning of which possibly denotes 'strife borne of selfish contentiousness' (BDAG). 'Dissensions' was **διχοστασὶαι**, (plural) 'the state of being in factious opposition,' (BDAG). The origin of the word was from the literal idea of 'to stand apart,' which created tension from an ensuing and vocal dissension (Thayer).

The last word on the list in this verse was '**heresies**,' from **αἱρέσεις** (plural), 'an opinion varying from the true exposition of the Christian faith' or 'heresy' (Thayer), or with 'a negative connotation, a dissension' or 'a faction' that had arisen from a heretical sect' (BDAG).

5:21: "...envy, drunkenness, revelries, and the like; of which things I said before to you, even as I said before that those who are practicing such things will not inherit the kingdom of God."

'Envy' was **φθόνοι**, a synonym of **ζῆλος**, which was similar in meaning, but the exact differences were unknown (see Thayer). 'Drunkenness' was **μέθαι**, the plural for **μέθη**, related to any intoxicating drink (Thayer). 'Revelries' was **κῶμοι**, or wild parties: 'feasts and drinking parties that are protracted till late at night and indulge in revelry' (Thayer). BDAG defined it as 'excessive feasting.' Paul concluded this vice list by declaring that those practicing such things will not inherit the kingdom of God. Paul had warned them before about this kind of conduct.

5:22: "But the fruit of the Spirit is love, joy, peace, longsuffering, gentleness, goodness, faith...."

The positive fruits were presented to offset the overall negative tone of the lengthy vice list. There were nine virtues that were recommended in verses 22 and 23.

5:23: "...gentleness, self-control, against such things the law (does) not (speak)."

The law dealt primarily with negative behavior.

5:24: "And those who are of Christ [Jesus] crucified the flesh with its passions and its lusts."

The crucifixion was applied to every believer, and the resulting effects were a considerable diminishing of those passions and lusts, often a radical 180 degree transformation.

5:25: "Since we are living in the Spirit, let us also conform ourselves to (the) Spirit."

"...If we are continually living in the Spirit...." 'Living' was ζῶμεν, a present active progressive verb, representing a continuous action. The 'active' voice indicated that believers (those living in the Spirit) had access to the action of conforming themselves to the Holy Spirit. This contract verb should not be a subjunctive mode, even if the spelling of the present subjunctive is exactly the same as the present indicative. The exhortation should probably read to live 'in the Spirit,' with the 'locative dative,' and probably not with the instrumental dative, 'by means of the Spirit.' This phrase represented the protasis (the condition which would result in a conclusion, the apodosis).

The twin actions were displayed here as two steps of deepening trust in the Holy Spirit. The first, **"Living in the Spirit"** was a prerequisite to the second action: **"let us also conform ourselves to (the) Spirit."** The first action could have represented conversion, since believers began their walk with the Spirit at conversion. But since the idea of 'living' indicated a 'continuous action,' not an instantaneous one, then this action is better understood as a Christian, but one who was not fully mature.

"...Let us conform ourselves...." was στοιχῶμεν, 'conform to His standards' or 'follow the Spirit' (BDAG), a hortatory subjunctive mode, which included a challenge to the author, resulting in a gentle command. 'Conform' was to 'be in line with the Holy Spirit as a standard to live by.' It involved 'conforming, holding onto, agreeing with, following, and adjusting the believers' lives to the image of Christ.' This phrase was the apodosis, or final stage of maturity of the believer. In this stage of growth the believer not only was well adjusted to the awareness of the Holy Spirit, but had a strong bond of communication with Him. However, it must also be recognized that a believer will only reach final maturity at the Parousia (the final return of Christ).

The Challenge for believers here was for them to reach to out toward the final fruit of advanced maturity with the 'fruits of the Spirit,' listed in verses twenty-two to twenty-three. The fruits of (conforming to) the Spirit were: **"love, joy, peace, patience, kindness, goodness, faithfulness, gentleness, self-control"** which could not be obtained by following the law, only through the development of a believer's growth by submitting to the Holy Spirit.

5:26: "Let us not become boastful, challenging one another, envying one another."

There are three more vices to avoid: 'bragging about one's gifts,' 'provoking one another,' or even by privately or publicly 'expressing envy against one another.'

'Bearing Burdens' Galatians 6:1-10:

6:1: "Brothers, even if a man may be caught beforehand in some trespass you yourselves who are spiritual restore such a person in a spirit of gentleness, considering yourself, lest you also may be tempted."

Paul now turned to those Galatians that perhaps had responded positively to the Judaizers, or if they were at fault in other wrongdoings. How should the churches of Galatia handle those guilty of certain sins? The restoration process was outlined below.

"Brothers, even if a man may be caught beforehand in some trespass…." Paul gave an example of a person caught beforehand in some sin or heretical issue. Now that person wanted to be reinstated to the church. How should that be accomplished?

"…you yourselves who are spiritual restore such a person in a spirit of gentleness…." Paul recommended a gentle and forgiving approach. He identified the best persons to handle the issue were 'spiritual' individuals, not necessarily church leaders. He addressed those persons with the emphatic 'you' in the plural, ὑμεῖς, perhaps indicating the convening of a small group meeting.

"…considering yourself, lest you also may be tempted." Their attitude must be humble, because they could be in the same situation in the future. 'Considering' was σκοπῶν, from σκοπέω, which meant, 'to observe,' but also indicated a 'careful scrutiny,' as opposed to a simple glance (Thayer).

Christians who counseled other believers had to know themselves well, and realize that some situations may even 'tempt' them. 'Tempt' was πειρασθῇς, from πειράζω, 'to test one's faith by enticement to sin' (Thayer). Note the passive subjunctive, indicating someone else may be in control of the tempting (Satan?); the subjunctive mode was the mode of possibility, not certainty. Therefore, Christian counselors were advised to be humble, understanding, and introspective when counseling such a person.

6:2: "Bear the burdens of one other, and thus fulfill the law of Christ."

Although the following advice could refer to general situations, it was also quite possible that Paul was still speaking about the counseling session noted above. The context here seems to suggest the latter.

"Bear the burdens of one other…." Counselors also must be selfless and caring about others during such a session.

"…and thus fulfill the law of Christ." When done properly, a good outcome was likely, which was a fulfillment of the 'law of Christ.' The 'law of Christ' was a rebuttal to the Judaizers who blamed Christians for being 'lawless,' since believers did not recognize the OT law as a requirement for salvation.

6:3: "For if anyone thinks (himself) to be something while being nothing, he is deceiving himself."

Paul will again address this issue of the 'nothings' and the 'somethings' again in I Corinthians 1:28. Christians should recognize that they were undeserving 'nothings' that God had chosen to 'adopt' as 'children of God.' But Christians should not revel in that choice, and think they were the 'somethings,' to whom others should 'bow before.' In God's eyes believers were the 'somethings.' In the believer's eyes and in the eyes of unbelievers in general, they were the 'nothings.' 'Deceiving' was φρεναπατᾷ, 'to mislead by an appeal to the mind' (Thayer). It was also a present progressive active indicative verb indicating a 'continual' act of self-deception.

6:4: "But let each one examine his own work, and then he will have rejoicing for himself alone, and not in another."

"But let each one examine his own work…." 'Examine' was δοκιμαζέτω, a present imperative active verb, from δοκιμάζω, 'to make a critical examination of something to determine genuineness,' or 'put to the test,' (BDAG). Notice that in this verse, the person should continually (present progressive imperative) examine his 'work' to determine genuineness, not the reality of his/her faith. In other words, Christians should re-evaluate their work in order to learn, not only the effectiveness of the counseling session, but also its authenticity from Scripture: was the advice given based on objective Scriptural evidentiary truth?

"…and then he will have rejoicing for himself alone, and not in another:" If the advice passed the test, then there was reason for rejoicing. However, that rejoicing must be internal, not an outward expression that would lead to pride and arrogance.

6:5: "For each one shall bear his own load."

Now Paul seemed to transition to a general concept of bearing one's own burden. Each Christian had a specific set of circumstances that he/she must carry. That 'load' may have been due to the believer's sin before conversion; it may be the effect of sin after conversion; or it may be God's way of training and causing growth within the believer. 'Shall bear' in the future tense was βαστάσει, from βαστάζω, 'to sustain a burden,' or 'to carry' something heavy (BDAG).

6:6: "And let the one who is being taught the word share with the one who is teaching, with all good things."

The imperative verb here was Κοινωνείτω, from κοινωνέω, meaning 'to make a contribution, or share,' (BDAG). Here Paul was establishing the right of evangelists and ministers to be supported financially by the church.

The term used for 'teaching,' (BDAG), was κατηχέω, a late Greek word, not used in the LXX, and only found in the NT eight times, four by Luke, and four by Paul. Its derivation, according to Thayer, came from the meaning, 'to charm, or fascinate, with a resounding sound.' The image must have impressed both Paul and Luke when they compared the 'resounding' blend of sounds when a preacher or teacher was proclaiming the gospel. The 'preaching' was both instructive and fascinating to both Paul and Luke. The first time the word was used in this verse was the present passive participle, κατηχούμενος, representing the person 'being taught.' The second time it was used was the substantive participle, κατηχούντι, a dative (of advantage), singular, present tense participle, indicating the 'teacher.' The person being taught had the obligation to share 'all good things' with the teacher, who was making such charming and fascinating sounds while teaching or preaching.

6:7: "You do not mislead yourselves, God is not being mocked. For whatever a man may sow, this also shall he reap."

"You do not mislead yourselves; God is not being mocked…." The 'you' is often omitted by translators, because the people being addressed in a command was 'understood.' But we included it in the translation because it was embedded in the verb and it indicated a plural subject. 'Mislead' was πλανᾶσθε, from πλανάω, 'make no mistake' (BDAG). The present tense was likely progressive, indicating a continual watch was required, and a middle voice was preferred over a passive. 'Mocked' was μυτηρὶζεται, (passive) 'turn up the nose at' God (BDAG) 'without a consequence' (see vs. 7b). In the OT, the word in the LXX was used to 'mock' God's messengers (Bruce, p. 264). This word was a NT hapax, only used here in the NT.

"...**For whatever a man may sow, this also shall he reap.**" This general truism confirmed that the truth uttered in verse 7a had a definite consequence, whether they mocked God by ignoring Him, or by their conduct, or by their heretical beliefs which resulted in ignoring the gospel. However it was expressed, sin will be punished.

6:8: "Because the one sowing for his flesh shall reap from the flesh corruption, and the one sowing in the Spirit shall reap eternal life."

Paul clarified verse 7b with a metaphoric expansion. 'Flesh' was the 'unregenerate human.' They sowed for the sake of their own carnal desires, and they will so reap the consequences.

6:9: "But let us not grow weary while doing the beautiful thing, for we shall reap in our own time if we do not lose heart."

The hortatory subjunctive, ('let us' was a polite way to express a command: the writer was challenging himself as well). ἐγκακῶμεν, always with the negative, do not 'lose courage' (Thayer). 'Beautiful thing' was καλός, 'beautiful,' or 'well,' expressing a high degree of aesthetic beauty.

6:10: "Therefore, as we have opportunity, let us work the good to all, and especially to the households of the faith."

Paul's conclusion: 'Let us work the good toward all, especially to the believers, and their households. 'The good' is ἀγαθός, 'inherently good.' 'Opportunity,' is ὡς καιρός, 'as (we have) time.' 'Let us work' is ἐργαζώμεθα, especially indicated a high priority, expressed as a hortatory subjunctive, the 'gentle command.'

'Bearing Burdens' Galatians 6:11-18:

6:11: "Behold what large letters I wrote to you with my hand."

Paul at times did add a postscript in his own hand. The effect would personalize the original message to the church and authenticate it as coming from Paul. Here he wrote in especially large letters for reasons no one knows. He may have had an injury to his hand, his eyesight could have been impaired, or, he just didn't realize that his script was so large until he finished the sentence. It was also possible, but unlikely, that he wrote the entire letter himself, without the aid of a secretary, or amanuensis (Bruce, p. 268).

6:12: "As many as want to make a good showing in the flesh, these are compelling you to be circumcised, only in order that they may not be persecuted by the cross of Christ."

The Judaizers demanded that the Gentile believers be circumcised, possibly due to the pressure being applied by Jewish Zealots in Judea, known troublemakers of the period who hated Roman (and foreign) influence, and demanded strict Pharisaic religious standards on synagogues. They were a powerful and dangerous group when they policed the areas where synagogues (or churches) were found. The Judaizers who visited the Galatians churches were only interested in collecting evidence of church members who were circumcised, so they could convince those who sent them that the Christians were submitting to circumcision. 'Compelling' is ἀναγκαζούσιν, to 'force or compel by the standards of custom or tradition' (BDAG). The purpose clause, **"only in order that they may not be persecuted by the cross of Christ"** indicated that the Judaizers were subject to persecution (by the Zealots or by their church leaders). To avoid persecution they had to submit physical evidence that the male members in the Galatian region were being circumcised. But, according to Paul, that evidence was only 'to make a good showing in the flesh, and would invalidate the vital meaning of Christ's death on the cross.'

6:13: "For those who are circumcised are not keeping the law, but they want you to be circumcised in order that they may boast in your flesh."

But Paul declared here that those people in the home churches who sent the Judaizers, and the Judaizers themselves, were not keeping the law, and therefore they were left exposed to God's ultimate judgment. All they had for boasting purposes, were handfuls of 'evidence' that some Galatians were circumcised. That level of boasting resulted in arrogance and vanity.

6:14: "But may it not happen for me to boast, except in the cross of our Lord Jesus Christ, through Whom the world has been crucified to me, and I to the world."

Paul declared here that the only boasting that was beneficial was boasting about the 'cross of Jesus' which enabled Paul and all believers to personally

51

participate in the effects of Christ's suffering and, thereby, obtain Christ's rewards, metaphorically described for Paul (and all believers) being 'crucified to the world,' with all of its alluring temptations and gross misinformation.

6:15: "For neither is circumcision anything, nor uncircumcision, but (what is vital is) a new creation."

Therefore, circumcision or even being uncircumcised has no effect in the fulfilling of God's demands. They are without purpose and accomplish nothing. What is vital, however, is the accomplishment of the new birth, described here as a 'new creation,' καινὴ κτίσις, an act that results in a transformed life and a new relationship with God the Father and His son Jesus, the Messiah.

6:16: "And as many as walk according to this rule, peace and mercy (be) upon them, and the Israel of God."

Those who walk according to this rule, rather than the rule of circumcision and trying to impossibly satisfy the law of God, Paul closed his letter with this address: 'peace and mercy (be) upon them,' these who are the true Israel of God, not imposters trying to get in through the back door, which, incidently, was sealed shut.

6:17: "From now on let no one trouble me, for I bear in my body the marks of the Lord Jesus."

Paul earned his stripes from preaching the message of Jesus the Messiah: 'Come unto Me, all you who labor and are heavy laden, and I will give you rest' (Matthew 11:28). **"...Marks...."** was στίγματα,' which meant, 'a mark, brand,' (BDAG), that was used by slave owners to 'brand' their 'mark' of ownership on the body of the slave with a red hot branding iron.

6:18: "The grace of our Lord Jesus Christ (be) with your spirit, brethren: Amen.

Paul closed with this message to the Galatian believers by mentioning the grace of the Lord Jesus: 'may the special grace that belongs to the Lord Jesus Christ (be) with your spirit.' The unmerited favor (grace) of Jesus was shown to each believer at conversion; but it continued to activate and energize the soul of every believer from time to time. Paul wanted the Galatian believers to experience that activation and vitality as they mulled over these closing remarks.

Galatians
Recommended Bibliography Commentators

Abbreviations:

BRUCE *The Epistle to the Galatians, A Commentary on the Greek Text.* By F.F. Bruce, Paternoster Press and Eerdmans Publishing Company, Grand Rapids, Michigan, 1982, reprinted, 1998.

WITHERINGTON *Grace in Galatia, A Commentary on St. Paul's Letter to the Galatians.* By Ben Witherington III, William B. Eerdmans Publishing Company, Grand Rapids, Michigan and T & T Clark, LTD, Edinburgh, Scotland, 1998.

(Both books are recommended for their extensive bibliographies and thorough research)

CHAPTER 2
I THESSALONIANS

Illustration 2:
Inscription of King Philip's wife, 'Thessalonika'

The founder of Thessalonica was King Phillip, who named the city after his wife, Thessaloniki. This was an inscribed base of a statue of Thessaloniki, from about BC 175, found in the area of the ancient Agora and part of a group of statues of the family of Alexander the Great. The inscription: ΘΕΣΣΑΛΟΝΙΚΗΝ ΦΙΛΙΠΠΟΥ ΒΑΣΙΛΙΣΣΑΝ, reads, 'Thessaloniki, of Philip (the) Queen." The statue could have been a representation of an unknown goddess, or more likely, of Thessaloniki herself, with the date of the inscription about two centuries after her, and Philip's, death.

CHAPTER 2
I Thessalonians, circa AD 50

Anticipating the message of I Thessalonians: *After encouraging them, Paul gave a warning to the lazy, then exhorted them to remember their training, and think about their bright future at the coming of Christ.'*

I THESSALONIANS
Introduction

Date and Circumstances of Writing:

Date of Writing: about AD 50: Bruce's date of AD 50 seems accurate for the situation (p. xxxiv). Paul, having fled the persecution that had arisen from unbelieving Jews in Thessalonica, went on to Berea, where the Jews were much more responsive than Thessalonica. However, after some initial success at the Berean synagogue there, Jews from Thessalonica heard about Paul's presence at Berea, and caused an uproar there also. On their arrival, Paul was sent on to Athens while Timothy and Silas remained in Berea. On his arrival at Athens, Paul sent those who accompanied him back to Berea with word for Silas and Timothy to join him at Athens as soon as possible (Acts 17:1-15).

The Circumstances of the writing. Since Paul was forced to leave Thessalonica prematurely, he realized that he needed to give the Thessalonian believers much more instruction about certain elements of the faith which he did not have time to explain. Also he was concerned about the outcome of the persecution that had arisen causing Paul to be rushed out of the city. Therefore, at some time, either when Timothy joined him in Corinth, or at Athens, he sent Timothy to see if the uprising at Thessalonica had settled down, and check on the status of the church there.

(I Thessalonians 3:1-6). Meanwhile, Paul preached a sermon to the philosophers on Mars Hill in Athens, formed the nucleus of a church, and soon departed to Corinth, where he taught in the synagogue there until Timothy arrived not long after with favorable news about the Thessalonian church. He then wrote I Thessalonians, followed sometime after by the second letter to them (Acts 17:16 to 18:4).

The Text

I Thessalonians Chapter 1: Verses 1 - 10:

1:1: "Paul and Silvanus and Timothy to the church of the Thessalonians in God (the) Father and (the) Lord Jesus Christ, grace to you, and peace."

"Paul and Silvanus and Timothy...." Paul, now in Corinth, had both his major team members, Timothy and Silas with him again, with good news about the status of the church in Thessalonica.

"...to the church of the Thessalonians in God (the) Father and (the) Lord Jesus Christ, grace to you, and peace." The 'in' here, could be translated as a 'locative' preposition, or an 'instrumental' preposition. The 'locative' dative would indicate the church in Thessalonica was 'in' God the Father's and in the Lord Jesus' presence. Taken 'instrumentally,' the church could be viewed as existing 'by means of' the twin efforts of God the Father and the Lord Jesus Christ. In this context, the locative is favored.

1:2: "We are thanking God always for all of you, making remembrance of you in our prayers, constantly..."

Paul had two declarations to reinforce to the Thessalonians: first, 'we are thanking God always for all of you.' Secondly, 'we are making remembrance of you in our prayers.' The term, 'constantly' we take as the adverb connected with the participle in verse 3.

1:3: "...remembering your work of faith and your labor of love and your perseverance of (the) hope of our Lord Jesus Christ before God and our Father."

Since Paul was now writing with the knowledge of their status from Timothy, he could be very precise as to his prayers for them. Three items are called out here by Paul: Their **"...work of faith...."** in the midst of persecution was the first. 'Faith-activated labor,' in spite of persecution, was what Paul had modeled, and what he had told them to expect. It was a labor, not to earn salvation, but because salvation was already assured.

Their **"...labor of love...."** was the second. Not only were the Thessalonians spreading the word, but they were doing it in a spirit of the 'agape' love, which had a sacrificial element, as well as a selfless and a godly aspect to its definition. It was a 'Christ-like love.'

The third recognition was **"...your perseverance (of) the hope of our Lord Jesus Christ in the presence of God and our Father.'**

'Perseverance' was ὑπομονῆς, meaning literally, 'to remain solid under any circumstance,' or 'the capacity to hold out or bear up in the face of difficulty' (BDAG). The object of that perseverance was 'the hope' ἐλπίδες, meaning 'an assurance or guarantee') of a future coming of the Lord, and the fulfilling of all His promises.

1:4: "Having known, beloved brothers and sisters, your election by God our Father,"

The 'subject' of the participle, 'having known' referred to the missionaries, Paul and his assistants. They observed the telltale signs of many authentic conversions in Thessalonica. This was a kind of knowledge that came easily by observation, the **οἶδα** kind of knowledge that came via seeing the results of true repentance. It was not the higher order thinking kind of knowledge that came from the application of serious mental study, γινώσκω. The perfect tense participle, **εἰδότες**, from **οἶδα**, indicated a past action of 'knowledge' that was acquired at the scene of their conversions. Paul affirmed his confidence that these attributes they were revealing in verse three were the results of having known by an experiential knowledge that they were truly, the 'elect' (ἐκλογήν), which meant, a 'special choice' (BDAG), by 'God the Father.' That 'knowledge' was the driving force behind Paul's exhortations.

1:5: "...because our gospel did not occur to you by word only, but also by power and by the Holy Spirit, and by a deep assurance, even as you know what kind of men we were among you for your sakes."

Paul gave the reason here that their conversion produced such a radical transformation in their lives: the 'gospel' was not just a word that was delivered by Paul, but it included three objective ingredients that transformed the lives of those who believed. The first result of the gospel as the 'power' (δυνάμει), of God (implied) that accompanied salvation. The second result was very evident to the believers and those who knew them. It was by the powerful activity of the Holy Spirit. The third result of the gospel was the profound assurance that resulted from accepting the gospel message. 'Assurance' was πολλῇ πληροφορίᾳ, 'being in a state of complete certainty,' (BDAG). That powerful impact of the gospel message was validated, not only by Paul and his missionaries, but pagan friends of the new converts. That witness of their acceptance of the gospel also was a confirmation of the kind of people Paul and his associated were; they had no material gain, or even fame by preaching the gospel. They were simply 'givers' of the truth of God. Furthermore, they sacrificed their lives doing it.

1:6: "And you yourselves became mimics of us and the Lord, having received the word with much affliction, with (the) joy of the Holy Spirit,"

The emphatic 'you' stressed the fact that they became imitators of Paul and his associates: they all suffered persecution as a result. The 'joy' they experienced was produced by the Holy Spirit in spite of the persecution.

1:7: "So that you became a pattern for all the believers in Macedonia and in all Asia."

The suffering became a pattern for others, and was talked about by Christians everywhere.

1:8: "For from you the word of the Lord sounded forth not only in Macedonia and [in] Achaia, but in every place your faith toward God has gone out, so that we have no need to speak of it."

The Thessalonians let the word out (ἐξήχηται, 'to sound out with a loud trumpet blast, (BDAG), only here in the NT, in spite of the local persecution which they endured. They became examples in southern and northern Greece.

1:9: "For they themselves declare concerning us what manner of entry we had in you, and how you turned to God from idols to serve the living and true God…"

Their conversions became well-known all over Greece, and they let Paul know their impressions. Believers in Corinth, Athens, and Berea were very impressed by the remarkable life transformations that occurred in Thessalonica.

1:10: "…and to wait for His Son from heaven, whom He raised from the dead, even Jesus, who delivers us from the wrath which is coming."

'Waiting' was ἀναμένειν, 'expecting' (BDAG) the Parousia to come imminently. The present progressive tense of the infinitive indicated that the 'waiting' was as a *continual* part of their lives. 'Christ's coming again' was also a vital part of the entire early church. It still is, or it should be, for Christians today.

'Recollections of our Visit'

I Thessalonians 2:1–12:

2:1: "For you yourselves have known, brothers and sisters, that our visit to you has not been without result,"

"For you yourselves have known, brothers and sisters…." Here, Paul was quick to remind the Thessalonian believers of the success with which his team presented the gospel when they first arrived. The emphatic 'you yourselves' was αὐτοὶ in the plural, called them as a whole to remember the original response Paul's team received on arrival. 'Have known' was οἴδατε, from οἶδα in the perfect tense, a past action, with continuing results, even into the present.

"**...that our visit to you has not been without result,**" 'Has not been' was γέγονεν, from γίνομαι, 'to become,' here in the present intensive perfect tense, a past action with the stress on the *continual* action, stressing that there were indeed *continual* results of their visit. Their arrival created a profound influence on those many people who accepted the Lord; it even had continued to be influential to the present time of Paul's writing. The believers there 'had known that fact,' making any persecution bearable.

2:2: "**...but having suffered beforehand and treated shamefully, even as you know in Philippi, we were emboldened to speak the gospel of God to you under (the condition of) great stress.**"

"**...but having suffered beforehand and treated shamefully, even as you know in Philippi....**" Two major things happened at Philippi that impacted their visit at Thessalonica. First, they suffered a physical beating by the magistrates, rendering them weak and physically in pain. Second, the punishment was illegal because they were Roman citizens (Silas was also a Roman Citizen, see Acts 16:37). 'Treated shamefully' was ὑβρισθέντες from ὑβπίζω, 'to treat someone in an insulting and spiteful manner,' (BDAG), which only explained part of the meaning, because this 'shameful treatment' (the word comes into English as 'hubris,' an excessive arrogance), was conducted illegally, all in a shame culture. The magistrates could have lost their careers, their prestige, as well as suffering the same beating, had the word gotten out that they whipped Roman citizens. The Thessalonians knew of Paul's weak physical condition on arrival.

"**...we were emboldened to speak the gospel of God to you under (the condition of) great stress.**" One might think that the missionary team of Paul and Silas would have been influenced to take some weeks off to heal their wounds after that beating. The beating actually inspired them to speak more boldly: 'we were emboldened' was ἐπαρρησιασάμεθα an aorist indicative middle voice, with the implication that a 'benefit would result in' the action 'to speak the gospel.' 'Under (the condition of) great stress' was ἀγῶνι, with a meaning likely near the English derivation, 'agony,' or 'under the stress of great opposition,' (BDAG).

2:3: "For our exhortation (was) not out of deceit nor impure motives or by means of guile,"

Many of the traveling teachers who earned a living by teaching philosophy or rhetoric were deficient in these areas. Paul and Silas were not like them. They were genuine. They were givers of a treasure that was unspeakable; they gave from their hearts, selflessly, and without asking for financial support.

2:4: "But even as we have been tested by God to be entrusted with the gospel, even so we continually speak, not as men pleasers, but (we speak) to God who tests our hearts."

'Testing' here occurred twice. The first time was δεδοκιμάσμεθα, a present perfect intensive passive voice, indicating that God 'continually,' tested their hearts. The issue was not critiquing the effectiveness of their speech, nor any philosophical analyzing. The second 'test' was δοκιμάζοντι, the present *progressive* active indicative tense indicating that God 'continually' tested their hearts in an active sense. The continuous testing by God was a guarantee that the apostle and his team were thoroughly genuine, adequate to preach the gospel and not cater to man's vanity or pride. 'Entrusted' was πιστευθῆναι, 'trustworthy.'

2:5: "For neither at any time did we use flattering words, as you have known, neither a cloak for covetousness - God is our witness."

The Thessalonians were very aware of the style of preaching that Paul and his leaders used. They differed radically from the sophists of the day who used flattery and scamming techniques to win points and degrade their opponents. The approach of Paul's team was honesty and truth.

2:6: "Nor did we seek glory from men, either from you or from others, when we might have made demands as apostles of Christ."

The sophists sought fame however they could, even if it involved pretense to fame; Paul could have even asked for financial support, which he wisely decided not to do in many occasions, as here in Thessalonica and later in Corinth.

2:7: "Being able to make demands as Christ's apostles, but we became gentle among you, as a nurse caring over her own children."

Paul's characterized his approach to the Thessalonians as very gentle, as a nurse would care for the children of the house, even though he wanted them to know that he had the authority as an apostle of Christ to ask for support.

2:8: "So affectionate (were we) of you, we were well pleased to impart to you not only the gospel of God, but also our very lives, that you became beloved to us."

'Affectionate' Ὁμειρόμενοι, only used here in the NT, 'to have a strong yearning for,' (BDAG). 'Impart' was μεταδοῦναι, a compound present progressive infinitive, μετα, 'with' + δίδωμι, 'to give,' 'a continual kind of giving.' 'Lives' was ψυχάς, sometimes meaning 'soul,' but here it was used as 'lives,' particularly since the preaching of the gospel could threaten their lives, but not their 'souls.'

2:9: "For remember, brothers and sisters, our labor and our toil: working night and day so as not to be a burden on any of you, we preached to you the gospel of God."

Since Paul made no demands of support on them, the team was forced to work hard to support themselves. Here, it seemed, that the issue at stake was that Paul did not want to be a burden on the poor saints of Thessalonica. Thus, he resorted to working, probably as a tentmaker, the trade that he was trained in, as he also did in Corinth. In Corinth, however, he likely refused support for a different reason. There were wealthy Christians in Corinth, but if they spent money for services rendered, they demanded a patronage relationship for the person they gave support to, and the strings attached could have been very onerous, often requiring 'supporters' to parade as a group, publically defending the character of their patron on a regular basis. Paul would have had to publically show support for a patron, who often had shady ethics and morals, often twice a day, with other responsibilities as well. This situation would not have worked for him even in ideal circumstances, which were not always available.

2:10: "You are witnesses, and so is God, how devout, just, and blameless our behavior was toward you believers;"

Paul had a blameless reputation which he carefully guarded. He was Christ's ambassador; and he was constantly under scrutiny by critics.

2:11: "...even as you know, as a father does his own children..."

He was a 'father' to the believers in Thessalonica, and elsewhere.

2:12: "...thus we exhorted you, encouraged you, and charged you, that you are to walk worthy of God who is calling you into His own kingdom and glory."

All three verbs here were synonyms. 'Walking worthy of God' was what God expected of His children.

'We are Grateful for You' I Thessalonians 2:13-20, to 3:1-7:

2:13: "And for this reason, we ourselves also are thankful to God always, because, having received the word of God, hearing from us, you received (it) not (as) the word of men, but even as it is truly (the) word of God, which also is being activated in you who are believing."

Paul expressed here the basis for his grateful attitude about the Thessalonian church. The original reception to the gospel was ideal: they accepted Paul's word as the word directly from God, Himself. When that word was applied to their hearts, Paul was very pleasantly surprised that it was genuine, precisely because it produced a changed life in the believers. 'Activated' was ἐνεργεῖται, meaning that the Word of God was 'effective within the life of the believer' (BDAG). The Word produced a power that altered the life of the believer through the dynamic workings of the Holy Spirit. That result was what Paul noticed among the believers in Thessalonica as a result of their conversion, and it was confirmed when they faced the obstacles of persecution and triumphantly persevered.

2:14: "For you yourselves became imitators, brothers and sisters, of the churches of God being in Judea by means of Christ Jesus, because you also suffered the same things at the hand of your own countrymen, even as (they did) by the Jews,"

'Imitators' was μιμηταὶ, 'mimics' in the sense of following the same pattern of the Judean churches (Bruce, p. 45), when they were persecuted by unbelieving Jews. This compared the persecution that was inflicted on the Judean churches, and was now inflicted on the Gentile churches in Thessalonica. Both groups were persecuted in the same way, authenticating the firm foundation which was now in evidence.

2:15: "who also killed the Lord Jesus, and the prophets, and drove us out, and (who) are not pleasing God, and contrary to all mankind,"

Jews of old were consistent in their persecutions: the Lord Jesus was murdered by them; so were the prophets of the OT. Even Paul was driven out in Thessalonica and Philippi by the Jews. These Jews were contrary to all mankind, and not as intended originally by God the Father. 'Not pleasing to God' was ἀρεσκόντων, 'to be acceptable;' they were continually (present progressive tense) *not* acceptable to God.

2:16: "…hindering us to speak to the Gentiles in order that they might by saved, for them to fill up their sins always. But the wrath overtook them to the uttermost."

The sentence from verse 14 continued in verse 16 to include the efforts by the Jews to prevent Paul even to speak to the Gentiles about salvation. The 'cup' that was filling up was already to the brim. 'Filling up' was ἀναπληρῶσαι, a compound verb, ἀνα + πληρόω, where the ἀνα intensified the filling 'to the brim.' The verb was also a present infinitive, indicating a 'continual' action.

2:17: "But we ourselves, brothers and sisters, having been orphaned from you for the time being face to face, (but) not in (our) hearts, we endeavored to see your face more eagerly with great desire."

With very affectionate language, Paul described his longing to visit the believers in Thessalonica, described his absence from them as being 'orphaned,' face to face, even though they were in the hearts of Paul and his team.

2:18: "Therefore we wanted to come to you, even I Paul, time and again, but Satan hindered us."

Because of his longing to see them again, Paul made a number of attempts to visit them again, but he was hindered by Satan. He did not enumerate any of those details.

2:19: "For what is our hope or joy or crown of boasting? Is it not even you in the presence of our Lord Jesus Christ at His coming?"

Paul, in this verse, iterated how much the believers there meant to him personally. They were Paul's hope, joy, and crown of boasting. The idea here was that his motives were not trivial; his hope and joy were involved in their spiritual success. The 'crown' for which he could boast related to the victory gathering in the presence of Christ at His Parousia ('coming again'). He was profoundly motivated by Christ.

2:20: "For you yourselves (are) our glory and our joy."

Paul's sole motivation was enveloped in the spiritual progress of the Thessalonians, not for fame, glory and joy over his own achievements. These Thessalonians were at the center of his world.

I Thessalonians 3:1-7:

3:1: "For this reason, no longer enduring, we resolved to be left alone in Athens…."

3:2: "...and we sent Timothy, our brother, and fellow-worker of God in the gospel of Christ, in order to establish you and encourage (you) concerning your faith,"

Since Paul made the case of his concern about their love and welfare, he explained that his actions proved his point.

'We' indicated that his staying in Athens alone was a joint decision, probably with Timothy and Silas, when the three were together in Berea. Paul would stay in Athens by himself, and, according to Luke's account in Acts 17:14, Timothy and Silas would stay temporarily in Berea. But when Paul arrived in Athens, he sent a message to Timothy and Silas to join him as soon as possible in Athens, likely after Timothy was sent briefly back to Thessalonica to check on them. The three were reunited in Corinth, rather than Athens, after Paul's message to the Philosophers on Mars Hill (Acts 18:5 records the reuniting of the three in Corinth). 'Enduring' was στέγοντες, 'unable to bear,' (BDAG), and the present tense participle was progressive, indicating a 'continual' action was meant. Paul was continually grieving over the status of the Thessalonians until Timothy returned with the good news.

3:3: "...that no one be perturbed during these troubles. For you yourselves know that for this you are appointed:"

The purpose clause here indicated that Paul's planning was designed not to cause anyone 'to be perturbed' σαίνεσθαι 'to cause to be emotionally upset,' or 'agitated,' or 'deceived,' (BDAG) by their persecutions. Paul then reminded them that they were 'appointed' (BDAG) for persecutions. Note the intensive pronoun 'yourselves' for emphasis.

3:4: "...For also, when we were with you, we warned you beforehand that we are destined to suffer trouble, even as it also occurred and you know (it did)."

Paul repeated his warning of the persecution issue when he was with them originally. They must expect it.

3:5: "For this reason, I myself, while no longer enduring, sent to know your faith, lest perhaps the Tempter may have tempted you, and our labor may be in vain."

Here Paul informed them of the reason for sending Timothy to check on them. These were real possibilities that Paul had to discover. It would involve a change of traveling plans had he learned that the believers had serious issues. He was very willing to return to Thessalonica if it was necessary. Their welfare was very important to him. He was not saying here that he was concerned that his 'labor' might have been wasted. He was doing the great commission that Christ demanded of him. Their eternal welfare was at stake.

3:6: "But now, when Timothy (just now) arrived from you, and announcing to us to us (your) faith and your love of us, and we have our good recollection always, while longing to see us, even as we (long) to see you."

Paul here revealed his great relief when Timothy returned with the joyous news that they had stood firm in the midst of persecution. That news impelled him to want to see them.

3:7: "For this reason, we were comforted, brothers and sisters, about Relief at the good news resulted in comfort to this hard-working team. The story had to be told.

'We are Grateful for You'
I Thessalonians 3: 8–20 to 4: 1-8:

I Thessalonians 3:8-20:
3:8: "Because we now live since you are standing firm in (the) Lord."

Paraphrased: 'We can now breathe easier since you are standing firm in the Lord.' 'Standing firm' was **στήκετε**, 'be firmly committed in conviction or belief,' from **στήκω**, which was a late form from **ἕστηκεν**, the perfect intensive tense from the main verb, **ἵστημι**. The verb **στήκω** was first found in the NT, (BDAG), where it was used eight times. Using **στήκω**, the present progressive tense (rather than the perfect tense, **ἕστηκεν**), and the action was durative: 'standing firm continually.'

3:9: "For what thanksgiving are we able to pay back to God concerning you for all the joy by which we are rejoicing on account of you in the presence of our God…"

3:10: "…night and day praying superabundantly to see your face and to bring to completion any deficiencies of your faith?"

'Pay back' was **ἀνταποδοῦναι**, meaning 'to repay,' or 'to practice reciprocity with respect to an obligation,' (BDAG). Or, paraphrased, 'What degree and kind of thanks are we able reciprocate to God for this abounding gift from Him of relief over your tenacity over persecution?' Paul wondered out loud what it would take to give God a response to His answer to prayer for the Thessalonians during this period of crisis. In **verse 10** he was now praying night and day for the opportunity to see them face to face in order to restore any deficiencies of their faith, to further protect them the next time they might face persecution. Paul continued to reveal his joy over their spiritual health during the persecution. 'Praying' **δεόμενοι** was a present tense progressive participle stressing a durative, or continuous, action. The content of his prayers was two-fold: First, to 'see' their face, and second, to bring to completion any deficiencies in their faith. 'Deficiencies' was ὑστερήματα, 'a defect that must be removed so that perfection can be attained,' (BDAG). The adverb, 'superabundantly,' modifying 'praying,' was **ὑπερεκπερισσοῦ**, 'quite beyond all measure,' (the highest form of comparison imaginable),' (BDAG).

3:11: "Now may God Himself, even our Father and our Lord Jesus direct our way to you…"

'Direct our way' was **κατευθύναι**, an optative form of the verb, expressing a wish. The word meant 'to direct,' or 'the removal of the hindrances of coming to you' (Thayer). The subject of the verb, 'direct,' was two-fold. First, 'God Himself' was the first Person to whom Paul addressed his wish. The intensive pronoun 'Himself' suggests that Paul had the boldness to address God the Father *Himself* for the granting of his wish. The second person addressed here was 'our Lord Jesus Christ,' linked by the copulative, 'and' (**καὶ**). Both, or either, could have granted Paul's wish.

3:12: "and for you to expand and abound in love for one another and for everyone, even as we (abound in love) for you,"

The wish from verse 11 continued, expanding Paul's wish for the Thessalonian believers in two more requests. The first one was for the believers to 'expand,' also an optative wish: **πλεονάσαι**, 'to multiply quantitatively,' (Thayer), as fruit expands in the fields. The second wish, from **περισσεύσαι** was also an optative 'wish' form of the verb, and meant 'to abound' qualitatively, 'to be extremely rich in quality,' particularly with an abstract object, such as 'love' or 'grace,' (BDAG). Both optative verbs applied to the agape love, which had a specialized definition, apart from pagan Greek: 'a Christ-like love.' This special 'love' was the operative force in the growth of the believer, one of the principle goals of sanctification. The believer was not to be static in his or her growth, but actively involved in the expansion of the agape love dimensionally, applied both to other believers, and even people outside the faith. Paul modeled this love to them and expected them to be expanding in this special virtue.

3:13: "to stabilize your hearts blameless by holiness in the presence of God, even our Father, at the Parousia of our Lord Jesus with all his holy ones [Amen]."

A purpose clause for the agape love in verse 12 followed Paul's wishes for their advancement: that their hearts might be so well-developed to be blameless by means of 'sanctification' in the presence of God. When did Paul expect this 'blamelessness' to occur? He expected it to occur during the Parousia (Christ's coming again). In other words, this 'holiness,' or 'sanctification' process was a lifetime work of God in the lives of His people. But by the time their lives were over, and at the Parousia, the achievement of 'perfection' with respect to holiness, will have been achieved. This idea will be further explained in chapter 4 by Paul as he expounded the Parousia in more detail. 'To stabilize' here was στηρὶξαι, from στηρὶζω, the meaning of which could have come from the construction trade (Thayer), who suggested a meaning of 'a support' for a wall, etc. Mostly it was applied to people who were well grounded in personal virtues or regarding the moral conduct of their lives.

'Reminders of Past Training' I Thessalonians 4:1 to 12:

4:1: "The rest, therefore, brothers and sisters, we ask you and appeal to you by means of the Lord Jesus, in order that even as you received from us how it is necessary for you to walk and to please God, even as you are walking, in order a that you may further bound (in this kind of conduct)."

These were instructions that Paul and his team had explained when he was with them. They were now reminders as appeals by Paul to continue to grow in the moral virtues of Christianity. 'Abound' here was the same verb used in 3:12, περισσεὑητε, only here in the subjunctive active meaning: 'that you may abound richly' in moral conduct.' Choices had to be made by believers to lean on the Holy Spirit for help in making those changes.

4:2: "For you know what exhortations we gave you through the Lord Jesus."

Paul had already briefed them on this issue when he was with them. They 'knew' what exhortations he had given them. **'Exhortations'** was παραγγελὶας, an official declaration from a person of authority.

4:3: "For this is the will of God, -- (involving) your sanctification -- for you to abstain from sexual immorality,"

The action that 'produced holiness' within a believer with the active assistance of the Holy Spirit resulted in this word for 'holiness,' ἁγιασμός, having a unique definition in our literature, (BDAG). This 'sanctification process' was the active moral guide in cases of sexual immorality in a lax society.

4:4: "...that each one of you (is) to know how to exercise self-control over your own vessel in holiness and honor,"

That 'moral guide' functioned to establish 'self-control,' κτᾶσαι, a present progressive ('continual control'), infinitive with a middle voice, with the infinitive meaning, 'to gain control over his own body,' (BDAG). The middle voice suggested that the person had some participation in the action, and acted in his own interest, a 'reflexive middle.'

4:5: "not with passionate lust, like the Gentiles also (practice) who have not known God,"

The negative was identified with pagan morals.

4:6: "...not go beyond and defrauding his brother in this matter, because the Lord (is) an avenger regarding all these things, even as we told you before and vigorously warned you."

'Go beyond' was ὑπερβαίνειν, with respect to sexual immorality, (Bruce, p. 84). 'Defrauding' was or πλεονεκτεῖν, 'exploiting' (BDAG) his brother, refers to cheating on his brother's wife. **'Avenger'** was ἔκδικος, 'exacting a penalty from (ἐκ) someone' (Thayer). This was the essence of what they were told before by Paul and his associates.

4:7: "For God did not call us to uncleanness, but to sanctification."

'Uncleanness' was ἀκαθαρσία, 'a state of moral corruption' (BDAG) was not what the believers were called to accomplish.

'Holiness,' or **'sanctification,'** ἁγιασμός (see verse 3) was what God called them in which to be actively engaged.

4:8: "Therefore, the one who disregards (this exhortation) is not disregarding man, but he is disregarding God who [also] has given His Holy Spirit into you."

'Disregarding' here, ἀθετέω, was repeated three times for emphasis, and revealed that the believer who disregarded this exhortation was not disregarding Paul as a man, but he or she was disregarding God who gave the Holy Spirit to him or her, for the express purpose of altering old lifestyles to conform to God's will and His character. How dare they consider such a possibility!

'Loving One Another and the Lord's Coming'
I Thessalonians 4: 9-18:

'Loving One Another' I Thessalonians 9-12:

4:9: "Concerning brotherly love, you have no need (for me) to write to you, for you yourselves are God-instructed to love one another,"

The area of 'brotherly love' φιλαδελφίας, was well-practiced by the Thessalonian believers, but Paul included the exhortation anyway for the sake of new converts who might read this letter, and to stimulate the Thessalonians to grow even more (see verse 10). 'You yourselves' was made intensive though the use of two pronouns, αὐτοὶ and ὑμεῖς. 'God-instructed' θεοδίδακτοι, was an adjective that contained a verbal force ('being instructed by God'); it was also only used here in the NT. The implication was that the believer was not only in communication with God, but was being instructed by God, or more precisely, the Holy Spirit, since the Holy Spirit indwelled the believer and was in communication with each one.

4:10: "...For you are also doing it for all the brothers and sisters in Macedonia. But we are exhorting you, brothers and sisters, to abound even more..."

'Macedonia' was northern Greece, which included Thessalonica, Philippi, and other cities and towns as well. Their love was expansive, and it extended to other communities, not just confined inwardly to those in their own neighborhoods. But Paul wanted the believers to reach out 'qualitatively' (see 3:12), not just 'quantitatively' using the verb, περισσεύειν, a present tense infinitive indicating a 'continual action.'

4:11: "...and also to aspire to be quiet and to practice your own affairs, and to work with your own hands, even as we commanded you,"

Paul had always been careful to explain to his churches that Christians were not to be political agitators. God was in control of the political destiny of the Roman state. They could pray for the state, and support the state through taxes; but they were not to be involved in riots or revolts. The idea of 'living a quiet life,' ἡσυχάζω, was expressed in the present progressive tense infinitive, which required a *continual* life of quietness. Therefore, they were to 'aspire' φιλοτιμεῖσθαι, 'to consider it an honor to aspire' (BDAG) to this kind of life. 'Practice your own affairs,' πράσσειν (present progressive tense) τὰ ἴδια, 'a *continual* activity of being about your own business, not minding other people's affairs.' 'To work with your own hands,' did not mean, in that context, 'manual labor,' but labor, whether in an intellectual career, or as a merchant, in contrast to the Roman upper classes and wealthy aristocrats who did no work at all. These instructions were not new here: but he repeated them for emphasis.

4:12: "…in order that you may walk becomingly toward those outside (the faith), and that you may lack nothing."

The purpose clause here gave two reasons for the injunctions in verse 11. First, that manner of life would be most influential to those who were not believers. 'Becomingly' was εὐσχημόνως, a compound verb, εὐ, good, + σχῆμα, 'a way of life,' or 'a way of life that was perceived outwardly as excellent' (BDAG). This kind of conduct was expected to be 'continuous,' from the present progressive tense of the verb, 'walk,' περιπατῆτε. The subjunctive mode indicated that this kind of 'walk' was not only possible, but achievable to the believer as a matter of choice, since the subjunctive was the mode of probability (Wallace, p. 461). That did not mean that assistance to make the choice was not attainable, because the Holy Spirit may be needed to offer His strength and power to effect that choice.

Second, 'That you may lack nothing.' If the Thessalonian believers worked as they should have (vs. 11), rather than wait for the Parousia, they would not have been a financial burden on the resources of the church.

The Parousia: (The coming of the Lord'): I Thessalonians 4:13-18:

4:13: "But we do not want you to be ignorant, brothers and sisters, about those who have fallen asleep, lest you may grieve, even as the rest who are not having hope."

It was not certain whether the Thessalonians communicated with Paul about this issue. Some of them may have lost believing loved ones, and they grieved excessively over their loss, not unlike their pagan counterparts. This section opened a major issue about the loss of believing friends and relatives. 'Ignorant' was ἀγνοεῖν, a compound infinitive verb α + γινώσκω, 'not know,' with the word 'know' meaning, a knowledge that could not 'grasp(s) the significance or meaning of something,' (BDAG). 'We' spoke not just from Paul, but also all the leaders with him, to add mutual support and significance to this charge. Paul affirmed that Christians may grieve temporarily over the loss of a believing loved one, but the grief should not be excessive or last over a long period of time, as often occurred when unbelievers lost their loved ones. There was no hope for them that they would ever be reunited with their loved ones. 'Fallen asleep,' was κοιμωμένων, the 'sleep of death' (BDAG).

4:14: "For if we believe that Jesus died and rose again, so also will bring those who sleep with Him."

'We believe' was πιστεύομεν, a present progressive tense verb indicating a 'continual belief' was intended. This belief was based on Christ's death and resurrection: if He was raised from the dead, then all believers will have the same experience of resurrection. Further, Paul noted that Christ would come for them personally. 'He will bring,' ἄξει, the future indicative from ἄγω, to 'lead or bring,' (BDAG). Christ will personally escort those who have died in the Lord at the Parousia, and from there, to heaven.

4:15: "For we say this to you by means of the word of the Lord, 'We ourselves who are remaining at the coming of the Lord shall by no means precede those who have fallen asleep:"

This affirmative charge by Paul made this revelation: 'I say this by means of the word of the Lord,' which indicated that this statement was authentic and was derived directly from the word of the Lord which was conveyed to Paul. The Parousia itself, however, will be well organized. The 'dead in Christ' will be raised before those who were still alive on the earth at the Rapture. The dead have first priority at the Parousia. Whether, at the resurrection of the dead, believers will be seen coming out of their graves by people alive on the earth was possible, but speculative and unknown. After they were raised, then they would be followed by those believers who were still alive on the earth at the time of the Parousia. The time for each resurrection event could be seconds or minutes in length.

4:16: "Because the Lord Himself by means of a word of command, with the voice of an archangel, and by a trumpet of God, shall descend from heaven, and the dead in Christ will be raised first,"

Three events will precede the Parousia. The first announcement will come from the Lord Himself, that is, the Lord and no other representative. He will give out a military shout. Then the next voice heard will be the voice of an archangel. This will be followed by the trumpet of God, blowing the military signal of His coming. Christ will escort the dead into the heavens, repeating the order of events in verse 15.

4:17: "Then, we ourselves, who are remaining alive, shall be carried away in the clouds for a meeting of the Lord in the sky; and thus we shall always be with the Lord."

Then, the final part of the Parousia will occur. Those believers who were alive on the earth will then be escorted personally by the Lord for a meeting in the sky. From that time on, believers will always be with the Lord.

4:18: "So comfort one another with these words."

'Comfort' παρακαλεῖτε was a present progressive command: 'continually comfort.'

'The Timing of the Lord's Coming'
I Thessalonians 5: 1-11: The Events Leading to the Parousia:
5:1: "But concerning the times and the seasons, brothers and sisters, you do not have a need (for me) to write to you,"

Paul had already given instructions about being prepared for the day of the Lord. This was just a reminder. 'Times and seasons' χρόνων and καιρῶν, where χρόνων referred to chronological time of the calendar: hours, days, weeks, months, years, and καιρῶν, which considered time 'with the implication of being especially fit for something and without emphasis on precise chronology,' (BDAG), as in certain seasons of the year, or a key to events: 'planting time,' or 'harvest time,' etc.

5:2: "...for you yourselves know perfectly well that the day of (the) Lord comes as a thief in the night."

They 'knew perfectly well,' ἀκριβῶς οἴδατε, because they were so well trained in the events of eschatology (the end times). The key part of eschatology was to be always prepared for this long anticipated event, where God and Christ would intervene in history to bring to a close the age of grace. Paul did not want any believer, at any time, to be unprepared for this cataclysmic event. It was the greatly anticipated event that drove them to achieve great things for God, both qualitatively in their own growth, and quantitatively, in expanding the gospel message to others.

5:3: "Whenever they may say, 'Peace and security,' that sudden destruction arrives on them, as birth pangs on a woman with child, and they cannot escape."

For the unbelievers, this same event will bring surprise, terror, shock, and dread of the ensuing events.

"Whenever they may say, 'Peace and security'...." These were the two conditions that unbelievers did not possess. 'Peace' was εἰρήνη, a peace that was only derived from knowing God and the Lord Jesus. It was not available to unbelievers. 'Security' was ἀσφάλεια, 'a security from enemies or dangers,' from the verb, σφάλλω, meaning 'to cause someone to fall,' so when the alpha privative is added, 'safe from falling or failing,' (Thayer). The Day of God's judgment will come at a time when unbelievers feel especially secure.

"**…that sudden destruction arrives on them, as birth pangs on a woman with child….**" 'Sudden,' αἰφνίδιος, 'sudden and unexpected,' (Thayer). Paul described the event like the sudden birth pangs just prior to the birth of a child. 'Destruction' was ὀλεθρός, 'destruction, ruin or death,' (BDAG). It was from the Classical Greek, ὄλλυμι, 'to perish' or 'die,' often horribly, (Liddel and Scott).

"**…and they cannot ever escape.**" 'Escape' was ἐκφύγωσιν, 'To flee from danger' (BDAG), an aorist subjunctive active, but accompanied by two negatives οὐ μή, indicating no possibility of escape.

5:4: "But you yourselves, brothers and sisters, are not in darkness, in order that the day may overtake you as a thief:"

The encouraging element to this news was applied to the believers at Thessalonica and believers everywhere. They were not in 'darkness,' where unbelief dwells, with all the attendant circumstances of violence, suffering, and punishment. They were well prepared by Paul so that this marvelous event could never overtake them suddenly with fear and dread. καταλάβῃ, 'to catch by surprise,' (BDAG) 'as a thief in the night.' The verb, 'catch,' was an aorist subjunctive, indicating that the possibility of being caught by surprise does exist, but not for those who are anticipating it.

5:5: "For you yourselves are sons of light, and sons of the day. We are not of the night, nor of darkness:"

'**You yourselves**' was the intensive pronoun, 'you' (ὑμεῖς, added to the text for emphasis). The plural addressed the believers at Thessalonica and all subsequent readers of the text who are Christians. That believers were 'sons of light and sons of the day,' revealed that they were described as sons of God, who was light, and they were also described 'as sons of light' because they were continually anticipating that coming day, and they were radiating that light. Believers were not victims of the night, nor were they people of the darkness; they belonged to the Day of the Lord.

5:6: "So therefore, let us not sleep as the rest, but let us stay awake and let us stay alert."

Since they were of the Day of the Lord, they needed to be encouraged to continually walk as if that Day could come at any time, because, metaphorically, if they slept, they were incapacitated. 'Let us stay awake and stay alert,' γρηγορῶμεν and νήφωμεν, were both hortatory subjunctives, the most gentle of commands, because they included the writer, Paul, ('us') as well as those addressed in the letter. Those 'who sleep,' καθεύδωμεν, in this extended metaphor, represented either carnal believers, or, more probably, unbelievers, who were totally unprepared for that day.

5:7: "For those who sleep, sleep at night, and those who drink, drink at night."

Those people who were incapacitated by sleep, occurred during the night, just as those who were drunk with alcohol: they 'lived' for the nighttime hours.

5:8: "But let us ourselves, who are of the day, be sober, putting on the breastplate of faith and love, and a helmet of the assurance of salvation:"

'Let us, ourselves' (ἡμεῖς) was also the emphatic pronoun, 'ourselves.' 'Let us be sober,' νήφωμεν, was another hortatory subjunctive, meaning, as in verses 6 and 7, to be 'free from every form of mental or spiritual drunkenness,' or 'self-controlled,' (BDAG). The metaphor now extended to military imagery: 'putting on' ἐνδυσάμενοι, as in 'putting on' or 'wearing' (BDAG), two kinds of defensive armament: θώρακα, 'breastplates' protecting the vital organs of the heart, stomach, and intestines, and περικεφαλαίαν, 'a helmet, protecting the head.' The **'breastplate'** was metaphorically described as associated with faith, while the **'helmet'** was associated with 'the hope of salvation,' or, better, the 'assurance of salvation.' Both were defensive weapons which provided critical protection against injury or death during the battle. This military metaphor was also found in Ephesians 6:11-18, which may extend back into the OT to Isaiah 59:17, 'where Yahweh himself put on righteousness as a breastplate and wore the helmet of salvation on his head....' (Bruce, p. 112).

5:9: "Because God did not appoint us for wrath, but for (the) acquisition of salvation through our Lord Jesus Christ..."

The reason why believers should be sober, and put on this armor of God, was because God did not want believers to experience His wrath at the end of time. He provided the acquisition of their salvation through the work of Christ on the cross. **'Appoint'** was ἔθετο, from τίθημι, 'to consign someone to something,' (BDAG). **'Acquisition,'** was περιποίησιν, the 'experience of an event of acquisition,' (BDAG). God appointed the acquisition of salvation for believers. That appointment came through faith in Christ Jesus.

5:10: "...who having died for us, in order that, whether we are awake or asleep, we may live together with Him."

Verse 10 was an elaboration of verse 9, explaining how that salvation was made effective. Christ died for us; that is, He died in our place. The purpose of that death made it possible that believers may live together with Him. The **'may'** marked the subjunctive mode in the verb, indicating that salvation 'may' happen, but only if it was acted upon.

'May live' was ζήσωμεν, from ζάω, 'to live.' What had made this verb meaningful, however, was that believers may not only 'live,' but live 'with Him,' whom believers have learned to love. 'Awake' or 'asleep' was used metaphorically here, meaning 'alive' or 'dead.' Whether the believer was still alive at the Parousia, or had died before the Parousia, he or she will not miss out on eternal life.

5:11: "Therefore, encourage one another and build up one another, just as you are also doing."

Paul's concluding words about the Parousia was this exhortation: **'encourage'** παρακαλεῖτε 'to come alongside another and utter words of encouragement,' and **'build up,'** οἰκοδομεῖτε' an architectural term, meaning to 'to construct or improve the building.' Both are present tense commands, meaning 'a continual action.' These were needless commands, Paul recognized, for they had been doing those things already, perhaps for months.

'Final Exhortations'

Chapter 5: 12-28

5:12: "Now we ask you brothers and sisters, to know those laboring among you and who are caring for you in (the) Lord and instructing you..."

Paul petitioned the Thessalonians to get to know the leadership of their church within three of their functions: "Now we ask you brothers and sisters, to know ...." Paul addressed here the church members in general. 'Ask' was ἐρωτῶμεν, 'to make a request for something to take place,' (BDAG). He asked them in a polite way to 'get to know '(εἰδέναι from οἶδα), 'become familiar' with one group of leaders who were active in their growth in the Lord in three distinct ways. The plural definite article (τούς) of the first participle should be included with the two other participles (Bruce, p. 118).

"...those laboring among you...." 'laboring' was κοπιῶντας, 'one who exerts oneself physically, mentally, or spiritually, work hard, toil, strive, struggle' (BDAG). The intensity of the labor was always implied with the use of this word. The continuous action of the labor was indicated by the use of the present tense of all three participles.

"...and who are caring for you in (the) Lord...." 'Caring for,' was προϊσταμένους from προΐστημι 'those giving aid, or caring for others' (BDAG). As part of their hard labor these leaders were giving out spiritual or physical care-giving to the church members.

"...and instructing you..." The 'instructing' here was νουθετοῦντας, 'to counsel about avoidance or cessation of an improper course of conduct, admonish, warn, instruct,' (BDAG). The 'instruction' related to the conduct of the believer, especially a new convert, who needed some personal guidance related to the new way of life that was expected to follow conversion. This was especially needed in a pagan culture where certain practices were acceptable in the pagan society, but not in the Christian community. The new converts needed to develop a new set of mores to replace those into which they were born.

5:13: "...and hold them in very high esteem and love because of their work. Be at peace among yourselves."

The church members were to highly value the services of these leaders. 'To hold' was ἡγεῖσθαι, 'to consider or regard' (BDAG). 'High esteem' was ὑπερεκπερισσοῦ, 'to the highest degree possible,' (BDAG), an adverb modifying the infinitive, ἡγεῖσθαι. The workers who performed this task were evidently highly gifted in their various tasks. Paul wanted the church members to be very grateful and express love to them for their service. Their title was unimportant compared to their hard work: the quality of their work was the important thing, which was a reversal of the value system of the Graeco-Roman culture, where their title was everything. 'Be at peace' was the verb form of the noun, 'peace,' εἰρηνεύετε, 'cultivate' or 'keep peace and harmony' (Thayer) 'among yourselves.'

5:14: "Now we admonish you, brothers and sisters, warn those who are disorderly, comfort the fainthearted, help the weak exercise patience toward all."

The 'admonish' here was in contrast to the polite form of 'ask' in verse 12. Here, Paul was also addressing the same group (church members) that he addressed in verse 12. Only here, he expected the members, on occasion, to do the 'warning' that the church leadership was doing in verse 12. The same verb was used: **νουθετεῖτε**, only here it was in the present imperative mode expressing a command: 'admonish, or 'instruct, with regard to counseling.' Paul was charging them to perform the functions of the leaders, when the occasion warranted, rather than rely on an overworked staff. All church members were considered workers by Paul.

Some of the members were **'idle,' ἀτάκτους**, 'to be out of step and going one's own way, *insubordinate, disorderly,*' (BDAG). But there were to be no social classes of a 'non-active laity' versus a 'professional clergy.' All members could contribute as a team. Other responsibilities that the members could contribute were: 'giving comfort to the fainthearted,' **παραμυθεῖσθε**, 'to cheer up' or 'console' someone, (BDAG), in this case those who were discouraged, **ὀλιγοψύκους**, literally, 'a person reduced to a small soul,' as when tragedy struck, and a person was reduced to a depressed state. 'To help' was **ἀντέχεσθε**, 'to have a strong interest in,' thus 'assist the weak,' which was, **ἀσθενῶν**, 'weak in faith,' or 'weak in body due to age or illness' (BDAG). 'Exercise patience toward all,' **μακροθυμεῖτε**, 'have patience' toward everyone (BDAG). The verb also can convey, with a more literal meaning, 'a long fuse with respect to temper.'

5:15: "See that no one may render evil for evil, but pursue what is good at all times [also] for each other and for all (people)."

Ὁρᾶτε, 'See to it,' was the introductory command for nine more imperatives, mostly in short phrases, from verses 15 to 22. They were all present progressive tense verbs indicating that Paul's intent was for the believers to assimilate these commands as continuous and habitual patterns of activity into their lives.

'May render' was **ἀποδῷ**, 'pay back in a negative sense, evil for evil,' (BDAG). The subjunctive mode indicated that this would be a choice that would have to be made by the believer in order to change the cycle of evil in the world view philosophy.

"...but always pursue what is good [also] for each other and for all (people)." 'Pursue' was **διώκετε**, 'strive for, seek after, aspire to' (BDAG). The object of the verb, 'pursue,' was the phrase 'what is good.' The adverb, 'always,' modifies 'pursue:' 'always pursue what is good.' The application of this virtue was also mentioned: 'also for each other, and for all (people),' Christians or not.

5:16: "Rejoice always!"

In the Greek, 'always' preceded the verb: 'always rejoice.' The order of the Greek words suggested that the verb was to be emphasized: Always Rejoice! Throughout the NT, as well as the OT, the theme of rejoicing rippled through text after text, helping new believers realize that, despite adverse circumstances, God's people had many reasons for joy as they served the Lord. That joy was not confined to the Psalms in the OT or Philippians in the NT. It ran throughout the Bible, based on the salvation promised in the OT, and carried out through Christ in the NT. Nor was that salvation the only reason for joy: for Christians it was the loving care and guidance of the Holy Spirit within each believer that stimulated joy and promoted satisfaction on a daily basis. 'Always' indicated action, despite circumstances.

5:17: "Pray incessantly!"

'Praying' was προσεύχεσθε, where the 'προσ-' was directional and the action involves a 'good' ('ευ') communication (to God). 'Incessantly,' was an adverb modifying 'pray' that revealed that prayer was to be done 'without an intermission.' Prayer was the believer's communication link to God; here it emphasized that the 'when' of prayer had no limits: it was to be done continually. Elsewhere in the NT and OT, there were further instructions about the nature of prayer, found in any concordance. Here, Paul only stressed the 'when' of prayer: without stopping.

5:18: "Be thankful in everything, for this is God's will for you by Christ Jesus."

'Thankful' was εὐχαριστεῖτε, 'to be grateful,' or 'to feel grateful' or 'to give thanks.' The Greek word has been transliterated into English in the word 'Eucharist,' which meant the celebration of the Last Supper in churches today. The Greek word literally meant, 'good grace,' or 'the goodness of God's grace' verbalized in an action verb. God punished the Israelites in the desert for not having a grateful attitude. Believers thrive on developing a positive spiritual gratitude in their behavior and conduct. Why? Because it *is God's will for every believer.* How? It occurred by Christ working within believers through the efforts of the Holy Spirit. The 'attitude of gratitude' was to be applied to everything.

5:19: "Do not quench the Spirit,"

This was one of three negative commands: verse 19; verse 20; verse 22. 'Quench' was σβέννυτε, 'to stifle, quench, or put out the fire.' The Holy Spirit was engaged in the process of producing holiness in every believer. It was possible to put out His fire that produced sanctification. In the Greek, the object of the verb was placed before the verb, indicating the emphasis lied on the Holy Spirit, as the target of the 'quenching.' He illuminated and energized the believer with God's fire; if the believer chose to pour water on that fire, the consequence of that action, if not corrected with repentance, yielded spiritual weakness and total disability.

5:20: "Do not despise prophesies,"

'Despise' was ἐξουθενεῖτε, 'to reject something, as beneath one's consideration.' As pointed out by F.F. Bruce, (p. 125) who stated, "There may have been a tendency in Thessalonica, as later at Corinth, to value more spectacular gifts above prophecy, hence the warning that prophecy must not be depreciated, but heard with respect due to the Spirit, whose voice is communicated through the prophet." Something similar may have already occurred in modern Christianity with regard to the major prophetic writing of the NT, the Book of Revelation by the Apostle John. While not despised, it has been neglected to some extent. The same might be said of OT prophets as well, especially Daniel and a number of others.

5:21: "But test all things; hold fast to the good,"

'Test' was δοκιμάζετε, 'to make a critical examination of something to determine genuineness, put to the test, examine,' BDAG). Something that has been tested and found to be false was ἀποδοκιμάζω, 'repudiated by testing,' much like gold was tested to determine whether it was genuine. What Christians were to test, Paul stated clearly here: all things. That is, all ideas that may conflict with Scripture; all people that make claims. That was not to indicate that Christians were to be paranoid; but they were to realize that the Devil still roamed freely in this world, deceiving many. The testing process will uncover false claims; it will also uncover genuine articles: in that case, the believer was to cling to those truths. **'Hold fast'** was κατέχετε, 'hold fast, adhere firmly, retain firmly,' (BDAG). Paul encouraged his believers in Thessalonica to cling to the good, that which passed the test of authenticity. The verb δοκιμάζω was related to the verb, δοκέω, meant, 'to consider the possibilities,' or 'to think rationally,' all related to a skilled and trained mind.

5:22: "abstain from every appearance of evil."

This was the last of the negative commands. **'Abstain'** was ἄχεσθε, 'to avoid contact with,' or 'refrain from.' 'From every appearance of evil' was ἀπό: 'from,' παντός: 'every,' εἴδους: 'kind,' or 'appearance.' Εἴδους was from the verb, Ὁράω, 'to see.' 'Evil' was πονηροῦ, 'pertaining to being morally or socially worthless …degenerate,' (BDAG). 'Appearance' indicated that even some conduct that may be questionable, which may look to some people like evil, and it should be avoided.

5:23: "And, may the God of peace Himself sanctify you completely, and may your spirit and soul and body be preserved blameless at the Parousia of our Lord Jesus Christ."

The verb ἁγιάσαι, was an aorist optative, indicating a 'prayer-wish' for the Thessalonians, an action that involved the will, and the meaning was 'sanctify,' (BDAG), which also carried the meaning of 'making holy,' a gradual, but progressive action, produced by the Holy Spirit in the believer's life after conversion. 'Completely' was ὁλόκληρος, being 'complete in all its parts… without blemish or defect' (Thayer), which represented not only the goal of sanctification, but also the final act of Christ at the Parousia for this transformational process. The word only occurred here in the NT, technically known as a hapax legomenon, or literally from the Greek, 'once in a writing.'

The second major verb in this verse was τηρηθεὶη, an aorist optative passive from τηρέω, meaning 'preserve or keep' (BDAG). As an aorist 'prayer wish,' it was here expressed in the passive voice, indicating that the action will be performed by someone else (the Holy Spirit), if the request was granted. The substance of the prayer-wish involved each believer's 'spirit, body, and soul,' in order that these parts of the believer's existence may be preserved 'blameless' at the Parousia of the Lord Jesus Christ.

5:24: "The One who calls you (is) faithful, who also will do it."

God the Father was the Person who calls (καλῶν, a present progressive participle) every Christian, not only to a successful completion of the sanctification process, but also who oversees the process of preservation for the believer through every crisis down to the end result of the Parousia. The last verbal phrase was intended to be a final word of encouragement. He will also activate the twin actions of sanctification and preservation for every believer: He alone had the power to accomplish these tasks. 'Do' was ποιήσει, 'to activate' (BDAG), expressed here in the future tense, as a promise from God that He will produce these powerful results. That process did not depend on the believer.

5:25: "Brothers and sisters, pray also concerning us."

Paul did not neglect Paul's need of prayer for himself and his leadership staff. He was not without spiritual and physical requirements in the work of the gospel. They could contribute by partnering with Paul in an objective way. They needed his prayers; Paul also needed theirs. 'Pray' was in the present progressive tense of the command form, middle voice, suggesting that a benefit would result for the person praying. Προσευχέσθω, used here in the command form, 'is the general term for pray' (Thayer). It was also the communication link to God that believers had as His children. They could and should utilize it to pray for other believers. Paul was not exempt from that need.

5:26: "Greet all brothers and sisters with a holy kiss."

The kiss was used as an activity of believers upon meeting for the communion, or even when they met at an assembly (Bruce, p. 134). It was initiated as a token of the agape love between men or between women of the church, before a service at one of the house churches, or, as here, as a term of affection and greeting on other occasions. It was described as a 'holy' kiss, perhaps to separate it from a familial or romantic kiss.

5:27: "I charge you by the Lord that this epistle is to be read to all the holy brethren."

Since there were other house-churches in Thessalonica, Paul wanted to be sure that the letter was distributed to all the house-churches in the city, not overlooking any of them. The term, 'charge' signaled that a serious tone was indicated here, amplified by the singular subject rather than the typical plural subject. 'Charge' was ἐνορκὶζω, and was only used here in the NT, which 'involved a person taking an oath' (BDAG) to perform the task of distribution, perhaps indicating that Paul was fearful that other groups might be neglected in the distribution of his letter (Bruce, p. 135).

5:28: "The grace of our Lord Jesus Christ (be) with you. Amen."

The final benediction, here cited by Paul was common in his letters. But that fact should not be viewed as a trite closure without meaning. The 'grace' was χάρις, a noun, although there were two verb forms of the idea of 'grace,' χαριτόω and χαρίζομαι, both referring to a gift, freely given. The noun, χάρις, has generally been understood as 'gift given to someone who did not deserve it, or an 'unmerited favor' in Christian circles. But it meant, more technically, 'the practical application of goodwill' (BDAG), that God and Christ have, and share with all believers. Paul was requesting that he wanted Christ to continue showering that marvelous process in the lives of the believers at Thessalonica.

CHAPTER 3
II Thessalonians, circa AD 50

Anticipating the Message of II Thessalonians: *A final warning to the lazy, and "Who told you that the Second coming of Christ had already occurred?"*

II THESSALONIANS

'God's Final Judgment at the Parousia' II Thessalonians 1:1-12:

Circumstances of the Letter: This letter was written sometime after I Thessalonians. But the tone of the letter seems somewhat muted, when compared with the exuberant enthusiasm of the first letter, about which various scholars have commented (Bruce, p. 143). This argument rests on a careful comparison between the lack of excitement displayed in the similar language of verses 2 and 3 here with the nearly identical 'thanksgiving' phrases of I Thessalonians 2 and 3, which were much more exuberant in tone. But if there was some time lapse between letters, long enough to receive a response of the first letter, then Paul might have understood the Thessalonian situation more clearly, and his 'muted' response here may have been due to that reason.

1:1: "Paul and Silas and Timothy to the church of the Thessalonians by our God (the) Father and (the) Lord Jesus Christ…"

If either Timothy or Silas had delivered the first letter, and then returned with an update on the situation there, the result might have called for a change of tone. This idea will be explored as we proceed throughout this letter in order to look for supporting evidence of Paul's tone.

1:2: "…grace to you and peace from God [our] Father, and (the) Lord Jesus Christ."

This section differed from the shorter version in I Thessalonians 1, which stopped with the word, 'peace.' Here, the grace and peace were identified as coming from God the Father and the Lord Jesus Christ. This more detailed version of the introductory remarks may have suggested less emotional anguish than that displayed in the first letter.

1:3: "We are always owing a debt of gratitude to God concerning you, brothers and sisters, as it is fitting, because your faith increases abundantly and the love of every one of you multiplies for one other,"

As mentioned above, the language here seemed also to represent a cooler tone that the first 'thanksgiving' phrase of the first letter. **"...We owe...."** was ὀφείλομεν, 'we are obligated by a debt owed,' (BDAG) seemed quite detached, when compared with the εὐχαριστοῦμεν, "We are thanking God always...." in I Thessalonians 1:2, and reinforced by verse 3.

However, Paul recognized here their faith had 'increased abundantly,' ὑπεραυξάνει, 'increased wonderfully,' or 'abundantly' (BDAG). He also complimented them by saying, **'the love of every one of you *multiplies* for one other.'** 'Multiplies' was πλεοανάζει, 'abundance, 'or 'to become more and more,' (BDAG). Here, one wonders whether this letter was, indeed, more 'detached' than I Thessalonians. The articulation of their 'abundant faith' and 'multiplying love' were very objective reasons for rejecting the 'detached' viewpoint, although more evidence may lie ahead.

1:4: "...so that we ourselves boast about you to all the churches of God for your patience and your faith with all your persecutions and your troubles by which you are enduring,"

'Boast' ἐγκαυχᾶσθαι was presented as a 'result infinitive,' meaning 'to be proud of someone, and express oneself accordingly,' (BDAG), a NT hapax legomenon, used only here in the NT.

'We ourselves' was the subject of the verb, expressed in the accusative case in this construction, **'αὐτοὺς ἡμᾶς'** literally, 'ourselves we.' The term 'ourselves' expressed a strong emphasis on the 'we,' indicating that Paul and his leadership team were all involved in 'being proud' of them. Not only were they proud of their spiritual progress in the faith, but they spread the word to all Christian visitors who stopped at Corinth to visit Paul. The objective reason for their 'pride' mentioned here was for their patience and strong (implied) faith in spite of the serious persecutions and trouble that they suffered. Both were strong indicators that they were maturing in the process of sanctification, and Paul wanted them to know how proud they were of this fact.

'Patience' was ὑπομονῆς, literally, 'to remain under' some serious trouble without showing anger or a negative attitude.

1:5: "a certain indication of the righteous judgment of God (on the persecutors) so that you may be counted worthy of the kingdom of God, for which also you are suffering,"

This sentence started with verse 3 and will continue to verse 10, revealing a very complex set of ideas. Here, Paul had shown the results of that persecution:

first, it activated the righteous judgment of God on the persecutors, and second, it demonstrated that the Thessalonians were counted worthy of the kingdom of God. God's action in their behalf was demonstrated in both results.

'Counted worthy' was καταξιωθῆναι, 'to be consider worthy to receive some privilege, benefit, recognition' (BDAG), in an aorist passive form, indicating that the 'worthiness' was brought about, not by the extraordinary resources of the individual believers, but by the action of the Holy Spirit working within them. That was the reason of their success.

1:6: "...since it is righteous from God's point of view to repay your troubles by troubling those who trouble you..."

'From' was παρά, meaning: a 'marker of one whose viewpoint is relevant, in the sight or judgment of someone,' (BDAG).

'Repay' was ἀνταποδοῦναι, 'to exact retribution, repay, pay back,' (BDAG).

"...From God's point of view...." was a vital concept. Believers must relearn many things in order to be in line with God's point of view. That is why some Christians may ask, 'why me?' when confronted with persecution, illness, or trials. They do not have God's point of view. Others may ask 'why' when they do not understand God's Word, or His precepts. There are many things that believers do not understand; some things they may discover as they grow in Christ; other things they will learn only at the Parousia, when they are transformed. Believers must learn patience and be willing to wait in order to grasp the full intent of God's purpose for the many questions they want to ask. Faith involves the willingness to wait for answers. From God's point of view, God will repay those who persecute Christians: sometimes they will be repaid within the lifetime of the persecutor; sometimes it will be repaid at the final judgment: trouble repaid with more serious trouble.

1:7: "...and (it is righteous from God's point of view to repay) you who are being troubled with relief (together) with us, by the revelation of the Lord Jesus from heaven with His powerful angels..."

Paul, as missionaries, had suffered the same kind of persecution. How Paul found relief from the pain of suffering was the contemplation of the Parousia, when all believers will find satisfaction from their earlier suffering for Christ. That was, from God's point of view, a just compensation for those troubles. Paul was in effect saying: 'Join the club.' We know what you have gone through. But the just judgment of God will make things right at the Parousia.' Verse 6

84

introduced the first revelation of God's point of view for the persecutors, Verse 7 continued the same idea for believers, hence a repetition of the phrase.

1:8: "...with flaming fire, handing out vengeance to those not knowing God and to those not listening to the gospel of our Lord Jesus,"

This verse elaborated in detail of the events after the Parousia, when the final judgment of God will be meted out to the persecutors. However, these were specific statements of judgment applying, in general, to all unbelievers: Jews and Gentiles alike, much like the prophecies of Daniel in the OT. 'Vengeance' was ἐκδίκησιν, 'penalty afflicted on wrongdoers,' (BDAG). The repetition of the article τοῖς indicated two separate groups of unbelievers: those 'not knowing God' and those 'not listening to the Gospel of Christ.' Both are judged alike.

1:9: "...such ones will pay (the) penalty, eternal destruction from the face of (the) Lord (Jesus) and from the glory of His power,"

This verse continued to describe the details of the punishment. 'Will pay' was τίσουσιν from τίνω, used only here in the NT, meaning, 'to experience retribution, pay, undergo a penalty,' (BDAG). That penalty was eternal destruction, ὄλεθρον αἰώνιον or 'eternal death' (BDAG). The person from whose face they will be removed was the Lord Jesus. They will also be removed from the beautiful glory of His power which they will not witness, only the effects of that power.

1:10: "...whenever He may come to be glorified with His holy ones and to be marveled at by all those who will believe, because our witness to you was believed in that day."

This phrase completed the long sentence started in verse 3. At the Parousia, Christ will come in power and glory, raising the dead in Christ first, then raising those believers who remained on the earth. His 'holy ones' were both groups of believers. The Thessalonian believers were among that group because they believed the testimony of Paul and his assistants when they were converted.

'In that day' could refer to the verbs, 'glorified and marveled,' (Bruce, p. 153), or the phrase could refer to the time the Thessalonians first believed, when Paul and his team first arrived there from Philippi, (probably the latter).

1:11: "For which end we are always praying for you, that our God may count you worthy of His calling, and He may finish every good desire, and work of faith by means of power,"

"**...For which end....**" was the purpose Paul and his team were constantly praying for them, that is, 'for the blessed end result of the Parousia that will occur for believers.' Paul and his team were constantly praying for them. The content of the prayer was in three separate areas. First, that God may count them worthy of His calling. 'Worthy' was ἀξιώσῃ, 'consider worthy, deserving' (BDAG). They were initially considered worthy by Christ when their conversion occurred. They were especially worthy when they suffered for Him. Second, that God may finish every good desire to please Him.

'Finish' was πληρώσῃ from πληρόω, 'to bring to completion that which was already begun, complete, finish,' (BDAG). This phrase represented the third purpose for their prayers, that 'He may finish (every) work of faith,' not to gain salvation for them, but as a grateful response to the salvation they already had. How could all this happen? It occurred by the power provided by the Holy Spirit.

"**...By means of....**" was 'the instrumental use' of ἐv, rather than a marker of 'kind or manner,' (BDAG).

1:12: "In order that the name of our Lord Jesus may be glorified by you, and you (are glorified) by Him, according to the grace of our God and of our Lord Jesus Christ."

"**...So that....**" was ὅπως, a 'marker expressing purpose for an event or state, *in order that,*' (BDAG). The purpose of Paul's prayer for them in verse 11 was in order that the Lord Jesus and His name may be glorified by their life work for Him. When that happened, then they would be glorified by Christ Himself.

The '**by**' in '**be glorified *by* you**,' was the instrumental use of ἐv, representing the individuals used in glorifying Christ: the Thessalonians themselves and their life's work in spreading the gospel and training the saints. Because of their admirable actions under such stress, Christ will glorify his busy children by the personal response of Christ Himself, both in this life, and in the next. This whole process would occur as a result of the grace, ('the unmerited and undeserved mercy') of God the Father and also the Lord Jesus Christ.

'Lawlessness and the Elect' II Thessalonians 2:1-17:
2:1: "Now we are earnestly asking you, brothers and sisters, concerning the Parousia of our Lord Jesus Christ and our gathering together with Him,"

Now Paul probed more deeply into the Parousia in order to keep heretics from leading them astray. "We are earnestly asking you…." was ἐρωτῶμεν, 'make a request,' or 'ask a question,' (BDAG). The 'Parousia' ('the Coming' or Rapture) and the 'gathering together' were tied together by the conjunction, 'and,' indicating two separate events that will happen at the same time.

'Gathering together,' was ἐπισυναγωγῆς, 'an assembly, meeting together to one place,' ἐπι meant, here, 'to' (Thayer). That 'one place' is difficult to comprehend in human terms, since the numbers of believers at the Parousia must be in the many millions. However, this was one of those situations that believers were to take by faith, not by human reasoning. God will provide a meeting place suitable for His purpose within a context that will be appropriate for the occasion, an example of 'divine physics' that mankind cannot grasp because of the limited human capability. That will all change at the Parousia.

2:2: "…for you are not to be soon shaken from the mind or troubled, neither by a (prophetic) spirit nor by (a spoken) word nor by letter as if from us, as though the day of the Lord already arrived…"

The negative purpose clause was introduced by an εἰς τό + infinitive clause, σαλευθῆναι, 'to disturb inwardly, to shake,' BDAG).

'From the mind,' was ἀπὸ τοῦ νοός, with the implication that the mind might be seriously shaken if they would learn that the Parousia (scheduled prior to the 'day of the Lord') had already happened, and not only were they not taken, but they found themselves in the beginning of the tribulation.

Verse 2 was a warning by Paul suggesting that the 'Day of the Lord story' had been fabricated as an attempt to deceive them: either by a (prophetic) spirit, or by a spoken word delivered by someone they trusted, or by a misleading letter allegedly from Paul and his team. This attempt to deceive them may have been reported to Timothy as he delivered the letter of I Thessalonians. When Paul heard of this rumor, this had to be one reason he wrote the second letter. It may also explain the difference in the tones of the two letters, since Paul was likely incensed at what he heard, and he wanted to send the appropriate warning quickly.

2:3: "(See to it) that no one may deceive you in any way. Because unless the rebellion may come first and the man of lawlessness may be revealed, the son of destruction (the Day of the Lord will not come),"

The added phrase, 'the Day of the Lord will not come' corrected a 'broken sentence,' (called an anacoluthon), not uncommon in Paul's writings

(Wanamaker, p. 244), which, in this case, resulted in a missing conclusion; thus, it was a sentence fragment. It seemed that when Paul was under stress, broken sentences were more common, even though he was dictating virtually all his letters to one or more of his co-workers, who may not have been as fluent in Greek as he was, or they were not thinking of the content as they wrote.

The argument against the willful heretical teaching that agitated the Thessalonians so greatly was carefully chosen by Paul. He would not to try to convince them of the early warning signs of the Parousia that they might have missed. There were none. He chose to show them that, despite the fierce persecution they suffered, the Day of the Lord had not yet arrived, which would come after the Parousia. There were specific prophetic warnings in the OT to which Paul could have used to refute the erroneous arguments of the heretics. If he could convince them that they were not in the initial stages of the Tribulation, then it would have been easier to convince them that they did not miss the Parousia, which was described in I Thessalonians 4:16 as a sudden event with no advance warning. Did they miss it? One can imagine their shock in that situation. But it just did not occur yet. His argument was supported by facts they had been taught earlier; he was convincing and gentle.

So Paul pointed out that here was an order of events that would precede the Day of the Lord. He outlined them briefly: first, there must be a large scale 'falling away' of believers; second, a political rebellion led by the Man of Lawlessness also was a required event (Bruce, p. 166). Neither of those events had yet happened: in fact, the churches were growing rapidly at that time. In addition, the Jewish Wars did not begin until AD 66, well over a decade after this letter was written. Even an appropriate candidate for 'Man of lawlessness,' the emperor Nero, was only about 13 years old at this time (ca. AD 51), and the emperor then was Claudius Caesar, who died in AD 54, and had no serious issues at all with the Christians. The emperor Caligula might have filled that description, but he died in AD 40. It was also very obvious to anyone in the Roman Empire that there was an unusual peace in the empire, later called Pax Romana, which lasted well into the second century. There were no foreign wars. Although current events could not prove that they missed the Parousia, Paul could demonstrate with authority that the Day of the Lord, the beginning of the tribulation, was certainly not under way.

'May deceive' was ἐξαπατήσῃ, 'to cause someone to accept false ideas about something, *deceive, cheat,*' (BDAG). Paul stressed that he did not want the believers to be deceived in any way possible about this vital issue. The verb was expressed as an aorist subjunctive (the mode of possibility), rather than the imperative (the command mode), but some translators insert a 'missing' verb, 'βλεπετε,' 'see to it,' as an 'understood' omission (Bruce, p. 166). This reference to deception, coupled with verse 2, demonstrated that false teaching was the source of the problem, whether it came from outsiders, or unbelieving acquaintances observing their fate, not unlike Job's 'friends.'

2:4: "...the one who opposes and is being exalted above everything named God or worshipped, so that he sits himself as God in the temple of God, showing himself that he is God."

The **'Son of Destruction'** (probably equivalent to the 'Man of lawlessness') was further described here as a possible political or military world leader who will cause great destruction upon society during that time. That destruction was not specified, but may have been due either to wars, or a massive famine, or both. Here, Paul added to the description by saying that this 'person' 'opposes,' ἀντικείμενος, 'one who not only opposes, but was probably 'God's end time adversary' (BDAG).

He was also a person who exalted himself above every aspect of God, or other 'gods,' or, by implication, above all other religions.

'Exalted' was ὑπεραιρόμενος 'to have an undue sense of one's self-importance, *exalted...elated.*' The preposition of the prefix was ὑπερ 'a marker of a degree beyond that of a compared scale or extent,' (BDAG). 'Surpassing the norm' was added to αἴρω 'to raise to a higher place or position,' (BDAG). The present progressive tense adds that his hyper ego and will be continuous and always visible. He will also be self - exalted to the extreme. As a result, he will have a throne mounted in the temple at Jerusalem (probably expressed literally), which will further exalt him. He will present himself as 'God' Himself in his own temple.

2:5: "Do you not remember that while still with you, I was telling you these things?"

Paul was gently scolding the Thessalonians here, because he had taught them all these things before. He was likely wondering why they were so naïve to believe such a lie that the Parousia had already occurred.

2:6: "And now you know what is holding (him) back, for him to be revealed in his proper time."

Paul here reverted to the main topic of the events that will precede the Day of the Lord, so they will be forewarned - again. They will know now what is holding back the Day of the Lord from occurring at this time. The timing was not correct for the Man of Lawlessness to occur. The above sequence of events must precede the coming of the Man of Lawlessness. The 'him' referred to the 'Man of Lawlessness' in verse 3. The one holding back the man of lawlessness was the Holy Spirit.

2:7: "For the mystery of lawlessness is already working: only he who now is held back until he may be removed."

Paul carefully pointed out that the 'mystery, or secret,' of lawlessness, the conditions of the arrival of the Man of Lawlessness, were already showing signs of appearing: 'working' was ἐνεργεῖται, 'the secret force of lawlessness is at work, *is in operation.*' But in the time period before the Man of Lawlessness these activities were very limited, and the 'Man' who will lead this rebellion against God had not yet appeared on the world stage. 'The one who is under restraint,' κατέχων, a present progressive active participle revealing that the Man of Lawlessness was 'continually held back until he may be removed.' The Man of Lawlessness had no choice. A greater power was holding him back. Although the participle κατέχων was not passive, this person knew his powers were being limited, and, for the time being, perhaps he hoped that future opportunities will be allowed during the Tribulation for more devious activities.

"...May be removed...." [The subject 'he' referred to the Man of Lawlessness] was the phrase, ἐκ μέσου γένηται, with an aorist subjunctive passive verb (not middle in this context), indicating that the Man of lawlessness and his influence was limited by God for a time until that day approached. The literal meaning of the phrase was 'he may become removed from (the) midst,' referring to his removal by the Holy Spirit from the scene at the midpoint of the Tribulation (MacArthur, p. 279).

2:8: "And then the lawless one will be revealed, whom the Lord will destroy with the breath of His mouth and He will abolish (him) in the appearance of his 'Parousia,'"

At the very peak of his apparent liberty, the Man of Lawlessness, at his own 'Parousia,' will be destroyed by God or the Holy Spirit.

The verb, **'revealing,'** ἀποκαλυφθήσεται, meant, 'the mystery man will be revealed for all to see.' The verb was passive, indicating that God was the likely force behind the revelation. He lifted the veil to expose the Man of Lawlessness for the grossly evil individual that he really was.

The force behind the destruction was the 'breath of His mouth.' The 'breath of the Lord' was expressed in the OT as force of creativity, as in Gen. 2:7, where God 'breathed into his nostrils the breath of life,' or for the formation of the earth, in 2 Samuel, 22:16, 'Then the channels of the sea were seen, the foundations of the world were uncovered, at the rebuke of the Lord, at the blast of the breath of the Lord,' (NKJV). But the breath of God was also an image of God's judgment. In Isaiah 11:4, the prophet said, 'He shall strike the earth with the rod of his mouth, and with the breath of His lips shall He slay the wicked,' (NKJV). That power exceeded all the power known to man multiplied by millions. With that power, He created the universe and mankind; with that power he can destroy anyone: man, beast, or fallen angel. There was no limit to His power. He will use it here to destroy the Man of Lawlessness forever.

The verb for **'destroy,'** was ἀνελεῖ the future tense of ἀναιρέω, 'to get rid of by execution, *do away with, destroy*, usually by a violent death,' (BDAG). The term 'Parousia' was used as a parody of the Messiah's 'Parousia,' again in verse 9.

2:9: "…of whom the 'Parousia' (of the lawless one) is according to the working of Satan with all power and signs and false wonders,"

The power behind the Man of Lawlessness was now revealed to be Satan himself. During the brief period the Man of Lawlessness was roaming free, he was supported by three distinct reinforcing elements.

First, he had been given **'all power,'** πάσῃ δυνάμει, 'deeds which exhibit an ability to function powerfully, *deed of power, miracle, wonder*,' (BDAG). The 'all' magnified that power enormously.

Second, he had been given **'all signs,'** σημείοις, 'miracles worked by Satan or his agents to mislead God's people,' (BDAG).

Third, all **'false wonders'** will also be provided to his disposal. The adjectives 'all,' and 'false' applied to all three nouns with the meaning, 'everything belonging, in kind, to the same class designated by the noun, *every kind of, all sorts of*,' (BDAG), which would then mean, 'all types, or variations of false powers, false signs, and false wonders available to Satan or his agents.' The one purpose of these instruments was to expand the influence of the Man of Lawlessness throughout the whole world.

2:10: "...and with all (the) deceit of unrighteousness among those who are being destroyed, because they did not receive the love of the truth for them to be saved."

The Man of Lawlessness will use one more tool to achieve his ends: 'the deceit of unrighteousness,' to delude those who are perishing, if all the other tools fail. 'Deceit' was ἀπάτη, 'the introduction of every kind of wicked deception,' (BDAG). These tools were being allowed by God because the unbelieving remnants did not receive the love (agape love) of the truth, which would have saved them.

The verb, **'destroyed'** was passive, revealing that they were mere spectators in the event of their destruction; God was making it happen, not because God was vengeful, but because they rebelled against Christ's way of salvation, much like the rebellious Israelites in the desert.

2:11: "And for this reason, God will send to them the effect of delusion, which they may believe the lie,"

Here was an example of God contributing to their unbelief: He hardened their hearts and accelerated their fall into destruction. After signs of delusion already growing, God hastened that activity, qualitatively, and assisted them in that destructive pathway. The end result: that they may believe a lie and perish even sooner than they would have because of it. Their minds and their hearts were completely hardened, and so, easily crushed.

2:12: "...in order that all those who were not believing, but taking pleasure in unrighteousness, may all be condemned."

These rebels who have believed the lies, the effects of their delusion were now faced with the result of that way of life: eternal condemnation. They were given every chance to believe, but willfully they chose not to, and took pleasure in the effects of their choices be continually taking pleasure in unrighteousness. They crossed the line, and God contributed to their delusion; now they had to face the consequences of their evil choices.

'May be condemned' was the passive subjunctive verb, κριθῶσιν, 'the divine tribunal to administer justice which God brings upon sinners,' (BDAG). In this courtroom, there will be no plea agreements, no consideration of the origin of their failures, no rationalizing or blaming others for their poor judgment, because God is the Judge, who is all-knowing. Their guilt cannot be reasoned away. The punishment will be severe and final. There will never be any appeals or reduced sentences.

"Restoration and Renewal: Paul's Gentleness in dealing with his Naïve Flock:"

II Thessalonians 2:13-17:

2:13: "But we ourselves are always obliged to be grateful for you, brothers and sisters having been loved by the Lord, because God from the beginning chose you for salvation through sanctification by means of the Holy Spirit and belief in the truth,"

The reasons for Paul's belief in his gratitude for them are clearly stated:

First, they had been loved by God: 'loved' was ἠγαπημένοι, a present perfect participle that was intensive, where the action of the 'loving' was considered to be a *continuous* event, not merely a point of beginning in the past and a conclusion in the present with resulting effects: God's love for them was not interrupted by any 'bump in the road,' particularly this one.

Another reason that was active in Paul's mind was God's choice to bring salvation to them individually. This salvation was preplanned from the beginning, and included a process to perfect the failures of these believers by providing sanctification to them through the supervision of the Holy Spirit. How could Paul do otherwise than be grateful for their loving status in His family?

The third reason for Paul's gratitude for them was their 'belief of the truth.' 'Belief' was πίστει, 'a state of believing on the basis of the reliability of the one trusted,' (BDAG), in this case the objective genitive was the object of belief: 'truth.' Faith in God always rested objectively on a foundation of truth. The personification of that truth was Christ. The Thessalonians expressed the validity of that objective reality when they were converted.

2:14: "...for which reason He [also] called you through our gospel for (the) possession of (the) glory of our Lord Jesus Christ."

Paul also revealed to them that, for the reasons just stated they were 'called,' ἐκάλεσεν, 'choose for receipt of a special benefit or experience,' in this case, an official 'proclamation' to share in God's glory, (BDAG). The 'gospel' was the objective truth upon which their calling was based.

'Our gospel' was significant here. It was not just Paul's gospel. He always operated with a team of co-workers, who shared his mission, and contributed in the teaching and preaching of that gospel. They not only needed to be recognized as contributors to the gospel outreach, but Paul intended here to contrast his entire team against those who deluded them with their false claims. They were genuine; they were selfless; they were caring; they were knowledgeable. They were also devoted men of God.

'Possession' was a vital word here. It was περιποὶησιν, a compound noun, περὶ + ποιέω, 'to do something around oneself,' or, 'the experience of an event of acquisition, *gaining, obtaining*,' (BDAG). The believers were in the process of acquiring the 'glory of our Lord Jesus Christ,' beginning from the point of conversion. He was willing to share His glory with all believers, because they knew Him experientially (the γινώσκω kind of knowing), and they loved Him with all their hearts. These same virtues were also reciprocated to them by Christ through the Holy Spirit. 'Of (the) glory' was an objective genitive revealing the object of their acquisition: 'His glory.'

2:15: "Therefore, brothers and sisters, stand fast and hold the traditions which you were taught, either by the (spoken) word, or by our epistle."

'Therefore,' that was based on His calling and their precious acquisition of Christ (verse 14), Paul called them to perform two commands. First, Paul called on them to **'stand fast.'** This verb was στήκετε, from στήκω, a military term, 'to stand erect,' 'to keep standing firm,' (Thayer). During a military engagement, if the soldiers, as a group, broke and ran, that would spell disaster for the outcome of the battle. In the face of opposition, they needed to be disciplined to stand fast and face the enemy with a vigorous fighting spirit. Paul was calling them to do just that. Second, Paul asked them to hold on to their traditions in the future. **'Hold'** was κρατεῖτε, in the present progressive tense ('continually hold'). The verb meant 'to adhere strongly to, *hold*,' (BDAG). It implied the holding must be accomplished with the gripping power of a professional wrestler. Training for that kind of grip was required. 'Traditions' was παραδόσεις, a compound noun, παρα + δίδωμι, literally, 'to give over from beside another,' or 'the content of instruction that had been handed down, *teachings*,' (BDAG). This was the specific problem that they faced when they believed the lies of others about the Parousia which 'had already occurred.' They did not learn well enough, or forgot Paul's teachings about eschatology (the study of the end-times).

2:16: "Now, our Lord Jesus Christ Himself and God our Father who loved us and gave us eternal comfort and good assurance by means of grace,"

If Paul was exhorting them to several commands in verse 16, then the Thessalonians were going to need the direct assistance of the Holy Spirit to make it happen. Verses 16 and 17 represented a wish-prayer to God and Christ to assist. The first verb here, in the form of an aorist participle, ἀγαπήσας, 'the one who loved us with the agape kind of love,' as defined by the sacrifice of Christ, was singular here, possibly indicating that it referred to God only, not Christ (Wanamaker, p. 270). However, Hiebert provided an alternate view, 'It seems that the whole construction is intended to stress the unity of the persons in the Godhead,' (Hiebert p. 355). Therefore, God and Christ were addressed as One by Paul: equals in essence, in power, and in wisdom.

God and Christ not only loved the believers, but they gave them 'eternal comfort' and 'good assurance.' The first of these twin gifts was 'eternal **comfort,'** αἰωνὶαν, 'eternal.' The second was **παράκλησιν,** 'lifting another's spirits, *comfort, consolation,'* (BDAG). Note how anxiety-ridden the believers were when they thought that the Parousia had already occurred. Their anxiety was due to the lack of trust in the teaching that was passed down to them by Paul. God and Christ had promised them comfort that would last eternally, in every situation they faced. **'Good assurance'** was ἐλπὶδα, meaning 'the looking forward to something with some reason for confidence respecting fulfillment, *hope expectation,'* (BDAG), but 'hope' today in the language on the street means a vague wish that something good will come. The 'hope' of the NT was a strong assurance of fulfillment, a guarantee of results. The noun, **ἀγαθῆν** was the nature of that expectation, which was characterized by Paul as especially good, in the best sense of the word.

2:17: "…to encourage your hearts and strengthen you in every work and in every good word."

The conclusion of the wish-prayer was expressed added two more wishes as verbs in the optative mode:

'encouragement' and 'standing firm.' 'Encourage' was **παρακαλέσαι,** a compound verb, **παρά + καλέω,** literally, 'to call someone beside you for encouragement purposes,' or 'to instill someone with courage or cheer, *comfort, encourage, cheer up,'* (BDAG). The use of the noun form in verse 16 and the verb form here was an emphatic repetition. This was one virtue that the Thessalonians needed now, perhaps as much or more than the other requests.

The second verb, was **στηρίξαι,** from **στηρίζω,** meaning, 'to cause to be inwardly firm or committed, *confirm, establish, strengthen,'* (BDAG). They needed to be 'comforted' and 'established' in the faith. Both were vital to their spiritual maturity.

'Reinstatement as Equals and Warnings'
II Thessalonians 3:1-18

'Reinstatement as Equals' II Thessalonians 3:1-5:

3:1: "Finally, brothers and sisters, pray for us, in order that the word of the Lord may run speedily and may be glorified, even as (it is) with you,"

When Paul asked them to pray for 'us,' he was acknowledging them as equal partners of the gospel. The Thessalonians were undergoing persecution in northern Greece. Paul here in Corinth was likely embroiled in daily conflicts in the synagogue that would later explode into legal charges being leveled against him. But now, Paul, his converts, and his team were undergoing verbal accusations by the Jewish unbelievers of the synagogue in Corinth. By asking for prayer, the believers in Thessalonica, as poor as they were, could do something to help the newly arrived Paul and his associates. They certainly would be appreciative of Paul's needs, and could pray intelligently for solutions.

'Run speedily' was τρέχω, an athletic term, often associated with running a race in the games, meant, 'to proceed quickly and without restraint, *progress,*' (BDAG), relating here to the advance of the gospel with a continuous advance (present tense verb). Paul was making some progress, but the heat of resistance was also growing rapidly. The second prayer request was that the 'word of the Lord,' the gospel message, may receive the glory it deserved in these agitated debates, δοξάζεται, a present progressive tense verb ('continually') with a passive voice.

Paul recognized that, despite the persecution in Thessalonica, the believers there were advancing in numbers. Paul was recognizing their spiritual success in this area with the phrase, καθὼς πρὸς ὑμᾶς, literally, 'even as (it is) with you,' referring to both of the verbs mentioned above. They were advancing in the faith, at least in the one dimension of numerical expansion.

3:2: "...and in order that we may be rescued from absurd and evil men: for the faith (is) not among all men."

The purpose clause here ('in order that') introduced another area needed for prayer: They were faced with Jewish men who resisted Paul's gospel message, and Paul sensed that their rage might erupt in physical persecution. 'May rescue' was ῥυσθῶμεν, from ῥύομαι, 'to rescue from danger... *deliver,*' (BDAG). The early months at Corinth were dangerous times for Paul and his associates. Even later in his 18 month stay, and other visits to the city, Paul had to be careful because of the stubborn opposition.

The dangerous men that proved such a threat to Paul were described here in two characteristics of behavior. First, they were men who were 'absurd,' ἀτόπων from ἄτοπος,' 'pertaining to being behaviorally out of place, *evil, wrong, improper*,' (BDAG). This term could be used to describe persons (plural here) who were not behaving with reason, showing an outrageous behavior during a debate.

Second, they were described as inherently immoral men, πονηρῶν from πονηρός, 'degenerate,' (BDAG), possibly with bad language and a temper to match the description. The 'and' here, joining the two characteristics could represent a hendiadys (literally, 'one through two,'), two words describing men having one characteristic that was a combination of two descriptors. The combination of these traits could have made them very dangerous.

3:3: "But the Lord is faithful, who will establish you and guard you from the evil one."

Paul abruptly returned to his discussion with the Thessalonians, using the pronoun, 'you' which, because of the 'and' applied to both verbs, 'establish,' and 'guard.'

'Establish' στηρίξει, used before in 2:17 in the optative mode expressing a prayer-wish, was used again with the same meaning, but the tense and the mode were different, expressed in the future indicative. The indicative mode was the mode of fact: 'it is a fact that the Lord will establish you….'

'Guard' was φυλάξει, from φυλάσσω, to protect by taking careful measures, *guard, protect*,' (BDAG), and was also in the future indicative. What was the critical reason for these using these two verbs? The Thessalonians needed to be protected from the 'evil one' (πονηροῦ).

3:4: "But we have been persuaded by the Lord about you, that you are doing and will do the things we have commanded."

Paul may have conveyed the notion that their questionable actions in the recent past were a blight on their progress, and Paul may have acted like the 'critical parent.' But here, he allayed those notions with an expression of confidence. That confidence was based on Paul's knowledge of their positive response in situations like these. He was confident that they would respond 'to do' all the things he commanded of them. That confidence was positive, because he commended them for following his commands even now, despite their misunderstanding about the Parousia.

3:5: "Now may the Lord direct your hearts into the love of God and into the patience of Christ."

Paul used the main verb here as an aorist active optative, a verb form of a wish-prayer. The verb was κατευθῦναι, from κατευθῦνω, literally, 'to make a straight line....' (Thayer). But in this verse it meant 'direct our way,' (BDAG). Paul's wish was for two things to occur with respect to the Thessalonians. First, He requested that the Lord may direct their hearts into the protective sphere of God's love for them. We are taking 'of God' as a subjective genitive. Second, he requested that they may be directed into the sphere of Christ's 'patience' ὑπομονήν, 'the capacity to hold out or bear up in the face of difficulty, *patience, endurance, perseverance...*' (BDAG). Another meaning could be, 'patient waiting for someone or something, *expectation*' (BDAG), as in the Parousia. But since they were under persecution, and Paul already clarified their confusion about the Parousia, it may be more precise to adopt the meaning of this noun as 'patience under persecution,' rather than 'expectation' of the coming of Christ, (Bruce, p. 202).

'Of Christ' was taken here as a subjective genitive: 'that Christ's patience at the cross, as a model of suffering, may be directed into their hearts.'

'The Problem of the idle in the Church' II Thessalonians 3:6-15:

3:6: "But we command you, brothers and sisters, in the name of [our] Lord Jesus Christ, to keep you away from every brother walking in laziness and not according to the tradition which they received from us."

Amidst the wish-prayers and encouragement, Paul here turned to a formal command regarding some who were lazy, and not working. In I Thessalonians 5:14 Paul had warned those who were disorderly and not part of the team, to become active workers. Apparently, when Timothy delivered the first letter, he found that the lazy church members still did not want to participate in the work of the church, even after the letter was read to the assembly.

Therefore, Paul now must use consequences for those rebels with a formal command for the whole church: 'keep away from them, avoid contact with them until they change their flawed attitude.' The problem was considered so serious by Paul that he devoted the whole section of verses 6 through 15 to this single topic. The problem was compounded because the church was providing food to this group, and the real workers in the church were overwhelmed with the tasks at hand, while this group refused to work. 'In laziness' was the adverb, ἀτάκτως, 'in defiance of good order,' BDAG), and in more specific terms here as 'idleness.' See also 3:11.

3:7: "For you yourselves knew how it is necessary to follow us, because we were not disorderly among you..."

Paul had been a model for them, working as a missionary, by not using church funds to support himself. He expected the church workers who were provided food to 'earn their keep.' 'Follow' was μιμεῖσθαι, from μιμέομαι, and meant, 'to use as a model, *imitate, emulate, follow,*' (BDAG). It was an aorist infinitive deponent verb with an active meaning. By saying Paul and his team were not 'disorderly' among them, he meant that they did not ask for donations and live off the church. That was apparently altered by the church at Thessalonica so that the church would provide food for at least some of the workers, who were perhaps indigent (see verse 10).

3:8: "...nor did we eat free food from anyone, but with labor and toil, working night and day in order not to burden any of you:" Apparently, when

Paul arrived in Thessalonica and founded the church, he must have noticed that these people who were being saved were not, for the most part, among the wealthy class in the city. Paul would not become a drain on their limited resources. He did the same thing at Corinth, but for a different reason. There, it was a conflict with the traditions of patronage (see I Corinthians).

Paul did not say what work he did, but it was likely what he was trained in: a tent-maker. His team was possibly also working, for the 'subject' of the participle, ἐργαζάμενοι, 'working' was plural. The present tense of the participle ('continually') seemed to indicated long hours, perhaps 6 days per week, probably over the whole time they were there. The labor was apparently very hard, likely interspersed with ministerial duties.

3:9: "...not because we do not have authority (to demand it), but in order that we may give ourselves to you (as) an example in order to follow us."

In Luke 10:7, or Matthew 10:9, 10, Jesus established that authority for the disciples to receive food and drink for His traveling missionaries from the homes they visited, or by implication, from the churches after they were established. These truths were likely well known from the oral tradition that was disseminated from Palestine several decades earlier.

'Authority' was ἐξουσίαν, 'a state of control over something, freedom of choice, *a right to act,*' (BDAG). This principle of support was also well established in Hellenistic times by traveling philosophers in order to develop their careers in Greek or Roman cities of the time. This Graeco-Roman tradition made the idea of Christian missionary support outside of Palestine as an accepted model for the churches as they were developed in the first century AD. However, Paul varied his approach in this matter of support for himself, perhaps understanding that Christ's principle was not a demand, but a choice which could be made by each traveling missionary.

An **'example'** to which Paul referred here was τύπον, 'an archetype serving as a model, *type, pattern, model... or example*' (BDAG). Paul set the example of support by how he and his missionaries refused financial assistance. Each church could then choose to follow his pattern, or vary its application as they saw fit.

3:10: "For even when we were with you, we commanded you this: that if anyone is not willing to work, neither should he eat."

But as Paul discussed this issue of support of church workers, he demanded of them one principle: if a church worker or missionary refused to work while he was being supported by the church, then he should not receive his food allotment. Accountability was required.

3:11: "For we are hearing that certain ones who are walking among you in a disorderly manner, not working, but are busybodies:"

Here Paul revealed the source of this discussion: 'hearing,' that probably came from Timothy when he delivered I Thessalonians. When Paul mentioned this issue in I Thessalonians 5:14, he used the word, ἀτάκτος, 'in defiance of good order,' (BDAG), again in 3:6 as an adverb, and now here also as an adverb, 'in a disorderly manner.' Paul viewed this conduct as a serious violation of good church order. The meaning was also amplified by showing what these 'idle' workers were doing: they were 'busybodies,' here expressed as a present progressive tense ('continual action') participle, περιεργοζομένους, literally, 'working around,' rather than 'working on' the task assigned, or 'to be intrusively busy, be a busybody, a meddler,' (BDAG).

These 'workers,' perhaps decided to do something in response to Paul's first letter. Instead of just lying around doing nothing, they began circulating among the church members as 'social butterflies,' thinking they were at least doing something if anyone checked. Timothy must have seen them talking and quickly realized that the substance of the conversation had nothing to do with their assigned tasks. This news must have infuriated Paul when he heard it.

3:12: "But to such people we are commanding and exhorting by means of the Lord Jesus Christ, in order that while working in silence they may eat their own food."

In this verse, Paul outlined a specific demand of the church regarding these lazy recalcitrants. The command was formal and used two verbs: 'commanding,' παραγγέλλομεν, 'to make an announcement about something that needs to be done, give orders, command, instruct, direct,' (BDAG), and the verb, 'exhort' παρακαλοῦμεν, 'to urge strongly, appeal to, urge, exhort, encourage,' (BDAG). These verbs were presented in the present progressive tense indicative mode, indicating a continual action, as an official order and amplifying the order by naming the Lord Jesus Christ as the authority behind the demands.

3:13: "But you, brothers and sisters, do not grow weary doing beautiful works."

Here Paul abruptly changed his serious tone to reveal his softer side: a pastoral care for the church members. The verb, 'grow weary,' was ἐγκακήσητε, 'to lose one's motivation in continuing a desirable pattern of conduct or activity, *lose enthusiasm, be discouraged,*' (BDAG). The challenges of church pastoral work could drain pastors and church workers. Paul appealed to them not to lose heart in these very trying church responsibilities.

'Beautiful works' was καλοποιοῦντες, too often translated 'doing good works.' This participle, where the prefix καλός was the Greek word for something aesthetically pleasing, was 'beautiful,' not just 'good.' The normal word for 'good,' was ἀγαθός, 'something inherently good,' but not necessarily beautiful. The works that church members were called to do were 'beautiful' works, because they were accomplished for the glory of Christ. He made the drudgery of the work beautiful. An attitude shift was called for here to avoid burnout.

3:14: "And if anyone is not obeying our word through our epistle, note this one, not to intermingle with him, in order that he may be ashamed:"

Red flags were to be used for those members: 'note this one,' σημειοῦσθε, 'to take special notice of, mark,' (BDAG). Those who were not obeying the commands and exhortations of Paul's epistles needed special consequences.

Perhaps Paul had some idea by now that his letters were part of God's work, and the Holy Spirit was rendering assistance in word choice, structure, and idea formation. This was, perhaps, the dawning of the notion of the OT idea of God 'breathing out' Scripture through His writers (II Timothy 3:16) that Paul was now beginning to realize applied to his own writings. Regardless of that possibility, his own letters were to be taken authoritatively, and Paul laid out consequences for not following them. The main verb of the phrase, 'not to intermingle with them,' was συναναμίγνυσθαι, from συναναμίγνυμι, 'mingle, associate with,' (BDAG). The purpose of these consequences was also stated, with the phrase, 'in order that he may be ashamed,' a sure sign of a genuine Christian, rather than a wolf wearing sheep's clothing.

3:15: "…and do not regard him as an enemy, but admonish him as a brother."

Paul here qualified the conditions of the consequences to include the motive behind those restrictions. Those individuals were to be regarded as erring brothers, rather than enemies. 'Regard' was the verb, ἡγεῖσθε, from ἡγέομαι, 'to engage in an intellectual process, think, consider, regard,' (BDAG). 'Admonish' was νουθετεῖτε, 'to counsel about the avoidance or cessation of an improper course of conduct, admonish, warn, instruct,' (BDAG). 'Admonish' here was the thinking process that involved using discrimination about how an offender was to be treated. He was to be treated as a brother that failed. He was still a family member at this point. The idea was not to drive him away from the family with an angry demeanor reserved for enemies.

'The Conclusion of the Letter' II Thessalonians 3:16-18:

3:16: "And (may) the Lord of peace Himself always give peace to you in every place. (May) the Lord (be) with all of you."

The Lord who was the essence of peace will share His peace with believers. Paul was here requesting that Christ Himself, and no other, might provide that quality of peace, as the believer continually connected with the Holy Spirit in prayer and rejoicing. Paul was asking Christ, who expresses His will to the believer that He may be with them all.

3:17: "The greeting of Paul with my own hand, which is a sign in every epistle: thus I write."

Paul always wrote the last portion of the epistle with his own hand in order to authenticate it from any forgeries. His writing could be checked against other original letters to prevent that situation from occurring. Also, it was a personal touch to the readers.

3:18: "(May) the grace of our Lord Jesus Christ (be) with all of you."

The grace χάρις, although a noun, is an action word. It is the unmerited and undeserved favor of Christ showered upon believers, which He willingly shares with His children, providing a fitting conclusion to this letter.

Thessalonians
Recommended Bibliography Commentators

Abbreviations:

BRUCE   **Word Biblical Commentary, 1 & 2 Thessalonians.** By F.F. Bruce, Word Books, Publishers, Waco, Texas, 1982.

MACARTHUR   **The MacArthur New Testament Commentary, 1 & 2 Thessalonians.** By John MacArthur, Moody Publishers, Chicago, 2002.

WITHERINGTON   **1 and 2 Thessalonians, A Socio-Rhetorical Commentary.** By Ben William B Eerdmans Publishing Company, Grand Rapids, Michigan and Cambridge, U.K., 2006.

WANAMAKER   **The Epistles to the Thessalonians.** By Charles A. Wanamaker, New International Greek Testament Commentary, William B. Eerdmans and the Paternoster Press Grand Rapids, Michigan and Cumbria, U.K., 1990.

CHAPTER 4
I CORINTHIANS

Illustration 3: Corinth
The Emperor Nero Coin from Corinth, AD 67 or 68

[Drawing by J. Rouse]

The obverse of a silver coin from Corinth, Greece, minted about the same time the apostle Paul likely came through there on his way from Philippi to Nikopolis, on the Ionian Sea to meet Titus, his fellow-worker ministering in Crete at the time. The date of the coin is AD 67-68, which could match with the possible dates of Paul's and Nero's travels. Nero was attending the games in Corinth, with a large assembly of his Royal Military Guard traveling with him. It was not an ideal place or time for Paul; it was in Corinth that he was possibly arrested the second time. He also might have been turned in to the Roman authorities by the Jewish metalsmith, Alexander, who gave Paul much trouble years earlier at the riot in the theater in Ephesus (see I Timothy 4: 14-15). Nero here was just 33 years old, and this was just months before his death by suicide on June 9, AD 68. His features were rather grotesque here, showing his obesity without restraint (the coin was likely minted just after his death).

[Drawing by J. Rouse]

On the reverse, Nero's image was again on the Corinthian coin, this time within a temple in the civic center, likely Temple E, the Roman family Imperial Temple in the city. He was so honored by the Romanized city of Corinth because he participated in these games as a contestant, something the Roman upper class was very upset about. Also, he was allowed to win in every kind of contest that he entered. So he walked away with many prizes. Nero blamed the burning of Rome on the Christians three years earlier in AD 64, and the years between early 65 and 68, particularly in Rome, there were brutal imperial persecutions instituted by Nero. He found the Christians a convenient scapegoat, after the populace in Rome blamed him for starting the fire to build a magnificent new palace, begun just after the fire.

Illustration 4: Corinth
The Bema (The City's Open Law Court)

[Photo by J. Rouse]

This building was the Bema, or the regional court building located in the middle of the civic center. It was an open platform, without a roof, with a rectangular base that rose to about 12 to 15 feet in height from the ground of the open civic center area. On each side of the structure there were alcoves with built-in bench seats to accommodate the two sides of a judicial matter, which kept apart the two sides from fighting. Furthermore, Roman soldiers were present to keep the peace, or, sometimes, to punish the party who brought a frivolous law suit. In the center and front of the building, the judge would sit on the top level and the plaintiffs would plead their case on the ground level just below him. The structure had no roof, and there were two flanking curtain walls about 20-30 feet high in the rear of the back side, and on each corner, to enhance the prestige of the judge, and also, perhaps, to create an efficient sound production.

The Apostle Paul was brought before this court when the ruler of the Jewish synagogue in the city made a legal charge against Paul and his associates, near

106

the end of his 18 month stay in Corinth in the year AD 51, plus or minus one year, recorded in Acts 18:1-17. The first synagogue ruler of Corinth, Crispus, actually became a believer in the Lord, with his whole house. It was the next synagogue ruler, Sosthenes, who possibly was forced by leading synagogue Jews to bring legal charges against Paul to Gallio, the district judge over all of southern Greece. Gallio was a recent appointee of the emperor Claudius, and he had just arrived in Corinth. He was also a brother to the philosopher, Seneca, who later became virtual ruler over Rome from the death of Claudius in AD 54 until his retirement in AD 62. Gallio was the major legal official for the whole of Achaia, including Athens and southern Greece. When Paul was about to speak, Gallio pronounced the case dismissed, and the charge to be fraudulent, which activated a beating of the Jews by the Roman guards. Interestingly, just a few weeks later, before Paul left Corinth, Sosthenes also became a believer, and when Paul left Corinth for Ephesus, Sosthenes went with him, and served in the churches at Ephesus.

In the fourth century AD (circa AD 320), when Christianity finally became a legal religion, Christians of the time remembered the Bema incident and the structure. Church architects decided to take down the curtain walls and build a small church on the top of the platform, to show to all that Christianity triumphed over paganism, in spite of those two plus centuries of serious imperial persecutions.

Illustration 5: Corinth
The Bema: The West Waiting Room

[Photo by J. Rouse]

This photo shows the western alcove for litigants: There were two of these areas for litigants and their supporters, one on either side of the main structure. Paul and his friends would be seated during the legal proceedings which would take place at the top of the main structure, to the left of this photo. When the defendants were asked to speak, they would have been led to the front of the building where they could face the judge, in this case, the chief magistrate for southern Greece, Gallio, the brother of the famous philosopher Seneca, the current tutor of the teenage Nero, whose mother had just recently married the Emperor Claudius.

Illustration 6: Water, Water, Everywhere
Peirene Fountain: Civic Center Area

[Photo by J. Rouse]

One of the most necessary issues for ancient cities was water production. Corinth had a special gift for resolving water needs for cleaning, bathing, and drinking purposes. There was a natural underground river that ran for 7 miles from the mountain behind the city. That mountain was approximately 1800 feet in elevation, and on its top were several ancient temples, which were mostly small in size. Centuries before this fountain spring was built by the Romans, when the destroyed Greek city was renovated into a Roman city in BC 146, the inhabitants of Greek Corinth had learned about the rich source of water that flowed out of the mountain. In Roman times, the users of water could climb down the stairs and into a wading pool, seen here, and even climb into the underground chambers that fed the water into the pools. Corinth had a number of such water sources, spread throughout the city in various areas. Peirene fountain was built in a quatrefoil shape, somewhat like a four-leaf clover. At the apex of each of the four semicircular forms was a place for a statue of one of the gods.

Illustration 7: A Dining Sanctuary above the City
Temple of Demeter and Kore

[Photo by J. Rouse]

The Sanctaury of Demeter and Kore was excavated with extensive ruins which dated probably from early Greek times (7th century BC) until sometime in the fourth century AD when the structure was likely destroyed. Demeter was represented in Greek culture as the goddess of agriculture. Kore was the daughter of Demeter. The cult story generally reported that Kore was abducted by Hades, who raped her and kept her hostage, while her mother searched for her. The story involved Demeter's long search for her daughter, and finally, through the assistance of Zeus, Kore was reunited with her mother, at least for part of the year.

This story represented a common problem among women of the ancient world, who would all too often encounter men who would overpower them and rape them. Whether or not this sanctuary encouraged women to feast together as mother and daughter couples, or family related females is uncertain, but was entirely possible. No other sanctuary from the excavations uncovered as many dining rooms as this sanctuary.

The sanctuary complex exposed several dozen small 'dining rooms', which could accommodate no more than a few diners: perhaps, in most cases, just two. Other dining rooms were larger, likely for group events. This sanctuary was not the only one in Corinth which had dining rooms available for customers of the city. These dining rooms became a problem for Christians as Paul warned the Corinthian believers not to be seen eating in one of those sacred shrines by other Christians. I Corinthians 10:14-22.

Illustration 8: Corinth
Erastus Inscription
Erastus: Corinth City Official at Corinth, Friend of Paul and Timothy

[Photo by J. Rouse]

The close-up photo here spells out the name in Latin: (E)rastus. The message then explained that he paid for the construction of Theater Street to gain a political post, a common action for city government positions in that day. His name was mentioned three times in the New Testament: in Acts 19:22, Romans 16:23, and II Timothy 4:20. The span of time between these NT letters was about 17 years. It was possible that he obtained this post before he became a Christian, for there would have been civic duties that would have proved problematic for a Christian in pagan Corinth: meeting with other government officials in the dining areas of pagan temples, bowing in honor of other gods in meetings that he had to attend, not to speak of partaking of prostitutes in some of those meetings. It was likely that he resigned his office when he became a Christian and was then free to travel with Paul and his associates, which he seemed to do often. In the NKJV, Erastus was called the 'city treasurer,' which has not been confirmed, but possible. The block containing the first letter 'E' was not quite complete when the restoration of the area was accomplished, perhaps the first part of the letter was on another block not found in the excavations.

Theater Street was paid for by Erastus in order to acquire an important political post in Corinth. In that day, politicians were required to be rich and they had to perform civic responsibilities using part of their wealth to support the infrastructure of the city. This inscription was part of a park-like area below the theater. The street ran north and south ascending the hill that formed the bleachers of the theater. This street was covered with expensive marble. A 'step' across the street near the theater indicated that wagons were not allowed on this street.

Illustration 9: Corinth
Main Theater

[Photo by J. Rouse]

A view of the large theater, looking south, to the mountain behind the city is presented here. Theater Street ran north and south just to the left and out of sight in this photo. The bleachers have mostly disappeared over the centuries, but their general shape is visible in the photo. The circular wall at the base of the theater separated the audience from the arena area, marked by the sacrificial stone standing in the center. The photo was taken from the stage building area, now largely missing, where the actors would have presented the plays. Next to the theater across Theater Street were found ruins of a lunch counter for hungry audiences, before or after attending the programs. This theater was smaller than the one at Ephesus, accommodating only about 10,000 people. Proceeding south, just above the bleacher area, a smaller theater was also discovered in the excavations, built in the 2nd century A.D., after Paul's time. Corinth was a reasonably large city at the time of Paul's visit, estimated to have been about

50,000 people, spread over about eight miles from one end to another. However, Corinth was smaller in population than Ephesus, which had a population of about 300,000, and also Rome, which had about 1 million people.

Illustration 10: Corinth
A Synagogue Sign in Stone

[Photo by J. Rouse]

This stone was discovered in the rubble of the excavations in the civic center area, likely a reused stone during a later building project. The Greek letters in the photo show the last part of the word, 'synagogue Hebrew,' (–ΓΩΓΗ ΕΒ–, or in English, -gogue Heb–). Could it have been the sign that marked the presence of the NT synagogue? Critics of that view have pointed out that the letters were in a poorly carved state in Greek, and not in the neat and precise Latin letters that were found in the civic center area on other structures. However, the synagogues of the time were found in residential areas, not in the center of town. Possibly this crude sign found in the civic center marked a synagogue of an earlier time, reused perhaps in the rebuilding of a civic center structure, or as fill materials. Whether or not it was the sign marking the NT synagogue of the mid first century AD, is possible, but cannot be proven.

Illustration 11: Corinth
Lechaion Road looking North
'The Royal Road to and from Rome'

[Photo by J. Rouse]

Standing on the triumphal gateway, looking north, this monumental road led travelers from the harbor of Lechaion into the civic center area just behind where this photo was taken. This was the direction that visitors from Rome would have taken to enter the city center. The road was laid with marble, and was wider than other roads coming into this area, revealing a strong Roman influence and loyalty. The road also had barriers so wheeled vehicles were not permitted in this area. Vehicles bringing in supplies had to use the areas situated behind the shops. The view is looking north, and the ruins on the right and left of the road were shops for incoming and outgoing tourists. The triumphal arch, the base from which this photo was taken, commemorated the Roman conquest of Greece in BC 146, which leveled nearly all its Greek buildings to their foundations. Julius Caesar re-founded the city in BC 46. It was then repopulated by some of his Roman veterans and Corinth became a thriving Roman city in Greece that honored Roman culture, architecture and language, an influence that continued throughout the first century AD.

This road, called 'Lechaion Road,' led about a mile or so to the port town of Lechaion, one of the two major port towns of Corinth. The port area supported shipping from Rome and points west, and was made up of a man-made harbor and numerous warehouses. After Christianity was legalized in AD 322, a very large basilica church was constructed there, possibly over a pre-existing pagan temple. Although Corinth has been excavated extensively since 1896 by the American School of Classical Studies in Athens, the excavations have concentrated on the areas containing public buildings. Residential neighborhoods, for the most part, have been overlooked, being considered, understandably, to have a much lower priority.

Illustration 12
The Eastern Port of Corinth
Kenchreai

[Photo by J. Rouse]

This road was situated behind the shops of the main civic center of Corinth. The road led to the gate of the city walls and then on to Kenchreai, the second port city of Corinth. The view here was looking west to other ruins of the agora (civic center). To the right was the back of the civic center shops. Paul may have used this road when traveling from Kenchreai to the city proper.

[Photo by J. Rouse]

This is part of the remains of Kenchreai looking to the south and slightly east. One of the harbor moles can be seen extending into the sea. Over the 2,000 years since NT times, the Mediterranean Sea has risen, flooding many ancient seaport towns in the process. Much of the classical archaeological work on the mole and some other places, has been undertaken by underwater excavation equipment and techniques. A small temple of Isis was discovered on the mole, indicating that this site was the eastern port city of Corinth to points leading east, including Egypt, which the temple's presence honored. This town, unlike Lechaion, was mentioned twice in the NT, once in Acts 18:18, where Luke commented that Paul had taken a vow and had his hair cut at Kenchreai. The town was also once mentioned by Paul in Romans 16:1, where he mentioned Phoebe, 'a servant in the church in Kenchreai.'

Since the Peloponnesus was still attached to the Greek mainland through a thin area of land, ships from Rome had to venture around the dangerous waters south of the Peloponnesus. Consequently, the two ports became vital for shipping. Ships heading from Rome to points east would stop in Lechaion, unloading their cargo and passengers, and both would be transported overland to Kenchreai, about 6 miles from the civic center, where the passengers and cargo could board other ships heading east. The reverse was also true: ships heading west could avoid those dangerous seas, and unload passengers and freight at Kenchreai, where they would be transported overland to Lechaion and find ships going west. The thriving trade caused by this arrangement made Corinth a prosperous city throughout most of the Classical period.

Illustration 13
The Corinth Ampitheater

[Photo by J. Rouse]

This unexcavated amphitheater was located to the east and slightly north of the civic center, but within the city walls. As a Roman city in Greece, the

Roman settlers wanted all the reminders of home, including an amphitheater. 'Amphitheater,' by definition, was a 'double' theater shaped in an oval form. Various kinds of battles were staged in Roman amphitheaters, including gladiator battles, wild animal hunts and gladiator-animal fights, and wild animals devouring criminals convicted of capital crimes. In larger amphitheaters, as the Coliseum in Rome, sea battles were staged by filling the main floor of the amphitheater with water. These amphitheater events were sponsored by the Roman state, and they were considered a sport by the audiences. This amphitheater in Corinth was not built of marble, or even limestone blocks, but, from what was visible at the site, was made entirely of concrete. The bleachers extended around the edge of the oval; but, at one end, there was an underground area for animal cages, kept there until they were used in the performances. The amphitheater events were too brutal and bloody for the Greeks, and there were very few Roman-type amphitheaters built in Greece. This was one of those. The date is unknown, but it could have been constructed not long after the city was rejuvenated by Julius Caesar possibly as early as early as 40 to 20 B.C. A later date is also possible, ca. 200 to 300 A.D., arguing from the crudeness of the construction. However, marble overlays could have been used that did not survive the many centuries of earthquakes, and pilfering of fine marble was common for other uses. We favor an early date.

Illustration 14: Corinth
Amphitheater Comparison

[Photo by J. Rouse]

This was the underground cavern where the animals were caged. The builders, however, apparently did not realize that the Corinth area was earthquake country, and, in time, the ceilings fell to the ground, shown here as a massive number of giant slabs and small rocks.

[Photo by J. Rouse]

This is another amphitheater in Puteoli, Italy. This structure is not large, but the finished excavation and partial restoration revealed underground chambers, and the many rectangular 'openings' on the ground level were designed for the animals to be safely brought up from their cages below by elevator. The engineering was very complex and well thought out.

CHAPTER 4
I Corinthians, circa AD 55

BROAD VIEW:
CHRONOLOGY OF PAUL: AD 50 – 62

Chronology of Paul's Travels from AD 50 to 60:
Completing the Second Missionary Journey and Third

Feb., AD 50: Paul's first arrival in Corinth: (During the Second Missionary Journey).

Early July, 51 Gallio Trial: (Acts 18:12-17). This trial established the legal status of Christians under Roman law not only in Corinth, but probably in all of Achaia, including all of Southern Greece. The trial was likely near the conclusion of Paul's 18 month visit to Corinth.

Key Date: We believe that Gallio started his one-year term on July 1, 51 (Murphy-O'Connor). It was very likely that the Jews, learning of his arrival, wanted their accusation against Paul to be among the first cases on the docket that month.

Late July 51 through August

Paul left Corinth within a month, after the trial was over. He had spent 18 months in Corinth. Paul left with the intention to return to Syria which would close out his Second Missionary Journey. Aquila and Priscilla also closed their shop in Corinth, and the three left together to the eastern port of Corinth, leaving from Kenchreai.

Brief stop in Ephesus: Then they sailed on to Ephesus where Paul left Aquila and Priscilla. Paul evangelized a synagogue there, and the Jews vainly urged him to stay.

Spring, 52: After the brief stay in Ephesus, Paul sailed to Syria by sea, arriving in Palestine, thus completing his second missionary journey.

The Second Missionary Journey was recorded in **Acts 18:18-22.**

Fall to Winter 52: Paul started his **Third Missionary Journey** by going overland from Antioch to Ephesus. (**Acts 18:23**): Paul visited the churches on the way and arrived in Ephesus probably in the winter of 52. (**Acts 19:1**).

52 to 55: EPHESUS: Paul spent three years in Ephesus, two of those years in a rented or donated hall. **(Acts 19:1-20)**

Summer, 54: Paul sent a letter: 'the previous' or 'the severe letter' to the Corinthians, mentioned in **I Corinthians 5:9-10.** It was delivered by Titus, probably by sea. The issues in this letter were harsh, and on the return of Titus, Paul needed to clarify some issues in the Corinthian response. Consequently, he made the short second visit to Corinth by sea, inferred by the mention of a third visit **(II Corinthians 12:14).** Luke, in **Act. 20:1,2** established that Paul, after writing I Corinthians in Philippi was already headed for Corinth. Therefore there would be no reason for the second 'short' visit while in Macedonia (contrary to Harris, p. 57-58). Luke did not mention the second visit in Acts, which did not mean it didn't occur. It was not there probably because it did not rise to a major visit.

Spring of 55: Paul was delayed in his plans for the third visit Corinth because of Pentecost. He likely wrote I Corinthians during that time. **I Corinthians 16:8, 9.** Paul was further delayed because of the success of his mission in Ephesus, as evidenced by the book-burning of the valuable sorcery books among the converts.

Acts 19:11-20. Then another issue interfered with his plans to visit Corinth: the outbreak of the riot by the silversmiths in the theater.

Acts 19:21-41. When the civil disorder was over, Paul finally left Ephesus and traveled north to Troy.

Fall, 55: MACEDONIA to Corinth: Leaving Ephesus, Paul found a ship in Troas, which took him eventually to Philippi, **(Acts: 20:1).** There he stayed long enough to visit the church and meet the delegation who had delivered I Corinthians. Then he penned II Corinthians and sent it on ahead with Titus. On his way toward Corinth, he would also pick up the Macedonian collection for the poor believers in Judea.

Late Fall, 55: Leaving Philippi, he visited Thessalonica and possibly Berea before going on toward Corinth. He also visited Illyricum, a district north and west of Thessalonica at this time (Romans 15:19).

Late Fall/Spring, 55/57: CORINTH: Paul went to Corinth (overland, through Thessalonica, Berea, and Athens). He stayed in Corinth for 3 months, possibly writing the Book of Romans. Planning his next move, he wanted to go directly to Judea by sea, but unbelieving Jews laid plans to capture him on the road.

(Acts, 20:3). Changing his plans again, he decided to go overland through Macedonia again and back to Ephesus. However, Paul did not want to stop at Ephesus, so the ship continued on to Miletus, south of Ephesus. **Acts 20:17-38, II Corinthians 12:14.**

Spring 57 to Fall 60: In Judea, Paul was arrested and spent 2 years in prison, before being sent to Rome on appeal. **Acts 24:27.**

Spring 60 to Spring 62: Paul was sent to Rome, where he spent another 2 years under house arrest, before his trial. **Acts 28:30.**

Early Spring, 62: Paul's trial came up in Caesar's Court, and he was (probably) acquitted either by Burrus or Seneca.

Historical Broad View:
Emperor Nero Timeline

53 AD: Nero (age 16) married Claudius Caesar's daughter, **Octavia** (a second marriage for her), arranged by **Agrippina**, Nero's mother and now wife of Claudius, in order to put her son (by an earlier marriage) in line for the imperial succession.

54 AD: Agrippina murdered her husband Claudius Caesar with poison mushrooms. Nero was then proclaimed emperor. Since he was so young (17) and because Agrippina wanted him to succeed Claudius as emperor, she arranged (53 AD) for **Seneca** the famous philosopher to be his tutor before Claudius died. After the death of Claudius, Agrippina wanted to be the power behind the throne and she kept **Seneca** on as advisor and added another capable advisor, **Burrus**, head of the Praetorian Guard, to guide young Nero. Both Seneca and Burrus were successful in stabilizing the empire with judicious legislation and effective management strategies for the next 8 years.

55 AD: Nero began to show his true colors when he had his half-brother **Britannicus** murdered at a party where his family was gathered. Britannicus could have been a threat to Nero's rule as Caesar. In the same year, Nero sent his mother into exile so she would not present a threat to his rule.

58 AD: Nero began an affair with his best friend's wife (Poppaea), sending him off to a distant post so he could have the freedom he desired with her.

59 AD: Nero finally succeeded in murdering his mother, after four unsuccessful attempts.

60-62 AD: Paul's first 'imprisonment.' He wrote: Ephesians, Colossians, Philippians and Philemon.

62 AD: Burrus died of poison. He was replaced by **Tigellinus**, who had been exiled (AD 39) by Caligula for having an adulterous affair with Nero's mother. But because he had such a reputation for debauchery and depravity, Nero selected him to be his advisor. **Seneca**, after the death of **Burrus**, retired in disgust, and left the scene. With Seneca and Burrus both gone, Nero's world evolved into wild orgies, unstable legislation, arrests for treason and murderous intrigue. Nero Divorced Octavia, then had her murdered and married Poppaea. The hated laws of *maiestas* were reinstated (vague laws that gave willful emperors ways to terminate enemies legally).

62-63 AD: Through suspicion and poor advisement, Nero began a series of murders of potential enemies, including Roman Senators, wealthy nobles and others. Economic conditions worsened, so Nero would murder wealthy Romans and confiscate their properties. Enemies of Nero grew in number.

64 AD: (July, 64) **The great fire of Rome** destroyed over half of the city. Nero may have (?) climbed on the roof of a building and sang "The Capture of Troy" as the fire raged on. To his credit, Nero rebuilt a large portion of the city from his own funds. However, he also saved a large portion for his new palace (Domus Aurea) surrounding a man-made lake and massive gardens. Because of his palatial building project, residents of Rome had strong suspicions that he had set fire to the city intentionally. A rumor was spread (probably by Nero) that the Christians set the fire, starting the first of the imperial persecutions against Christians. Nero was becoming very bloodthirsty by this time, and was known to Christians as the (first) "antichrist."

65 AD: The Piso Assassination Plot was uncovered by Nero's agents. Nineteen people were murdered, all without a trial, and many on mere suspicion. Seneca and his nephew were among those who were forced to commit suicide. Seneca's brother, Gallio, managed to survive another year or two before he also fell victim to Nero. **The Persecution of the Stoic Philosophers** began.

66 AD: Nero murdered his pregnant wife Poppaea by kicking her to death when she complained about his coming home late from the games.

Fall, 66 AD: Nero traveled to Greece and attended the games as a contestant in chariot racing and singing events. The Roman people were outraged at the lack of respect and dignity he showed by participating in the games. Nero, on a whim, commanded three popular governors to commit suicide, also angering the local Graeco-Roman populace.

Early 68 AD: Paul's Death in Rome by beheading (the common and painless death sentence for Roman Citizens).

June 9, 68: The death of Nero: The Praetorian Guard and other rebel leaders revolted. Nero fled from Rome and attempted to commit suicide with his sword. His faithful secretary finished him off. He was 31 when he died. His last words were: "What an artist the world loses in me." The sociopath was finally gone.

NOTE: The above events represent only the tip of the iceberg for Nero's excesses and crimes. In Nero's case, "Absolute power corrupted absolutely."

Anticipating messages of I Corinthians:
"The Shame of the Cross; Divisions among you. Who were the nothings and the somethings? Paul Defended himself. Moral issues. The Master Architect and the Subcontractors."

Background: Chronology of Paul's Travels from 50 to 60 A.D., to the completion of the Second Missionary Journey:

Timeline: ca. Feb., 50 A.D. Paul's first arrival in Corinth: (During the Second Missionary Journey). Paul stayed in Corinth for eighteen months (Acts 18:11).

Early July, 51: The Gallio Trial: (Acts 18:12-17). This trial occurred likely at the end of his stay in Corinth and established the legal status of Christians under Roman law, not only in Corinth, but probably in all of Achaia, including all of Southern Greece, covering the major cities of Corinth and Athens.

Key Date: Gallio started his one-year term on **July 1, 51** (Murphy-O'Connor). It was very likely that the Jews, learning of his arrival, wanted Gallio to hear this case, and requested that it be placed among the very first cases on the docket.

From Late July 51 through August: Paul likely left Corinth within a month after the trial was over. He left with the intention to return to Syria which would close out his Second Missionary Journey. Aquila and Priscilla also closed their shop in Corinth, and the three left together to the eastern port of Corinth, Kenchreai, where they sailed to Ephesus. Before leaving Ephesus, Paul evangelized a synagogue there, and the Jews vainly urged him to stay. Paul left Aquila and Priscilla in Ephesus, and he then sailed to Syria arriving in Palestine, thus completing his Second Missionary Journey Acts 18:18-22, arriving in the late spring of 52 A.D.

Fall to Winter 52 Paul started his **Third Missionary Journey** by going overland from Antioch to Ephesus (Acts 18:23). Paul visited the churches on the way and arrived in Ephesus probably in the winter of 52 (Acts 19:1).

52 to 55: EPHESUS: Paul spent three years in Ephesus, two of those years in a rented or donated hall (Acts 19:1-20).

Summer, 54: He also sent a previous or a 'severe' letter to the Corinthians, mentioned in I Corinthians 5:9-10. It was sent by Titus, probably by sea. The issues in this letter were harsh, and on the return of Titus, Paul needed to clarify some issues in the Corinthian response. Consequently, he made the short second visit to Corinth by sea, inferred by the mention of a third visit (II Corinthians 12:14). Luke, in Acts 20:1, 2 established that Paul, after writing I Corinthians in Philippi, was already headed for Corinth. Therefore, there would be no reason for the second 'short' visit while in Macedonia (contrary to Harris, p. 57-58). Luke did not mention the second visit in Acts, which did not mean it didn't occur. It was not there probably because it did not rise to a major visit.

Spring of 55 Writing of I Corinthians: Paul was delayed in his plans for the third visit Corinth because of Pentecost. He likely wrote I Corinthians during this time when Paul was further delayed because of the ministerial success (I Corinthians 16:8, 9), evidenced by the (Acts 19:11-20). Then another issue interfered with his plans to visit Corinth: the outbreak of the riot by the silversmiths in the Theater of Ephesus. When the civil disorder was over, Paul finally left Ephesus and traveled north to Troy Acts 19:21-41.

Fall, 55: MACEDONIA to Corinth: Leaving Ephesus, Paul found a ship in Troas, which took him eventually to Philippi, (Acts: 20:1). There he stayed long enough to visit the church and meet the delegation who delivered I Corinthians. Then he penned II Corinthians and sent it on ahead with Titus. On his way toward Corinth, he would also pick up the Macedonian collection for the poor believers in Judea.

Late Fall, 55: Leaving Philippi, he visited Thessalonica and possibly Berea before going on toward Corinth. He also visited Illyricum, a barbarian district north and west of Thessalonica at this time (Romans 15:19).

Late Fall/Spring, 55/57: CORINTH: Paul went to Corinth (overland, through Thessalonica, Berea, and Athens). He stayed in Corinth for 3 months, likely writing the Book of Romans. Planning his next move, he wanted to go directly to Judea by sea, but finding out that Jews laid plans to capture him on the road (Acts, 20:3), he changed his plans again, and decided to go overland through Macedonia again and back to Ephesus. However, Paul did not want to stop at Ephesus, so he caught a ship which continued on to Miletus, south of Ephesus: Acts 20:17-38, II Corinthians 12:14.

Spring 57 to Fall 60: In Judea, Paul was arrested and spent 2 years in prison, before being sent to Rome on appeal. **Acts 24:27.**

Spring 60 to Spring 62: Paul was sent to Rome, where he spent another 2 years under house arrest, before his trial. **Acts 28:30.**

Early Spring, 62: Paul's trial came up in Caesar's Court, and he was (probably) acquitted either by Burrus or Seneca.

The Text:
'Greeting and Thanksgiving' I Corinthians 1:1-4:
1:1: "Paul, called an apostle of Christ Jesus by the will of God and brother Sosthenes..."

Paul was a 'called (an adjective, not a noun) apostle' (or better, a 'commissioned apostle') of Christ Jesus. The apostle Paul was 'owned' by Christ Jesus, a genitive of possession, a basic idea of the genitive. This 'commissioning' was accomplished by Christ, but was also under the authority of God the Father, representing an official act. It had God's stamp of approval regarding Paul's leadership role. (See Gal. 1:15, 16, and Acts 9:15, 16).

Sosthenes: (Acts 18:17) was designated as a brother. Was he the same Sosthenes who was the synagogue ruler when Paul went to trial? It is enticing to say yes. A possible (although admittedly speculative) scenario for identifying the two as the same person is postulated below. **First,** he must have been known to the Corinthian Christians because Paul did not give any further identifying characteristics. He just said, 'brother Sosthenes.' The Corinthian believers must have known him well. Second, as the Jewish ruler of the synagogue, he may have been forced to go along with the demands of the majority of the Jews, much like Josephus was forced to do at the beginning of the Jewish Wars against Rome in 66 A.D. The Corinthian Jews were likely in an emotional uproar, and possibly insisted on bringing Paul to trial. Therefore, he may have been at least sympathetic to Paul's gospel. **Third,** the charge was weakly written, indicating that Sosthenes, as one would think, the most intellectual of the group, should have had a stronger case. As a reluctant participant, it was possible that he intentionally held back when the writing took place. A lesson to be learned: a legal brief should not be written in the heat of emotion. **Fourth,** after he was beaten, he could have lost face among the Jews, and he could easily have started listening to Paul's message, and then converted, much like Crispus did before him. At the end of the trial, Paul may have stayed perhaps a few weeks at most before leaving for Ephesus, time enough to have had private meetings with Sosthenes (see Acts 18:8). **Fifth,** then it would have been wise for him to leave the area and accompany Paul when Paul left, a month or so after the incident. This is all quite speculative; but it is well within the realm of possibility.

1:2: The Addressees: "To the Assembly of God being in Corinth, having been continually sanctified by Christ Jesus, called holy ones, with those who called upon the name of our Lord Jesus Christ in every place, both their Lord and ours:"

That assembly was 'owned' by God the Father, (the 'of God' represents a genitive of possession). That unique society just happened to be in Corinth (It could have been from any place; Paul was not putting the Corinthian Christians above any other group of believers). Note the participle, 'being,' or 'existing,' οὔσῃ, a present progressive active participle indicating a continual action: they lived there. 'Having been sanctified,' was a perfect *intensive* participle indicating that Paul intended to stress the 'continual action of the process of sanctification,' which began with them at their own individual conversions.

The term 'sanctification' engaged the believer in a life-long process of becoming more and more Christ-like, using the term, ἡγιασμένοις, from ἀγαὶζω, 'to produce holiness.' This was done 'by Christ.' The instrumental use of ἐν is preferred, not the locative, which would have been 'sanctified in Christ,' even if it made sense. Christ was the acting agent in producing 'holiness' though the Holy Spirit. Those believers in that assembly were 'commissioned' (as) holy (set apart for Godly service). Therefore, both Paul and the Corinthian believers were 'commissioned:' Paul as an apostle, and the Corinthians were 'set apart for Godly service.' The term here may suggest that they were, perhaps, not quite living up to that commission, at least some of them.

The phrase 'in every place' indicated that Christians were everywhere equal in status, even if the Corinthians may have felt superior intellectually to the Christians in other places. Furthermore, the mention of 'other places' indicated that Christians were spread throughout the Roman Empire, and growing steadily. This realization may have had the effect of diminishing their feelings of superiority. They were in the minority. They should not feel unique or special when compared to other Christian groups.

1:3: "Grace to you and peace from God our Father and (from) our Lord Jesus Christ."

Paul used a standard greeting. They had done nothing extraordinary to deserve God's blessings of salvation or even gifts. 'Peace (to you)' was a special kind of peace that occurred in especially hard times as well as good times and to a degree that surpasses all understanding. Although this was a standard greeting, as above, there was also a subtle hint of what Paul would address in this letter using this word, 'peace.' Were they all at peace among themselves, and especially with God? This 'peace' surpassed the intellectual capabilities of believers and originated from two sources: from God the Father and from the Lord Jesus Christ.

Notice that God the Father and the Lord Jesus Christ were named in every verse. This continued through verse 9. Also Notice that the word 'called' (or 'commissioned') was frequent, occurring both for the Corinthian believers and for Paul. Paul was not different than the Corinthians: both were 'called,' although Paul's 'calling' indicated his rank: an 'apostle.' But they both had commissions; and they were both equally considered 'the called ones.' Again, the introduction provided another hint of the subject matter of the epistle: the 'call' (commission) of the Corinthians was to holiness (being set aside for service to God). Were they living up to their calling? Paul would address that issue in this letter.

1:4: "I am continually thanking my God always for you, based on the grace of God which was given to you by Christ Jesus,

What was Paul Thankful for? It was not for their labor of love or their 'good' works prior to their conversion. The verb, 'I am continually thanking,' was εὐχαριστῶ, 'to express appreciation for benefits, *give thanks, express thanks, render/return thanks,*' (BDAG). 'Continually' was from the present progressive tense of the verb indicating that the action was considered an ongoing process. Paul also revealed to whom he was thankful: to God, as undeserved and unmerited favor' that God had for the Corinthians, showered unreservedly on them when each one of them was individually converted. The Person of the Godhead that distributed that grace was the Lord Jesus Christ, who earned that right by His sacrificial death on the cross.

Paul, in expressing this gratitude to God for the Corinthians was an expression of Paul's own confidence in the genuineness of their own conversions. It would have had the effect of reinforcing their confidence that they were indeed, 'the children of God,' although they had done nothing in their former lives to deserve that distinctive title. That 'undeserved grace' was a gift from the God of the universe, who lived eternally in the heavens, totally unlike the 'dead' and powerless 'gods' they worshipped in their former lives. Paul was, with this statement of affirmation, building up their confidence and faith very early in this letter.

'More Reasons for Paul's Thankfulness' I Corinthians 1:5-9:
1:5: "...because in every way you were being enriched by Him, in every word and in all knowledge,"

This verse was a continuation of verse 4, revealing Paul's gratitude to God for the Corinthians. The 'because' reinforced Paul's gratitude with a result clause. 'As a result of their conversion,' Paul explained, they were 'enriched' by the Lord Jesus Christ.

'Enriched' was ἐπλουτίσθητε, 'to cause to abound in something, make rich, in imagery, of spiritual riches,' (BDAG). The verb was expressed in an aorist passive verb, indicating first, that the 'enriching' took place, as an aorist tense, in a single point of time (at their conversion). The verb was also expressed in the passive voice, indicating that it was an act of God who made the conversion happen. They were 'passive' as far as the conversion experience was concerned. The 'riches' involved were 'spiritual' riches, energized by the Holy Spirit working within them, which did not mean that they were not objective. The 'subjective' experience of conversion not only had an objective foundation, the Scriptural basis in the OT, now beginning to be expressed in the writings of Paul, and other writers, but that 'subjective' conversion experience resulted in a new objective world view, expressed in a new vocabulary and a new understanding of God's knowledge.

"...in every word...." ἐν παντὶ λόγῳ. 'In' referred to 'the realm or sphere of.' 'Every kind of word,' had to do with the kind of communication that was being developed within the new believer. The range and substance of their vocabulary has been permanently altered, as well as the subject matter. A new technical vocabulary will be required to learn, and a new theology will need to be formulated, both as part of the 'sanctification process' that began for them immediately after the point of conversion.

'In all knowledge' ἐν παντὶ γνώσει, expressed a 'new knowledge' about God they will need to learn, and how God had worked in the past with the Hebrew nation, and how that 'working' was represented as the 'Old Covenant' which must be integrated within the context of the 'New Covenant,' as part of God's plan, as well as the role that Christ played in the fulfillment and integration of that 'Old Covenant' with the 'New Covenant.' The noun, **γνώσει**, played a vital role in this 'new knowledge' into which the new believer had been introduced.

There were two words for 'know' in the Koine Greek of the time. The **'οἶδα** know,' and the **'γινώσκω** know.' The latter, very generally, was a kind of knowledge that was often used in higher order thinking skills, for example, by philosophers of the time. The 'οἶδα know' was commonly used for the kind of knowledge that did not necessarily require serious study, but was handed down from one generation to another, or by oral communication from one individual to another, although both words have various other meanings. The **γνώσει** in this verse was derived from the **γινώσκω** knowledge, representing the more sophisticated kind of knowledge. In addition, one must also realize that 'Christian knowledge' was overlaid on the pagan Koine Greek of the written and oral language of the time, requiring the study of the NT context of the word usage to separate the definitions of 'Christian knowledge' from the 'pagan knowledge' of that day. In the production of the NT, the position that is taken in this work is that 'All scripture is God-breathed,' from 2 Timothy 3:16, which applied at the time of Paul's writing this, to the OT, but as the canon of the NT was finalized, largely by Irenaeus in the early second century, A.D., was also applied to the NT writings. Consequently, the new Christians coming out of pagan Greek and Roman traditions of the time were introduced to a new vocabulary within a new world order, which implied new definitions for words currently in use as they became part of the vocabulary of the 'new man.'

The **γνώσει** was an early introduction in this letter to that new vocabulary that Paul would begin to use with the Christians of Corinth.

1:6: "...Even as the testimony of Christ was confirmed by means of you, ..."

'Testimony' was **μαρτύριον**, 'that which serves as testimony or proof, *testimony, proof*,' (BDAG), a legal term for 'courts of law.' Although the phrase, 'of Christ' could be an objective genitive ('the gospel or Holy Spirit was a witness to Christ, or about Christ,' Thiselton, p. 94), it seems more accurate to consider it to be a subjective genitive: 'the testimony that Christ gave when He was being judged, prior to His crucifixion.

The Lord claimed in His testimony that He was the Son of God and He was the Messiah (Matthew 26:64, 65; and Luke 22:67-70). The testimony was rejected by the ruling authorities; but His testimonial claim was demonstrated to be true. How? It was proven to be true by means of the Corinthians when they believed. The power of God working through those believers proved that that Christ was truly the Messiah. 'Confirmed' was βεβαιώθη, 'to put something beyond doubt, *confirm, establish,*' (BDAG). This was another legal term, where an attorney proved a point by citing objective proof. The Corinthians who believed, or any Christians, proved beyond a doubt that Jesus was the Son of God and He was the Messiah, because God worked in their lives to transform them into 'children of God,' with miracles accompanying the action, thus validating the Lord's claim when He was being judged years before. Paul rested his case. The proof was incontrovertible; the Corinthians proved the case. God was behind Christ all the way. By stating this verse, Paul lifted the spirits of the believers to a high level, in spite of issues that needed to be dealt with within this letter.

1:7: "...so that, as a result, you did not fall short with respect to any gift, while eagerly awaiting the revelation of the Lord Jesus Christ:"

Paul here introduced a 'result clause' to indicate that, as a result of being part of the proof that Christ was who He claimed to be, the Corinthians did not fall short of the gifts that proved the case. Various gifts of God were spread among the Corinthian believers. The 'you' was plural, indicating that Paul was speaking corporately here, to the whole church group, not to individuals.

'Fall short' was ὑστερεῖσθαι, 'to experience deficiency in something advantageous or desirable, *lack, be lacking, go without, come short of,*' (BDAG). As a group, they did not lack any of the spiritual gifts that were being distributed by God among the churches elsewhere. While basking in the beauty of those gifts, they also expressed a strong positive attitude about the return of Christ.

'Eagerly awaiting' was ἀπεκδεχομένους, 'await eagerly,' (BDAG), expressed in present progressive tense participle, indicating that they were continually and eagerly waiting for the Parousia.

1:8: "...who will also confirm you until the end blameless in the day of our Lord Jesus Christ."

'Confirm' was βεβαιώσει, the same word used in verse 6, 'confirm.' Christ, at the Parousia, will 'confirm' beyond any doubt that the Corinthians believers will be judged as blameless, because they accepted Christ as their shield and their righteousness. That did not mean that they will not be judged. In the Bema, the court of Christ for His children will be convened to pass out rewards, or withhold rewards, as they will be judged by the Lord.

'Blameless' was ἀνεγκλήτους, 'blameless, without reproach,' (BDAG). Believers will not be held accountable for any sins they committed, either before conversion, or after. Metaphorically, they will be wearing the robe of Christ which covered their sins. The penalty that should have been meted out to the Corinthian believers and all believers was paid for by Christ on the cross. He paid the penalty for the sins of all Christians, all believers, of all time. To be judged 'not guilty' of sin by Christ and God the Father was a reason for joy.

1:9: "God (is) faithful, through whom you were called into the fellowship of His Son, Jesus Christ, our Lord."

If God will confirm you blameless because of Christ, then He will carry through with His promise. If He confirmed you, rest assured, you were one of the called. 'Fellowship' was κοινωνίαν, "close association involving mutual interests and sharing, *close relationship....*" It was a loving relationship.

Issue One: Divisions within the Corinthian Church
'Paul's Plea to the Corinthians' I Corinthians 1:10 to 1:17:
1:10: "I exhort you, brothers and sisters, through the name of our Lord Jesus Christ, in order that you all may say the same thing, and there may not be a division among you, that you may be perfectly tuned up with the same mind and the same knowledge."

The seriousness of the plea was made clear by the appeal to the Lord Jesus with His full title.

'Perfectly tuned up' was κατηρτισμένοι, 'put into proper condition (of a trainer who adjusts parts of the body), adjust, complete, ...fix up any deficiencies in your faith or complete what is lacking in your faith,' (BDAG). The word was used for training athletes in the major athletic games in Greece. 'Muscle toning' was required for the athletes, and 'fine tuning' was required for Christian athletes who were in training for the 'big game' of life on the earth as God's ambassadors. That 'fine tuning' required unity of purpose and unity of thought.

The Plea: "...that you all may say the same thing...." was τὸ αὐτὸ λέγητε, literally, 'the same thing you may say,' an appeal to unity: they were saying different things.

"...that there may not be divisions among you...." 'Divisions' was σχίσματα, meaning a 'tearing apart.'

MICRO ANALYSIS OF THE TEXT

Word frequencies in verses chapter 1, verses 1-9:
"Called or Commissioned:"
  verse 1: κλητός "commissioned"
  verse 2: ἐκκλησία "called-out ones,"
    κλητοίς "commissioned,"
    ἐπικαλουμένοις "calling upon."
  verse 8: ἀνεγκλήτους, 'α' + 'ἐγκλήτους' meaning, "not called to account, or blameless."
  verse 9: ἐκλήθητε "commissioned" The Corinthians believers were "commissioned" for the purpose of being set apart for a Godly task. They were called to be active participants in the Christian 'war.'
Notice the frequency of the passive voice in the following verbs: (Things were done to or for them: they were only passively involved).
  verse 2, "having been sanctified" or "having been made holy."
  verse 4, "was given."
  verse 5, "were enriched."
  verse 6, "was confirmed in you."
  verse 9, "were called."

Compare Thessalonian believers with the Corinthians:

I Thessalonians 1:3: "Remembering ... your work of faith and labor of love," and verse 6: "You became followers...." The Thessalonians were very active, in spite of their persecution.

The Corinthians, on the other hand, were passive: reveling in the spiritual benefits, but sluggish in action. They were listeners of the Word, but not necessarily doers. This led to moral decay and a lowering of the standards of Christian living. It also allowed them to be unduly influenced by the Graeco-Roman culture all around them.

The Text Analysis of I Corinthians Continued:
1:10, continued: "…that you may be restored with respect to the mind…."

'The same mind' was νοὺς, the mind, 'specifically of the Christian attitude or the way of thinking,' (BDAG). The mind was always a major issue for Christians with problems. The noun νοὺς was used 24 times in the NT, 22 times by Paul, only once for John and once for Luke (Kohlenberger III, et al., p. 665).

"…and the same knowledge…." was γνώμη, a word related to γινώσκω, meaning the highest knowing of God and spiritual things that came from intense study and prayer. They were not unified in their knowledge; their theology was fragmented and flawed.

1:11: "For it was declared to me about you, my brothers, by those from Chloe, that there are contentions among you."

The source of this information came from believers who were connected to the house of Chloe. Chloe was not mentioned again in the NT, but she certainly was known to the Christian believers at Corinth, and was probably a respected believer, although that is not certain. She could have been a wealthy patron of the church or churches there, and employed a number of people, some of whom were Christian slaves or freedmen. Those people could have been commissioned by Chloe to bring this message of concern to Paul, who was now in Ephesus.

1:12: "Now I am saying this, that each of you is saying, 'I myself am of Paul,' or 'I myself am of Apollo,' or 'I myself am of Peter,' or 'I myself am of Christ.'"

The issue behind the contentious behavior appeared to be divided loyalties among the Corinthians. The divisions centered on personalities of the churches. These divided loyalties were splitting the church into factions that centered on the individual ministers of the gospel, and perhaps each one's individual style as a minister. The Paul Party: "I belong to the party of Paul." Notice Paul takes this, not as a compliment, but as a serious error. They could have been converts under Paul when he was in Corinth.

The Apollos Party: "I belong to the Apollos party" (Possibly attracted by his eloquence, not his message). The Peter Party: "I belong to the party of Peter" (Possibly Jewish Christians?). The Christ Party: "I belong to the Christ Party," an unknown group: a reaction to the others?

The Nature of the 'Parties:' the various groups mentioned here seemed to have been 'personality' cults, based not on theological differences, but on the different personalities of each individual. This 'split' was apparently based on the cult of the personality that was very evident in Corinth among the rhetorical teacher/student groups and especially patron/client relationships. Clients were slavishly loyal to their patrons. The secular students of the time were drawn to various teacher/orators, based on the individual flamboyance of the teachers, but not on the substance of their teaching. The students of these teachers were highly loyal to instructors, and would hurl insults at the students of the other teachers. This kind of personality cult led to the 'strife' that was tearing apart the church.

1:13: "Is Christ divided? Paul was not crucified for you, (was he)? Or were you baptized in the name of Paul?"

The results of these divided loyalties among the church provoked Paul to ask three rhetorical questions:

First, "Has Christ been split into factions?" Expected answer was: No.

Second, "Was Paul crucified on your behalf?" Expected answer was: No.

Third, "Were you baptized in the Name of Paul?" Expected answer was: No.

1:14: "I am thankful to God that I baptized no one, except Crispus and Gaius,"

Paul expressed his gratitude that he did not baptize many of the believers while he was in Corinth: (verses 14-16); he was glad he didn't because many others might have joined the 'Paul group.' Those Paul mentioned that he baptized were Crispus, the former synagogue leader, and Gaius, (full name: Gaius Titius Justus??). They were both Roman names. The mention of baptism in this context suggested that Paul thought that the rivalries were possibly based on strong ties of loyalty by whoever baptized them.

1:15: "…lest anyone might say that I baptized in my own name."

The idea of Paul baptizing people in his own name was repugnant to him. Christ should take center stage.

1:16: "And I also baptized the house of Stephanus. As to the rest, I do know if there was any other I baptized."

The house of Stephanas, a Greek name, had recently moved to Ephesus from Corinth, I Cor.16:17.

1:17: "For Christ did not sent me to baptize, but to evangelize, not with the wisdom of speech, lest the cross of Christ may be in vain."

The 'How' of Paul's Evangelistic Ministry:
(verse 17 b) ('οὐκ ἐν σοφία λόγου'):

'Not in Sophistic speech' or 'Not in wisdom language.' Either was possible and both would fit the explanation which followed: 'Lest the cross be made of no effect.' The 'cross' would be nullified, or hidden, either through the use of flamboyant Sophistic language, or by using human wisdom, both of which would 'fog' the message of the cross. Paul was not condemning articulate language in proclaiming the message of the cross (Apollos), as long as that language did not 'blur' the content of the cross. The *'cross'* was the message: it needed to be presented simply and with clarity, and without any pre-planned intention of inflating the status or eloquence of the speaker. Paul may also have been subtly referring to sermons which were significantly *off-topic* ('wisdom talk,' or 'a Sophistic debate,' rather than on solid Christian topics).

The Message and the Messengers
I Corinthians 1:18 to 1:31

'The Message of the Cross' I Corinthians 18-25:
1:18: "For the message of the cross is foolishness to those perishing, but to us who are being saved it is the power of God."

Paul stated a fact here that provided the theme of this section. The attitudes of the various cultures towards the Christians were expressed in some detail. In this introduction, Paul set the stage by explaining that the message (λόγος, meaning 'an extended communication, either oral or written, appealing to the mind,') of the cross generated two kinds of responses. One response to those who reject it was foolishness (μωρία, 'foolishness,'), because, for one initial reason, they failed to see the logic of following a dead leader. But that message' was more extensive and complicated, requiring a longer listening time to understand.

On the other hand, those who responded positively to this message of the cross, once applied to their lives, saw in this same message the power of God manifested on a personal level. 'Being saved' was σωζομένοις, a passive present progressive tense verb, meaning 'to save and preserve from eternal destruction,' (BDAG). These two responses were more fully explained by Paul in the following verses.

1:19: "For it has been written, 'I will destroy the wisdom of the wise and the understanding of the prudent I will declare invalid.'"

Paul quoted the OT prophet Isaiah (Is. 29:14) to connect the 'logos' of the cross to the OT Scriptures, where many passages were available to explain the coming Messiah, and His future redemptive work on the earth. This particular verse described the contradiction between God's wisdom and man's wisdom. God would 'make invalid' (ἀθετήσω, 'to reject something as invalid, *declare invalid, nullify, ignore*,' (BDAG), the understanding (σύνεσιν, 'the faculty of comprehension, *intelligence, acuteness, shrewdness*), (BDAG), of the 'prudent,' (συνετῶν, 'being able to understand with discernment, *intelligent, sagacious, wise, with good sense* (BDAG). Isaiah prophesied that God will destroy man's wisdom (ἀπολῶ from ἀπόλλυμι, 'to bring to destruction the wisdom of the wise,' (BDAG).

The highest form of man's wisdom was totally inadequate to grasp the wisdom of God. It could only be understood in a limited way when God breathed His life into a believer resulting in the transforming power of the new birth.

1:20: "Where (is) the wise man? Where (is) the scholar? Where (are) the debaters of this age? Did not God make foolish the wisdom of this world?"

Here, Paul quoted Isa. 19:12, 'wise'; Isa. 33:18, 'scholar'; Isa. 44:25, 'debaters.' The question, 'Where are they?' can be answered by viewing the OT record of Israel as they came into the land promised to them by God. They lay dead in the desert, having been judged by God for their unbelief and rebellion.

1:21: "For since, by means of the wisdom of God, the world did not know God through His wisdom, it pleased God to save those who are believing through the foolishness of preaching:"

Man was totally incapable of comprehending God by thinking, even by the most learned of men and women. God chose to be reached only through the medium of preaching, which, to the scholar, was a demeaning method of learning, subject to much to emotional reactions. Paul (Saul at that time) was the epitome of a scholar who tried to reach God with his flawed logic. He now had recognized that his 'wisdom' was an empty cup that a beggar uses. 'Know' God, was ἔγνω from γινώσκω, the highest form of knowledge expressed in the Greek language of that day. The world of people did not know God through man's wisdom; it could only be discovered by preaching, as the apostles were doing as they traveled the known world spreading that knowledge of God.

I Corinthians 1:22-25
Structural Analysis:
Parts of Speech, Antecedents and Words in Apposition
Grammatical Technique: Parallel Construction
Example 1: The Jews

Verse 22:	**"Since the Jews also are asking for a sign (a miracle) and the Greeks are seeking wisdom."**
The sentence subject:	**"JEWS"**
The verb:	**"ASKING"**
The direct object:	**"A SIGN"**

Example 2: The Greeks

The sentence subject:	**"GREEKS"**
The verb:	SEEKING"
The direct object:	**"WISDOM"**

Example 3

Verse 23:	**"but we ourselves are preaching Christ being crucified…"**
The sentence subject:	**"WE (believers)"**
The verb:	**"ARE PREACHING"**
The predicative nominative:	**"CHRIST CRUCIFIED"**

Example 4: Parallel Construction

Verse 24:	**"…but to them who are called, to both Jews and to Greeks, Christ is the power of God andthe wisdom of God:"**
The sentence subject:	**"(to believers) CHRIST"**
The verb:	**"IS"**
The predicative nominative:	**"THE POWER OF GOD AND THE WISDOM OF GOD"**

The Three Groups:
1. Paul, Peter, Apollos, Apostles, etc.
2. The Jews
3. The Gentiles (Greeks)

Three Different Observations about the Crucifiction:
1. Christ Crucified: Treasured (By Believers)
2. Christ Crucified: Scandalous (By Jews)
3. Christ Crucified: Foolishness (By Greeks)

Grammatical Technique: Apposition:

Words in 'apposition,' means literally, 'putting near,' and refers to words describing the antecedent. An 'antecedent' literally means 'the words going before.'

Example: The boy wore a baseball cap cocked to the side of his head, a red one: to the boy it was a sign of rebellion, because he knew that the hat's bill was intended to shade the eyes. The 'Antecedent' was 'HAT.' The words in apposition: 'red one' and 'a sign of rebellion.'

Antecedent in vss. 1:22-25: Christ (crucified)
Apposition Words 1. 'Embarrassment.' 2. 'Foolishness.' 3. 'Power.' 4. 'Wisdom.'

> Verse 24: **"But to them who are called, whether to the Jews or to the Gentiles, Christ (is) the power of God and the wisdom of God."**

To the "called ones:" Christ is the Power of God and the Wisdom of God. (The antecedent is "called ones")
DOUBLE APPOSITION USING INDIRECT OBJECTS: (to Jewish believers) and (to Gentile believers)
(The antecedent and subject of the sentence is 'Christ,' and is applied to both groups of believers)

Resumption of the Text: I Corinthians
1:22: "...for Jews also request a sign and Greeks are seeking wisdom,"
The Jews also had a limitation in their culture. They were taught to expect miraculous signs of a Messiah that would free them from Roman rule in a

present, physical sense. The Greeks, in their background of philosophical knowledge, expected the knowledge of God to fit the parameters of their particular philosophy, as Paul already learned when he preached to them at Athens, just before coming to Corinth. Both groups (Jews and Gentiles) resisted God's 'fine tuning' required unity of purpose and unity of thought to both cultural and historical traditions.

1:23: "…but we ourselves are preaching Christ being crucified, to the Jews a scandal, and to the Greeks, foolishness,"

So the conclusion that Paul reached was that the Jews considered God's message a scandal, and the Greeks saw that same message as 'foolishness.'

1:24: "…but to them who are called, to both Jews and to Greeks, Christ is the power of God and the wisdom of God:"

But to those in the minority of both groups, they saw this message of Christ as the 'power of God' and the 'wisdom' of God. The 'power' was δύναμιν 'the potential for functioning in some way, *power, might, strength, force, capability.*' (BDAG). By discerning the 'power of God,' the believer only viewed the power of God to transform his or her sinful life, which was a small portion of God's creative power. God not only shared His power with the believer, but He shared His wisdom, by lifting the veil of unbelief from the understanding of the old sin nature. Believers have the objective truth of God, as revealed in the Scriptures, and the ability to grasp those instructions with the aid of the Holy Spirit.

1:25: "…because the foolishness of God is wiser than men and the weakness of God is stronger than men."

Paul gave his reasons for the facts he described above. The 'foolishness of God's knowledge,' as the wise man of this world viewed God's knowledge, and the supposed 'weakness' of His knowledge was 'stronger' than men. God's knowledge operated on such a high level of advanced intellect, that man, even in his highest intellectual capacity, was not able to even begin to grasp the truths of God and His world.

Syntactical Analysis: The "Nothings" and the "Somethings"
I Corinthians 1:26-31:
   I. The Human Status of the Corinthian Believers verse 26.
      A. Not Many were wise by human standards (σόφος = "wise, related to "sophistry, or sophisticated")

B. Not Many were imbued with influential human power (δύνατος = "strong, powerful")

C. Not Many were "born to high-status families" (εὐγενεῖς = "well-born").

D. **The text did not say "not any."** We know there were some believers in these categories, because some well-to-do Christians provided their large houses for meeting places. We also know about Erastus, who was a prominent politician in Corinth, who was very wealthy and built Theater Street in fine marble at his own expense. A number of others could be mentioned as well.

II. **God's choices are not Man's choices: verses 27, 28.**

A. **"But God chose the foolish things of the world in order to shame the wise"** Paul didn't say "foolish people." He said, "foolish things." They were so low in status that they were below the level of human beings according to human standards of that day. Those low creatures were putting to shame the "wise" humans.

B. **"God chose the weak things of the world to shame the strong"** The "weak things," like the "foolish things" above, were the scum of the earth. They were putting to shame those who were powerful in the old system.

III. **"God chose the lowest social category of the world and those 'things' despised – those things which are nothing - in order to bring to nothing the 'somethings.'"** (vs. 28): a total reversal of the cultural standards of the day, whether Greek, Roman, or Jewish.

IV. **The Results of these Choices: verse 29. "So that, as a result, everyone may not boast before God."** (vs. 28: All humans were now reduced to two classes: "the **nothings**" and the "**somethings**.") The **nothings** were made into **somethings** by God, and the **somethings** were made into **nothings**, also by God. But the new 'somethings' did not have any basis for boasting. The believers (the made-over **somethings**) had no right to boast before God as being special, even if they had status in the "old" class system. The CLASS DISTINCTIONS practiced in the Graeco-Roman and Jewish worlds were no longer valid.

V. **The Place of "Wisdom" in the "New" Christian Society: verse 30. "But from Him** (God the Father) **you exist in Christ Jesus, who became wisdom for us from God** (the Father), **also righteousness, and sanctification and**

redemption," Two key elements are found here: Two key elements are found here: 1. Christians had their existence *in* Christ Jesus (the locative sense: "a place," not instrumental). 2. Since this existence was in effect, there were certain "gifts" that were presented to the believer: this was expressed in the text by the words, "for us" (not in us: ἡμῖν, here as a dative of advantage). Those "gifts" were: WISDOM, RIGHTEOUSNESS, SANCTIFICATION, and REDEMPTION. They came from God the Father because the believer was "in Christ," a place of safety and security. These four words are parts of the subject of the sentence (nominative case) and not only describe the essence of Christ (WISDOM), but also His work and gifts to believers (RIGHTEOUSNESS, SANCTIFICATION and REDEMPTION). The four "gifts" can further be described and applied to the believer:

1. **WISDOM:** The "nothings" became the "somethings" in God's eyes because they had been given one of Christ's inherent descriptors of Himself: **His Wisdom.**

2. RIGHTEOUSNESS: Being "in Christ," the "nothings" were "somethings" because they were acquitted, and had been imputed righteousness from God the Father. ("Just as if they had never sinned")

3. The "nothings" also had the gift of SANCTIFICATION: They had the unique ability among men to "draw near to God" by the process of being made holy. Again, the "nothings" became "somethings" in the eyes of God. But the old "somethings" of the world had now become the "nothings."

4. Finally, the "nothings" also had the gift of REDEMPTION: This word was connected to the slave market in that era: a price had to be paid to transfer ownership to a new "lord." Now the "nothings" were the "somethings" because they belonged to the Lord of the universe, paid for by Christ. The price: the Cross of Christ.

Resumption of the Text: I Corinthians 1:26

The "Nothings" and the "Somethings" I Corinthians 1:26-31:

1:26: "For look at your calling, brothers and sisters, that there are not many wise according to the flesh, not many powerful, not many well-bred:"

Paul called attention to the general population of the Corinthian believers. Were many upper class people among them, having sophisticated worldly wisdom, or those having great political power, or those having parents who are aristocrats in the society? No. They were generally common middle, or lower class people, who responded to the gospel message. Not many were wise by human standards, σόφοι, was 'wise, related to sophistry, or sophisticated.' Not many were imbued with influential human power, δύνατοι, meaning, 'strong or powerful.' Not Many were 'born to high-status families.' εὐγενείς, was 'well-born.' The text did not say 'not any.' There were some believers in these categories, because some well-to-do Christians provided their large houses for meeting places. For example, there was Erastus, who was a prominent politician in Corinth, who was very wealthy and built Theater Street in fine marble at his own expense. A number of others could be mentioned as well (Gaius, Stephanas, etc.).

1:27: "But God chose the foolish things of the world, in order to bring to shame the wise, and God chose the weak things of the world, in order to put to shame the powerful,"

Paul now introduced a metaphor of the 'nothings' and the 'somethings.' The words used here to refer to the 'foolish' are τὰ μώρα, 'foolish things' are 'foolish attributes applied to people.' However, if this phrase was considered as a metaphor, then the neuter plural became 'things,' lower than human life. God then chose the very lowest form of objects, below people, to put to shame the wisest of humans. In addition, again in a metaphorical sense, He chose the weaklings of this world to put to shame the strong and powerful. All humans were now reduced to two classes: "the nothings" and the "somethings." But God did not choose those who were the 'somethings' in the sight of men. Instead, He chose the 'nothings' to represent the God of the universe.

1:28: "…and God chose the base things of the world and the things which are despised, the nothings, in order to bring to nothing the somethings…"

Now Paul added another dimension to the above metaphors. They were 'base things' γένης, 'not of noble birth,' (BDAG). They represented the lowest forms of the social classes. They were the ones 'not of noble birth.' They were lowly commoners. They were selected over the people of noble birth. The 'despised' was another dimension of these metaphors. 'Despised' was ἐξουθενημένα, a perfect passive intensive participle, indicating that the idea of 'being despised' was a continual process: it was always there. Further, the participle was neuter, correlating with the 'things' (below humanity) which were being despised. In addition, Paul indicated that the 'nothings' were those things being 'nothing,'

148

τὰ μὴ ὄντα, literally, the 'things not existing.' They were even lower than the plant life: they did not exist, and they were treated that way in their respective cultures. The reason for God's choices within this group of 'things,' was to put to shame all those who considered themselves to be 'somethings.'

1:29: "...so that all flesh may glory in the presence of God."

The **nothings** were made into **somethings** by God, and the **somethings** were made into **nothings**, also by God. Neither group had any basis for boasting. The believers (with a few made-over **somethings**) had no right to boast before God as being special, even if they may have had status in the "old" class system. The CLASS DISTINCTIONS practiced in the Graeco-Roman and Jewish worlds were no longer valid. This especially elevated the divisions in the Corinthian church and the factions. Believers who thought that their groups were superior to the other groups were boasting about their *superiority*, and were typical of the Corinthian pagan and Jewish value systems within the system of the worldly 'somethings.'

1:30: "But from Him (God the Father) you yourselves exist in Christ Jesus, who became wisdom for us from God (the Father), also (He became) righteousness, and sanctification and redemption,"

This section was fully developed above in the syntactical analysis section. In essence, Christ made believers into a new social order by lending believers Christ's own attributes of wisdom and righteousness, mingled with elements sanctification and redemption designed and carried out by Christ with the confirmation of God the Father and the Holy Spirit. The result of such a potent arrangement of attributes applied to believers revolutionized their existence and, from God's point of view, recreated them into unique 'somebodies.' They were recreated from nothing into something special and precious to God.

1:31: "...so that, even as it has been written, 'Let the one who glories, glory in the Lord.'"

'Glorying' was the opposite of boasting. One who glories, does it for the benefit of someone else, not himself or herself. It was a selfless activity. But it was more than that. One who glorifies God, praises Him for who He is, and what He has done for that person. What beauty lies in that person who glorifies God? He or she can only be one of the 'nothings' that God made over into one of the 'somethings' by using His creative power. That person had no ground to boast since God was the one who performed the miracle of life in him or her.

There was one exception to this rule about not boasting, however. Paul explained this exception by quoting Jer. 9.24: **"Let the one who is inclined to boast, boast in the Lord"** who, by implication, was the One who made believers, the '**nothings**,' into the '**somethings**.' What made boasting a sin was the object of the boast. Boasting in one's status was a sin; boasting in Christ was not a sin. Indeed, that kind of boasting expressed the highest form of praise to Christ and God.

'The Manner and the Content of Paul's Preaching' I Corinthians 2:1-8:

2:1: "After having come to you, brothers and sisters, Even I myself did not come with high-sounding language or announcing wisdom to you (about) the mystery of God."

How Paul, upon his arrival in Corinth, did <u>NOT</u> proclaim his message: First, he did not come to them in the conventional way of a sophist teacher or philosopher: not with 'high-sounding (υπεροχήν) language' (λόγου): or 'flowery speech,' common to the sophist teachers of the day. Second, he did not come with high-sounding (words of) wisdom (σοφίας), common among traveling philosophers of that time. 'Announcing' was **καταγγέλλων**, 'to make known in public, with the implication of broad dissemination, *proclaim, announce*,' (BDAG). Paul, unlike the common philosophers and sophists of the day, came to them with the message alone, not presented in a flowery manner, but the truth alone. The speaker was not central; the message of Christ was central.

What was his message? It was the **'mystery of God'** (μυστήριον) of God: **'mystery'** was equivalent to a revelation of God. That revelation centered on the incredible fact that the crucifixion was not an 'accident' in the heat of a mob's passion: it was the central 'mystery' in the OT Messiah passages (note especially the 'suffering Messiah') for those faithful ones who believed God in the centuries before Christ. But the use of this word suggested to some modern scholars that Paul was using a term that was charged with negative meaning: referring to the Graeco-Roman 'mystery religions' of the time. That may have been the reason that a scribe later (possibly) changed the spelling of the word to read, 'witness' (μαρτύριον), changing three letters. Both spelling traditions followed from that time (about AD 200). The preferred reading, however, is 'mystery,' μυστήριον.

2:2: "For I determined to know nothing among you except Jesus Christ and this One having been crucified."

Paul's Focus in his Preaching: Paul's deliberate decision at the very start of his ministry in Corinth was to preach Christ crucified. 'Not to know anything,' εἰδέναι, from the οἶδα kind of knowledge: 'to know something from the senses: hearing, seeing, etc.' In other words, he was determined not to be influenced by the messages of other Christian ministers that he may have heard or seen in the past. He chose to have a very narrow focus: Christ crucified. **'Except Christ Crucified.'** His focus was on the major foundation stone of the Christian faith: the crucifixion, a sacrifice by the 'Lamb of God' that had to be paid for sin in order to pave the way for redemption.

2:3: "And even I myself became to you in weakness, and in fear and in much trembling,"

Paul's lowly manner in public speaking was admitted. Paul agreed that when he came to them, about February, AD 50, he came '…with weakness' as opposed to the 'power' of the 'somethings' discussed in the first chapter. 'With fear and with much trembling,' indicated a spirit of *extreme humility* as opposed to the self-confidence and theatrical body language demonstrated by the sophist orators. Paul used 'fear' and 'trembling' two other times in order to explain to Christian slaves how to serve Christ (Eph. 6:5) and to the Philippians how to work out their own salvation (Phil. 2:12). This admission provided the foundational attitude expected of one of Christ's most diligent servants: humility.

Paul's Delivery:

2:4: "And my message and my preaching were not with persuasive, sophisticated words, but with (the) demonstration of the Spirit, and (the demonstration) of power,"

Paul's 'Message' and his 'speaking' were: "Not with persuasive (πειθοι[ς]) words (λόγοις) of the sophist (σοφίας)." The sophists, whose prime purpose in public speaking, was to persuade the audience <u>by any means possible</u>, often resorting to tearing down opponents by exaggeration and slander. On the contrary, Paul's message was accompanied by 'irrefutable proof' (ἀποδείξει) from the (Holy) Spirit, and with power,' δυνάμεως. There was *power*, despite the humility in Paul's overall demeanor. The contrast of Paul's delivery was very striking, when compared to the 'sophisticated and polished professional' speakers of the day.

151

2:5: "...in order that your faith may not be by wisdom of men but by the power of God."

The purpose of Paul's style of delivery: 'In order that your faith may not be [grounded] in the wisdom (σοφία) of men who were the real 'nothings' and pretended to be the 'somethings.' Paul wanted their faith to be grounded on the objective truth of God, who demonstrated His approval with power to create new life from 'nothing.'

'Paul's Audience and Content' I Corinthians 2:6-8:

2:6: "But we speak wisdom among the mature adults, but wisdom not of this age, nor of the rulers of this age who are being destroyed:"

'Mature adults' did not necessarily mean 'spiritually mature' adults. It probably referred to those Corinthians who were mature enough to initially accept the message and respond positively.

"But wisdom not of this age," This wisdom was a Godly wisdom from the God of the universe. It was very far removed from the philosophers or rhetorical teachers who babbled about nothing, which ranting could not even be compared with the wisdom of God, now being announced to the world by Paul and others.

"...nor of the rulers of this age...." The political leaders of this age and their 'wisdom' were being turned into the 'nothings,' along with their ravings about nothing of substance. Their "wisdom" did not count. It was reduced to "foolishness," along with the men of leadership who were the true nothings. Both would be utterly destroyed.

2:7: "...but we speak the wisdom of God in a mystery, having been hidden, which God determined beforehand, before the ages for our glory,"

"...we speak the wisdom of God in a mystery, having been hidden...." The subject of Paul's sermons was described very generally here as 'continually speaking' about the mystery of God. That 'mystery' was hidden from humanity until the NT age began with Christ's birth. Bits and pieces of the mystery could have been found in the Messianic prophecies of the OT, but the full impact of the disclosure occurred at the time of Christ, whom John the Baptist introduced as the Messiah. The full comprehension of the mystery is still hidden to the world, but vital parts of it have been disseminated by the apostles, who were then disclosing it. 'Having been hidden' was the verb, ἀποκεκρυμμένην, 'to hide or conceal,' (BDAG). It was a perfect tense participle, probably extensive, emphasizing the consummation of the event and its effect upon mankind.

"…determined beforehand…." was προώρισεν, an aorist active verb, from προορίζω, 'Decide upon beforehand, *predetermine*,' (BDAG). This mystery was preplanned; it was decided before creation of the world for the glorious benefit of believers.

2:8: "…which none of the rulers of this age have known: for if they knew they would not have crucified the Lord of glory."

Because they did not know the identity of Christ, the rulers of the age unlawfully crucified the Lord Jesus.

'Knew' was ἔγνωκεν, a perfect intensive indicative active, where the 'intensive' indicated that their ignorance was continual. The 'γινώσκω' kind of knowledge was an experiential knowledge representing the most sophisticated form of the 'higher order thinking skills' in the Koine Greek language of that day. The rulers of the day, in the majority at least, did not have an experiential knowledge of Christ. Nicodemus was possibly the only exception of the 'rulers' on the Sanhedrin that may eventually have gained such an experiential knowledge of Christ.

The Manner and the Content of Paul's Preaching

'The Revelation Explained' I Corinthians 2:9-16

2:9: "But even as it has been written, 'That which the eye did not see, and the ear did not hear' also it did not enter upon the heart of man, the things which God prepared for those who may love Him."

Paul likely quoted from Isaiah 64:3, 4, coupled with Isaiah 65:17 (Thiselton, p. 264-5). The content of the quotation expressed the vast difference that existed between God's thinking and man's, even among OT men of God and even Christians of Paul's day, let alone the unbelieving Jews and Gentiles who represented the 'natural man.'

The verb in the phrase, **"…for those who may love Him…."** was ἀγαπῶσιν, 'love, or cherish,'(BDAG), expressed in a subjunctive present progressive active participle 'cherishing' as a continual action. The subjunctive mode participle suggested that the limited scope of the individuals addressed were believers in Isaiah's day, having had 'an experiential love of God' replicating Christ's love for believers, obtained at conversion. Others were excluded from that promise until they were converted. For those believers, the promise of the verse was profound, and was intended to overwhelm the believing reader, and perhaps, to entice others to join the ranks of the believers addressed here. The human senses could not even imagine what God had prepared, ἡτοίμασεν, 'prepared,' (BDAG), an aorist indicative active verb, which was a punctiliar act: emphasizing a singular, one-time action that occurred in the past, rather than a process that occurred over time, as expressed by the present progressive tense. The 'things,' ἃ was plural, indicating that there were many things that were promised for the believers that will overwhelm and transcend their minds, or even their hearts. The surprise is yet future, but it is something for which to anticipate and relish.

2:10: "But God revealed to us through the Spirit: for the Spirit examines all things, even the deep things of God."

'To us,' here, included all believers. The source of that knowledge was the Holy Spirit, who, because of who He is, conveys this understanding to every believer. The verb, revealed, was ἀπεκάλυψεν, 'to cause something to be fully known, especially of divine revelation of certain transcendent secrets, *reveal, disclose, bring to light, make fully known,*' (BDAG). The punctiliar, aorist active verb here was a parallel to 'prepared' in verse 9, indicating that the revelation was punctiliar, and instantaneous at conversion, when the Holy Spirit was initially introduced into the believer's life. The influence of the Holy Spirit in an individual's life was derived from the connection that the Holy Spirit has with Christ and God the Father. The Spirit 'examines' ἐραυνᾷ, 'to make a careful or thorough effort to learn something, *search, examine, investigate,*' (BDAG). The present progressive tense indicated that the Holy Spirit continually examines 'all things,' in every situation that the believer may be in, to direct him or her along a proper spiritual path. He even examines the 'deep things of God' to apply the appropriate solution to the situations of the believers.

2:11: "For who of men knows the things of a man, except the spirit of the man which is in him? So also no one knew the things of God except the Spirit of God."

Paul's justification for the power of the Holy Spirit was the disclosure of the 'spirit' that inhabited man himself. The logic involved here was that even as a man's spirit had an instinctive understanding of the man or woman in whom that spirit dwells, the Holy Spirit fully knows the things of God. There was one major difference between the two kinds of knowledge, however. The 'spirit' of man's knowledge was the **οἶδα** kind of knowledge which was limited to the nature of man. The knowledge of the Holy Spirit was the γινώσκω kind of knowledge, implying that the two words must be defined differently in some way. We would suggest here that the οἶδα knowledge was a knowledge that was generally passed down from one generation to another; while the **γινώσκω** knowledge was a deep knowledge that was restricted here to the knowledge that was associated with God, to which the Holy Spirit had access because of His divine nature. The **γινώσκω** was presented here in the aorist punctiliar tense, indicating that this deep knowledge was not available to mankind as a one-time activity except to the Holy Spirit. He was uniquely qualified for that role.

2:12: "But we ourselves did not receive the spirit of the world, but (we received) the Spirit which is from God, in order that we may know the things freely given to us from God."

Paul explained here that believers did not receive (at conversion) the 'spirit of the world,' which came with the birth of the child. What believers received, was the Holy Spirit from God at the 'second birth,' or 'conversion.' The purpose clause revealed the reason behind that gift: in order that all believers may know 'the things freely given to us from God.' 'Know' here was the οἶδα kind of knowledge that was transmitted to believers through the second birth as part of their new 'nature.'

The subjunctive mode indicated that this 'knowledge' was potential, and not always accessed to its fullest extent by the believer. Much depended on the response and dedication of believers to the study God's word and mentally, and prayerfully, engages in its truths with the desirous attitude to continually learn what God has for them, to be used in service for the extension of the gospel. This kind of response after conversion was deeply conditioned by the attitude of the believer's heart and the depth of his or her love for Christ, which must grow concurrently along with that knowledge.

2:13: "Also we are speaking things, not by the teachings of human wisdom, but by the words taught from the Spirit, teaching spiritual things to spiritual people."

Paul here applied this new knowledge to himself and all other preachers of the gospel. Human wisdom was not part of their curriculum. This was a new approach to public speaking: these people were proclaiming a message taught by the Holy Spirit of God. The message was spiritual, and it was addressed to spiritual people. The last participle here, 'teaching,' was a compound verb, συγκρὶνω, σύν + κρὶνω meaning 'a joining together of interpretations' (guided by the Holy Spirit), presented in the active present progressive tense form, indicating a continual process of 'interpreting spiritual truths to those who possess the Spirit,' (BDAG).

2:14: "But the natural man does not receive the things of the Spirit of God, for it is foolishness to him and he is not able to know, because they are discerned spiritually."

There was something quite different about the curriculum that Paul and his associates taught. It was certainly different than the rhetors of the cultured city of Corinth and other Graeco-Roman cities of culture taught, where the value of the speech rested not on the substance of the speech, but how it was expressed, often with bombastic and denigrating techniques that pointed to the rival rhetors as incompetent. The message that Paul was talking about was of such a spiritual substance that the general audiences of that day could not understand it. That was because they would need a prerequisite experience of conversion before they could begin to understand the messages of Paul.

The 'natural man' was ψυχικὸς ἄνθρωπος, 'unspiritual man,' (BDAG). It was a man or woman who had not experienced the transformative and personal joy of salvation with Christ in order to obtain the benefits of Christ's sacrifice on the cross, known as 'conversion.' This experience included the gift of a new spiritual status as a 'child of God,' forever forgiven, when the Holy Spirit entered the life of the 'natural man' and altered his or her nature to be sensitive to the urgings of that Holy Spirit, including the gift of 'understanding spiritual things.' Communication with God was then possible, but not before. This new experience was described by the Lord Jesus to Nicodemus, a profoundly religious man and leader in the major council of the Jews in Jerusalem, the Sanhedrin, who was still a 'natural man,' in John 3:1-21. Jesus told him that he would have to be 'born again' in order to enter heaven. The phrase, 'born again' was another description of this personal transformation experience also known as 'conversion.'

2:15: "But the spiritual person discerns all things, but he himself is not being examined."

Paul here described the new skills of the 'spiritual person,' or the person in whom the Holy Spirit now dwelled to begin the process of making the individual 'spiritual.' 'Examine' was ανακρίνει, 'to examine with a view of finding fault, *judging, call to account, discern,*' (BDAG). Conversion brings a new set of values to the believer. With those new values, discernment was engaged in the believer in order to effectively 'walk the walk' of Christ, as well as 'talk the talk.'

A new worldview begins to develop that displaces the old value system. The verb, ανακρίνει also was in the present progressive tense, revealing that this 'discerning process' was continual.

At the same time, the believer was now not being examined in the sense of God finding fault with his or her new life. The same word, ἀνακρίνεται, was used here, but in the passive voice, indicating that someone else (God) was no longer looking critically at the 'new individual.' God the Father will no longer reject the 'new person,' as Christ 'rejected' Nicodemus, as unfit for heaven, until he was reborn.

2:16: "For who knew the mind of the Lord that he will instruct Him? But we are having the mind of Christ."

Paul here seems to quote, at least the idea, of Isaiah 40:13. The statement here seems to suggest the following expression: "Who was so arrogant to think that he would know the mind of the Lord and instruct Him?" A few people probably might. However, believers have the 'mind of Christ' simply because they have been transformed by the personal experience of salvation. They now have the Holy Spirit to guide them and communicate God's will to them. The Holy Spirit is, after all, the Spirit of Christ (Romans 8:9). Believers now have the 'Mind of Christ' because the Spirit of Christ dwells in them and communicates with them.

'**Knew**' here was ἔγνω, the past tense of γινώσκω, meaning 'fully know, by experience' the mind of the Lord. Only the believers 'experientially know' the mind of the Lord because they are taught the lifelong process of sanctification regarding the 'mind of the Lord.'

The Master Architect and the Sub-Contractors
I Corinthians 3:1-23

'The Sluggish Growth of the Corinthian Believers' I Corinthians 3:1-9
3:1: "Even I, brothers and sisters, was not able to speak to you as to spiritual persons, but as to carnal people, as babes in Christ."

Here Paul shifted the topic of 'spiritual believers' to 'babes in Christ.' He was now recognizing that these Christians, even after their conversion experiences, were still 'carnal creatures,' as they were before conversion. They still did not quite understand the language of the Spirit of Christ in their lives. Paul discovered that some of them seemed to have been converted, but were not showing the normative signs of 'transformation.'

This slow process was called 'grieving the Spirit,' Ephesians 4:30, as Paul would later write to the Ephesians as a negative command, 'Do not grieve the Spirit of God, by whom you were sealed for the Day of Redemption.' Some of the Corinthians were doing just that, and the others seemed to tolerate those defective and carnal lifestyles.

'To carnal people' was σαρκὶνοις, 'pertaining to being material or belonging to the physical realm, *material, physical, human, fleshly*,' further described as 'a short step to Paul's nuanced view of the human condition,' (BDAG).

3:2: "I gave you milk to drink, not solid food, for you were not yet able, but even now you are still not able,"

The baby metaphor seemed appropriate for the situation which unfolded since Paul left Corinth. Details of the 'carnal conduct' begin to be seen in the next verse. 'Solid food' represented the feeding of the Christian on the Word of God, and the resulting advance in communication with God and Christ through a more advanced prayer life. 'Not able' was used twice, first in the imperfect middle voice, ἐδύνασθε, 'you were not able,' a continuous past action. The second occurrence was δύνασθε, 'you still are not able,' in the present progressive tense middle voice. Both verbs indicated a continual action; the imperfect was a 'continual' lack of ability in the past; the second was a present progressive tense, a 'continual' lack of ability even now in the present. There was no change in their appetites.

3:3: "For still you are carnal (people). For where there are (signs of) envy and strife, are you not carnal and walking according to (the standards) of mankind?"

Paul charged them in an overall general sense of being carnal. Then he specified the reason for his broad accusation. They exhibited signs of envy and strife. 'Envy' was ζῆλος, 'intense negative feelings over another's achievements or success, *jealousy, envy*,' (BDAG). 'Strife' was ἔρις, especially in reference to positions taken in a matter, strife, discord, contention,' (BDAG). Although this kind of conduct was common for that day, Christians were expected to live on a higher plane. Greed and temper were expected to be controlled by submitting oneself to the Holy Spirit. There were no signs of maturing in Christ when these vices were reported to Paul.

'Walking' was περιπατεῖτε, a *continual* walking (present progressive tense verb). The vices mentioned would be explained more fully in the next verse.

3:4: "When anyone may say, 'I am of Paul,' and someone else may say, 'I am of Apollo,' are you not (carnal) people?

The application of those vices was now made clear. There were contentious divisions within the church based on divided loyalties over the popularity of the leaders. There were some in the church who did not like Paul and criticized him after Paul left Corinth. Apollos was at Corinth later as the overall church leader, or in one of the various house churches. Those church members began, in spite of Apollos, to assemble together in churches where either Apollos or Paul was considered the more effective speaker. They were judging church leaders as the rhetoricians of time were being judged, on the techniques of public speaking, rather than on the substance of the teaching. Such rivalry was immature, divisive, and carnal according to Paul.

3:5: "Who therefore is Apollo? And who is Paul? (We are) ministers through whom you believed, as the Lord also gave to each one."

Paul now qualified the leadership by identifying who these leaders were, from a Christian point of view. They were merely tools wherein the Corinthians became believers, nothing more. They were not to be exalted above their common, everyday positions of ministry. God was to be exalted for creating the transformed life and training leaders. It was not due to the leaders of the churches. The responsibility of Christian growth was within the responsibility of the individual believer. The Christians had all the necessary resources to grow in Christ, in spite of a minister who was considered 'average.' They were to advance in the faith, not because of the leader, but, sometimes even in spite of the leader. They were to lean on the resources given to them by the Holy Spirit at conversion. That alone would prevent contentious relationships to arise within the churches.

3:6: "I planted, Apollo watered, but God gave the increase:"

Paul used the metaphor of the farmer here. Paul himself was only partially responsible for the growth of the field. He planted the plants, nothing more. Apollos maintained the field through watering. Both were absolutely necessary in the process of Christian growth. But one was no more vital than the other. It was a team effort, where all team members were doing their part to develop a harvest. They were also equal in functions. One leader should not be elevated over the other.

'God gave the increase.' 'Increase' was **ηὔξανεν**, from **αὐξάνω**, or **αὔξω**, 'to cause to become greater in extent, size, or quality, *grow*,' (BDAG). The growth could have been either quantitative or qualitative. That 'growth' was the responsibility and action of God Himself, acting through the Holy Spirit, not the leaders of the various churches. They completely misunderstood the role and function of the church leaders.

3:7: "So then neither the one who plants is anything, nor the one who waters, but God who gives the increase."

Paul here summarized his remarks above. The leader had no inherent value but to perform a special function within the ministry. God gave, not only the initiation of their conversion, but also the continuing increase. **αὐξάνων** was the same verb as in verse 6, but here it was expressed as a present progressive tense verb, indicating an expected and normative, '*continual*' growth by God.

3:8: "Now the one who plants and the one who waters are one, and each one will receive his own reward according to his own labor."

Even the rewards were considered equal to Paul. The one who planted would not receive any higher reward than the one who watered. They were to be judged by Christ at the 'Judgment Seat of Christ,' known as the 'Bema' named after the Graeco-Roman courthouse within the cities where judgment was meted out by magistrates, often, as in Corinth, an open air structure. The standards of judgment by Christ did not depend on the quantitative results of the worker, as in an earthly workshop, but on qualitative considerations, such as persistence, having an uplifting attitude, leaning on the strength of the Holy Spirit, not oneself, and devotion and dedication to the task at hand. These were 'giving characteristics,' rather than 'getting.' 'Reward' was **μὶσθον**, 'remuneration for work done, *pay, wages*,' (BDAG). Work done for Christ will be paid back by Christ, not only in this life, but also at the Bema judgment in the next life.

3:9: "For we are the fellow-workers of God; you are God's field; you are God's building."

The reason for Paul's views about the unimportance of comparing one worker with another was based, not on the workers. The field represented the labor of the workers. Their growth was paramount to this whole process. Paul introduced another metaphor here by suggesting that the believers were similar to a construction project carried on by God Himself. Each block of the building must be lifted laboriously with ropes and pulleys to finish the structure. Growth in the Christian life occurred the same way.

***"The High Status Metaphor: Paul, the Master-Architect"* I Corinthians 3:10-11: 3:10: From a Lowly Farmer to a Master-Architect: "According to the grace of God given to me as a wise architect, I put in place a foundation, and another (person) will build (upon it). But let each one be careful how he will build (upon it)."**

The Source of This Profession: A Career from God: by the Grace of God Paul could not "earn the right" to become that architect. It came through GRACE (χάρις), unmerited favor. The 'Contract' of Paul's life as an architect was laying the first block of the foundation. This block set the stage for the rest of the first level of the foundation blocks. It had to be carefully selected and laid. In addition, the measurements had to be exact in three dimensions. Furthermore, the land beneath that block had to be specially prepared (reference: Vitruvius, the master architect of Augustus: ***If solid ground cannot be found [level bedrock], but the place proves to be nothing but a heap of loose earth to the very bottom, or a marsh [like the example in the temple of Diana at Ephesus], then it must be dug up and cleared out and set with piles of made of charred alder or olive wood or oak, and these must be driven down by machinery, very closely together like bridge-piles, and the intervals between them filled in charcoal, and finally the foundations are to be laid on them in the most solid form of construction."* (Vitruvius, the ten books on Architecture,** translated by Morris Hicky Morgan, 1960, from the original edition in 1914.), italics mine.

Notice that the first block was the major responsibility of the Master-Architect. The sub-contractors continued where the Master-Architect had begun. Apollos was the next sub-contractor who laid the next foundation stone, followed by others.

The warning to the subcontractors: "Be careful how you continue the building." The reference was to the builders who followed the Master-Architect at Corinth: not just Apollos, but especially those others after him. This was the setting of events that Paul was referring to, when the divisions occurred. Other "sub-contractors" came in and the alignment was skewed. They did not follow the example that either Paul or Apollos laid for them.

Laying the Foundation Stones: The limitations on the sub-contractors:

3:11: "For another foundation no one is able to lay down besides that which is already laid, which is Jesus Christ."

No one was able to lay another block beside the first one which has been laid…. The first stone metaphorically represented Jesus Christ, the 'cornerstone' of the entire foundation. What was added next was vital: it had to be done by cutting other blocks with the exact dimensions of the first, and setting them in place by carefully aligning the two dimensions of levelness with perfect precision, following the alignment of the first block.

The first block, Paul explained here, was the cornerstone that was carefully chosen by the Master Architect. It was the key block, that, if it was chosen carefully with no flaws and cut to exact dimensions, it would set the stage for a strong foundation for the superstructure. If the cornerstone was flawed in any way, the foundation would be flawed and the superstructure would eventually collapse. Christ was the perfect cornerstone and flawless in all respects. The building had a great start. But, the sub-contractors could destroy the foundation if they were not careful in the exact measurements of the additional blocks that were added later.

3:12: "But if anyone will build on the foundation (with) gold, silver, precious stones, wood, hay, straw…."

3:13: "…the work of each will become apparent, for the Day will make it clear, because it will be revealed with fire: and the fire will (perform the) same test of what sort it is."

3:14: "If any work endures (with) which he built, he will receive wages:"

3:15: if any work shall be burned, he will be punished, but he himself will be saved, but so as through fire."

The Materials of Construction: (a metaphor within the metaphor) verses 12-15:

The quality of the materials for the structure: The materials must be high-quality and appropriate. 'Gold' was the best of the best. It will not corrode over time and has been considered the finest and most beautiful of all the raw materials. 'Silver' was perhaps the second best. Although it corroded over time, it was a popular metal for jewelry. 'Precious stones' were also a valuable commodity. Coming down the list, there was wood, which was valuable for building roofs and carving statues and other objects of art. However, it was combustible and could rot over time. Therefore it had limited use. 'Hay' was highly combustible and would rot easily. It was not recommended for building materials, although, mixed with clay, it could be used to strengthen mud-bricks. The lowest item on the list of raw materials was straw for thatched roofs, which was a very poor choice of materials.

Believers should leave a legacy for Christ and God, something that might be a valuable contribution of their love for Christ, and what Christ has done for that them. There were some Christians who have, or are, leaving a legacy using the finest raw materials available, a work that required years of development, leaning heavily on the Holy Spirit to produce. Others had little or no resources to produce anything of lasting value. But their dedication was just as devoted and sincere. Although their works did not survive over time, their efforts will not be forgotten, and Christ will also provide them wages for their effort. Even gold, when melted by fire will reveal impurities. But it was the quality of the work that mattered, and for whom it was accomplished, rather than the preciousness of the materials. The 'fire' revealed the purity of the work by the Master Architect. He alone will determine the work's value and reward the builder accordingly. The Building Inspector evaluates the choice of materials by testing the material using fire in the light of day. If the fire burns up the material chosen for the project, the worker, or subcontractor, will suffer loss. His life will be spared, but he will experience a very narrow escape, 'the smelling of smoke' will be in his or her nostrils.

NOTE: The primary application of these metaphors seems to have been related to the 'subcontractors' in Corinth who allowed the pagan culture to influence the Gospel in varying degrees. Some, who modeled their message after the pattern of Paul, the "Master-Architect," will receive wages for the precision of their calculations, and choice of building materials. Those who went off-level and selected poor quality materials will not forfeit their lives (lose their salvation). But their work will suffer loss (i.e. it will not be certified, nor be allowed to stand), and they themselves will suffer for their carelessness. Preaching and teaching the Word accurately is a heavy responsibility, and there are rewards for faithfully following the Truth, and there are punishments for straying from that Truth, no matter how slight.

3:16: "Do you not know that you are the temple of God and the Spirit of God dwells in you?"

Paul here amplified the metaphors above by revealing a truth that they should have known. The 'know' here was the **οἶδα** kind of 'know' that was transmitted from one generation of believers to another. This was knowledge that Paul had taught them while he was with them. How soon they forgot. The Holy Spirit also dwelled in them to produce over time the work of sanctification by which the believer was made to appear, inwardly and outwardly, more Holy, even as Christ was Holy. 'Sanctify' ἁγιάζω, was derived from the stem, 'holy,' ἁγια- in its verb, adjective, and noun forms. More was expected of them than envy, strife, and divisions.

3:17: "If anyone corrupts the temple of God, God will corrupt this one, for the temple of God is holy, which you yourselves are."

Paul rendered a warning here to the trouble makers in the churches of Corinth. 'If you corrupt the other believers in the assemblies, God will corrupt you.' Be very careful. Each one of the believers themselves was considered a temple of God. 'Do not agitate or strike out against them.' They were precious in God's sight.

3:18: "Let no one deceive himself: if anyone seems to be wise among you in this age, let him become as a fool, in order that he may become wise."

Leaders had arisen in the Corinthian church who seemed to be outwardly wise. However, they were the very ones that started the divisions. Paul was warning the church members here to be careful about how they evaluated their leaders. Leaders could deceive themselves, with the effect of leading the whole congregation astray. Humility was preferable than convincing articulation and arrogance. 'Wisdom' came from feeling lowly and not making grandiose and outrageous statements.

3:19: "For the wisdom of this world beside God is foolishness, for the Scripture has said, '(There is One) who seizes with the hand the wise with their own cunning:"

Paul warned the congregations and leaders that the wisdom that the leaders there were flaunting was 'foolishness,' when compared to God. By quoting Job 5:13, Paul amplified that God had no patience with those who thought they were wise. In fact, God 'seizes them with His hand' (δρασσόμενος) by means of their own cunning. He did it on a continual basis, since the participle was in the present progressive tense. He continually made fools of them and their vaunted ideas. 'Cunning' was πανουργὶα, 'quite predominantly, and in our literature exclusively, in an unfavorable sense, *cunning, craftiness, trickery,* literally, a willingness to do anything,' (BDAG). These 'wise' men were ruthless charlatans.

3:20: "...and again, 'The Lord deeply knows the reasoning of the wise, that they are irrational.'"

Paul here quoted Ps. 94:11 to establish that the wise of this world had no reasoning power whatever, unless they were inspired by the Holy Spirit. The 'natural man' was not wise because they had a flawed mind. Their grandiose thoughts were empty words without content. 'Knows' was **γινώσκει**, a 'knowledge' well beyond the reach of the natural man. God Himself deeply knew the flawed dialogue of the 'wise' and had concluded that they were futile thoughts, empty of any meaning. God's deep knowledge was also continuous, active in every age, because the verb was present progressive in tense.

3:21: "So therefore, let no one boast in men: for all things are yours,"

This message was to the congregations, as well as the leaders. When this letter was read to the various churches, all the members and even the leaders who thought they were wise, holding positions that divided the churches, were warned to avoid such divisive rhetoric. The members could also play a part in deflating the babble of those leaders who refused to stop, by just walking out of the service. 'All things are yours,' that is to say, in the primary application, they had the power to stop such foolishness if they acted in concert, backed by prayer.

3:22: "...whether Paul, or Apollo, or Cephas, or the world, or life, or death, or things present, or things about to happen: all are yours,"

The secondary application of 'all things are yours' in verse 21, had spiritual connotations. All the ministers that came to them were theirs to enjoy and learn from. That also went for the material or metaphysical things of their surroundings: the world, life, death, or things present, or things which will happen in the future: all were benefits that God had bestowed upon His children.

3:23: "...but you are Christ's, and Christ is God's."

Paul concluded this section by announcing who belonged to whom. The church members belonged to Christ, and Christ belonged to God. They were a unified group of people that God owned; and He will look after them.

'The Real Apostolic Ministry' I Corinthians 4: 1-13

4:1: "Let a man so consider us as servants of Christ and managers of the mystery of God."

Paul began here to paint a picture of what the apostolic ministry was really like. The Corinthians perhaps thought that the apostles had a plush lifestyle.

Here he corrected that notion with 13 powerful verses that described the real life of the apostles. 'Servants' were ὑπηρέτος, 'one who functions as a helper, frequently in a subordinate capacity, *helper, assistant,*' (BDAG). 'Managers' was οἰκονομούς, 'manager of a household or estate, *(house) steward, manager,*' (BDAG). A 'helper' was not a grand title; nor was a 'steward,' who was but a manager of the house, protecting the assets, and following orders. This 'steward' was in charge of the mystery of God, communicating messages as needed to the churches, a 'messenger boy,' as it were. So these positions themselves were not important positions on earth, as far as human standards were concerned.

4:2: "As to the remaining (conditions of the job), here it is required among servants that one may be found faithful."

Further, these 'lowly positions' had strict prerequisites. The candidates were chosen carefully, and had to be faithful and diligent in carrying out their responsibilities. 'Required' is ζητεῖται, with a middle meaning of 'requiring,' (BDAG).

4:3: "But as for me, it is a small thing that I will be judged by you, or by a human court: but I am not even judging myself."

In his positions, only his bosses could judge his performance. He could not be judged by other people from even human courts. He could not even judge himself. There was a slight advantage to that system, however. His 'bosses' were Christ and God the Father. They would judge his performance without any prejudice or the taking of bribes. They also would know if he slacked off on the job. 'Judged' was ἀνακρίνω, 'to conduct a judicial hearing, *hear a case, question,*' (BDAG). It was used twice here, once in the future active case when Paul told the Corinthians that it was a small thing for him to be judged in the future by them. The second time in this verse the verb was in a present progressive tense, indicating that he was 'continually' not judging himself. He had the assistance of the Holy Spirit to communicate a course correction, or a 'misstep.' He did not need to waste time analyzing and struggling inwardly to reach the right decision. He was following orders one step at a time, and relying heavily on the Holy Spirit for assistance.

4:4: "For I know nothing against my conscience, yet I am not having been justified by this: but He who is judging me is the Lord."

Paul here explained further that he knew nothing inwardly that he might have done that would indicate a tactical error in his ministerial decisions.

'Know' was **σύνοιδα**, a compound verb **σύν + οἶδα**, 'to know together.' BDAG defined it as 'to be aware of information about something, *to know, be conscious of.*' The prefix 'together,' **σύν**, added the implied dimension of his mind, combined with his own conscience as a 'judge,' confirmed with the short phrase, '**by this**.' That combination of mind and conscience was inadequate. The 'Judge' must lie outside of Paul. He could not trust his own analysis, even his 'spiritual thought process,' linked together with his 'conscience' for 'justification' of his actions as a minister of God. The Holy Spirit would have to represent God in guiding his own awareness of any sin that he may have committed in his ministry.

"**...not having been justified....**" was **δεδικαίωμαι**, a perfect passive intensive participle indicating that the past action of 'justifying' Paul's actions were *continually* not being justified in the past just by internal evidence alone. He would have to rely on prayer and the Holy Spirit for guidance and direct intervention. He would leave the results of his ministerial work in the hands of God. He would certainly not rely on himself and his conscience, acting together, to determine whether his ministerial choices were justifiable.

4:5: "Therefore, judge nothing before the time, until the Lord comes, who will bring to light the hidden things of darkness and reveal the intentions of the hearts. Then each one's praise will occur from God."

Since Paul had the assistance of Holy Spirit, therefore the Corinthians should judge nothing before the time when all believers will be judged when the Lord returns. The hidden things will be brought to light for all to see. Even the communications of the hearts of believers will be made manifest. 'Intentions' was **βουλάς**, 'that which one thinks about as a possibility for action, *plan, purpose, intention,*' (BDAG). Paul did not expect any praise from men for any plan or project that seemed to be successful. He would let God and Christ handle that kind of evaluation. After all, men have only a very limited vision, and even believers do not have all the facts. So Paul recommended that the believers at Corinth refrain from making any criticism or praise about Paul's successes or failures, until that day.

4:6: "But these things brothers and sisters, I have transformed for myself and Apollos on account of you, in order that you may learn by us not to think beyond what is written, that none of you may be puffed up on behalf of one against the other."

167

Paul here explained to the believers of Corinth that he used himself and Apollos as examples of not evaluating the success or failure of ministerial decisions, even from their more accurate viewpoints. He stated that they should not think beyond what was written, or even something stated as an objective fact, or 'jump to conclusions,' because it could lead to errors of judgment, harsh criticisms, and even pride.

'Transformed' was **μετασχημάτισα**, 'to cause a change in a state or condition, *transform, change*,' (BDAG). Ministerial success or even failure, if known while the minister still lives, could operate to inflate his ego, or even deflate him into depression. Others, also, using the same criteria of evaluating others may also follow the same path, and be tempted to criticize others, thereby causing divisions.

4:7: "For who differentiates you (from one another)? And what did you have that you did not receive? Now if you did indeed receive it, why do you boast as if you did not receive it?"

To reinforce his remarks above, Paul asked a series of questions to them. The first question was, 'Who differentiates you from another?' In other words, who made you superior to someone else? Are you superior to another person? Paul's answer was expected to be, 'No one made me superior to anyone else.' 'I am not superior in any way to another minister, or any other person.' This was a question of 'humility,' or the lack of it, that contributed to divisions in the Corinthians churches. But that was only the first question.

The second question was, 'Let's say you might be gifted in some area; who gave you that gift?' Perhaps, if the person thought that he was a gifted minister, he might say, 'God gave me this gift.' Now the problem was compounded when the person answered that God gave him this gift. He must recognize that he had boasted in his gifted abilities to the point that those actions caused quarrels and divisions.

Paul now presented another question: 'Why do you act as if you had this gift all along because of your boasting about it?' Now the person must recognize that he was being proud and arrogant, and also lacked humility. He was acting as though God did not give him those gifts, but that he already had them, and his boastful attitude was, therefore, against God.

4:8: "You are already full! You are already rich! You have reigned as kings without us -- and indeed I could wish that you did reign, that we might also reign with you!"

Now Paul very skillfully turned to irony. The Corinthians were already full of material things, full of an over-realized power, of being puffed up to the point of being inflated balloons. They thought they were kings, and could rule as dictators. But, in reality, they were not kings, and their rule was beggarly. They certainly were not living to the same standard of life that the apostles were living, who, if anyone deserved to live as kings, it would have been the apostles. Paul facetiously said, 'You are living as kings, but without us.' They grossly missed the point.

4:9: "For I think that God has displayed us, the apostles, last, as men sentenced to death; for we have been made a spectacle to the world, even to angels and to men."

In contrast to the Corinthian Christian way of living, Paul described what a real apostle's life was like. Perhaps they could wake up.

'Displayed' was ἀπέδειξεν, 'He has made/exhibited us (as) the last ones perhaps in a triumphal procession,' (BDAG). Paul and other apostles were displayed as if they were being paraded as captives last in a triumphal procession, and were marching off to meet death. The metaphor image was not too far from reality, as the next verses will reveal. 'Spectacle' was θέατρον, 'what one sees in a theater, a spectacle,' (BDAG). The apostles were part of the cast, being killed for entertainment.

The spectators in this metaphorical triumphal procession were both angels and men, indicating they were observers gathered together to watch the apostles die.

4:10: "We are fools on account of Christ, but you are wise in Christ! We are weak, but you are strong! You are distinguished, but we are disgraced!"

This ironical metaphor continued here. Paul described the apostles as 'fools for Christ's sake.' But the Corinthians who were living lavish lifestyles, were living high, as wise men, lifted up by their own rich intellects and rhetorical gifts. The apostles were weak and sickly; but the Corinthians were strong, rich and powerful. They were also distinguished citizens of the city; the apostles were the down-and-out, the scum of the Roman world.

4:11: "To the present hour, we are hungry and thirsty, and we are poorly clothed, savagely treated and without shelter..."

Now Paul moved from metaphor to reality when he described the lifestyles of the apostles. For the very beginning until the time of Paul's writing and during many years, Paul's lifestyle continued to be impoverished. Food and drink were scarce, clothes were almost non-existent, and they were often beaten and without any shelter. The sad, but true, story continued.

4:12: "...And we toil, working long with our own hands. Being cursed, we bless; being attacked, we endure,"

They also worked from time to time with their hands, revealing the low social status that they occupied in the Graeco-Roman world. Paul was trained as a tent-maker, so he could earn money occasionally in that harsh trade. Paul's associates also suffered the same fate. But their attitudes were always positive and uplifting. When they were yelled at and reviled by a mob, they blessed them, when they were persecuted, they also blessed them. Above all, they endured all the pain of being outcasts; but they endured, for the sake of Christ and the gospel message.

4:13: "...being slandered, we exhorted (them). We have become as the garbage of the world, the shoe-scrapings of all things until now."

While they were being slandered, they responded with pleading and exhortation. 'Garbage' was περικαθάρματα, 'that which is removed as a result of a thorough cleansing, *dirt, refuse, off-scouring*,' (BDAG). The apostles were the filth of the world, and treated as such.

'Paul's Heart Revealed'
I Corinthians 4: 14-21

'The Father Metaphor' (I Corinthians 4:14-15):
4:14: "I am writing these things not to shame you, but as my beloved children, instructing (you)."

"...Not to shame you...." Paul was very sensitive to the believers in a shame culture. He did not want them to get the idea that he was shaming them. He had another purpose: As a 'father' to them (the one who 'fathered the church in Corinth,' not necessarily the one who led each one to the Lord), he had every right to 'warn' his 'beloved children.' 'Think of me as your beloved earthly father' (paraphrase). He wanted them to realize that his instructions, or warnings, came a loving father, not from a hypercritical parent who was a harsh disciplinarian.

The Caring Father versus the "House Servant"
'The Father Image' I Corinthians 4:15:

4:15: "For if you may have ten thousand teachers in Christ, (you do) not have many fathers: For by means of Christ Jesus through the gospel, I myself gave birth (to) you."

In first century life, a father was more important than a guide (παιδαγωγος, a slave, or a hired servant, who was in charge of the son or daughter while the father was out). The father gave instructions to the 'paidagogos' regarding the child's instruction, and was also accountable to the father for the child's training, *especially the moral training*. In addition, the 'paidagogos' could have been a disciplinarian, or a 'teacher,' but he was more often responsible for delivering the child to the teacher, and waiting for him while 'school' was in session, and then bringing the child back home again. But, as was sometimes the case in first century upper-middle and upper class homes, the 'paidagogos' was dispensable, and during the life of the child, there could have been several of these 'guides.' But Paul said, "**(even) if you had 10,000 'paidagogoi' in Christ, you may not have had many fathers**." 'Listen, therefore, to your father, not to the hired guides. I set the moral tone for the family: not the hired servants or slaves' (paraphrased). Therefore, the translation of 'paidagogoi' could be 'guides or trainers.'

Certainly, Paul was referring to a 'loving' father in this metaphor, who genuinely cared about his children, and wanted the best for them. But if the 'paidagogoi' failed in providing the proper training, they could be dismissed from their positions (implied). The 'paidagogoi' were represented in this metaphor as the prideful Corinthian leaders.

'Reinforcing the Family Image' Corinthians 4:16-21:
4:16: "Therefore, I beseech you, become mimics of me."

'Model your lives after me' or 'imitate your father, not your 'paidagogos.' You should bear the family image of your father, not the 'paidagogos.' 'He was just a hired servant, and not really part of the family (paraphrase).'

4:17: "For this reason, I sent Timothy to you, who is my beloved child and faithful in the Lord, who will remind you my ways which are in Christ [Jesus], as I teach everywhere in every church."

'Sent' was ἐπεμψα, 'sent,' an epistolary aorist tense: Timothy was the letter carrier, and by the time the letter reached Corinth, it would have been a past event.

Who was Timothy? He was the child they should model their life after, for he carried the image of his father exactly. Being the 'model' child, he was beloved and trustworthy. Timothy would cause them to remember Paul's ways. 'My ways' refers to 'conduct', including, but not necessarily, in this case, theology.

A Warning to the Boastful and Errant paidagogoi:

4:18: "As though (I were) not coming to you, certain ones have begun to be puffed up:"

Note the use of the plural, **paidagogoi**: there were more than one in Corinth: possibly as many as four, perhaps one for every house church. They thought Paul would not come for disciplinary purposes: "Paul was all talk." They were 'puffed up' in their pride, confident that Paul would not return.

4:19: "But I will come soon to you if the Lord may will, and I will know, not the word of those being continually puffed up, but the power:"

The conditions of Paul's coming to correct the problems with the 'paidagogoi' included three things. First, he intended to come soon. He was not timid in correcting this situation in a face-to-face encounter. But he was under the control of the Lord. He would decide the timing, perhaps making them a little nervous. Then Paul would learn of their boastful talk and their so-called power (or 'effectiveness').

Second, **"I will know...."** 'Know' was **γνώσομαι**, from **γινώσκω**, 'the deep knowledge,' not of their vain words, but of their power. He would come and put their 'so-called power' to the test. It was also a future tense verb, dependent on his arrival.

Third, **"I will not know the word of those who are puffed up...."** 'Puffed up' was **πεφυσιωμένων**, a perfect intensive participle, indicating that their condition was 'continuous.' The meaning of the verb was 'to cause to have an exaggerated self-conception, puff up, make proud,' (BDAG). They had a continually inflated view of themselves. Paul would not need to know their talk about their 'power.'

4:20: "For the kingdom of God (is) not with (a display of empty) speech, but with (effective) power."

Paul here asserted his authority as an apostle and declared that the essence of the kingdom of God was not in empty talk, or rambling speech without substance, but was grounded in God's power to make things happen on a divine level. How would they fare with that kind of evaluation?

4:21: "What do you want? Shall I come with a rod to you, or also with a spiritual love and gentleness?"

'Should I come as a father carrying a rod for punishment (paraphrase)?' 'Or should I come to you with a spiritual love and gentleness? It's your choice.' 'Love' was the deep Christian 'agape' love, ἀγάπη. 'Gentleness' was πραΰτητος, 'the quality of not being overly impressed with a sense of one's self-importance, *gentleness, humility, courtesy, considerateness, meekness.*' (BDAG).

Paul could come either way. He preferred the latter.

'A Major Moral Issue' I Corinthians 5: 1-13:

5:1: "Sexual Immorality is even being reported among you, and such immorality which (is) not (acceptable) even among Gentiles, that (a man) has the wife of his father."

Paul came to another issue that had been reported to him recently. This issue was very serious, and the church had not dealt with it. A young man began a sexual relationship with his father's wife, probably his second wife, not his mother. It was not considered 'immoral' by the church, and so nothing was done in terms of counseling or even setting guidelines. This kind of conduct was even considered immoral among non-believing Gentiles. When the word reached Paul, he was already writing I Corinthians in Ephesus, dealing with various other church problems. But he was, no doubt, furious at the implications for the churches of Corinth. He treated this issue as a serious problem, and immediately developed his response.

5:2: "And you yourselves have continually been puffed up, and not, rather, mourned, that he, having done this deed might be removed from among you?"

Church leaders who knew of the problem ignored it. They even sent communications to Paul bragging about the churches, assuming all was spiritually well on the home front among Corinthian Christians and the churches. Paul's response started in 5:1 and continued through the end of the chapter. He condemned their 'bragging,' and told the leaders that they were continually puffed up when they should have been mourning. 'Puffed up' was ἐστὲ πεφυσιωμένοι, a rare 'intensive' periphrastic participle construction that very strongly emphasized the **'continual'** nature of the **'proud bragging'** that someone had witnessed. The verb for πεφυσιωμένοι, had a core meaning of 'to cause to have an exaggerated self-conception, *puff up, make proud*,' (BDAG). This word was also used in 4:6; 4:18f; 8:1; 13:4; in I Corinthians, and once in Colossians 2:18. It was never used in the NT anywhere else. Paul was obviously very agitated.

5:3: "For I myself, although being absent in the body, but present in the spirit, have already judged the one who so (boldly) committed this deed as if present:"

Paul here revealed the seriousness of his proposed participation in dealing with this situation. He wanted the Corinthians to imagine that Paul's spirit was there in their presence when they would follow his instructions on dealing with the problem. That way, they would more likely do what Paul asked without hesitation.

5:4: "...In the name of our Lord Jesus Christ, when you and my spirit, after having been gathered together with the power of the Lord Jesus,..."

5:5: "...to deliver such a one to Satan for the destruction of the flesh, in order that his spirit may be saved in the Day of our Lord."

These two verses represented the conclusion of his recommended procedures in dealing with the issue. They were to deliver the person to Satan and eject him from the church. He was not recommending to the church leaders to kill the young man, but to have a service in the church with the young man present, where Satan was invited to take his body, so that his soul might be saved upon the Lord's return. That must have been quite a church service to watch.

5:6: "Your boast (is) not attractive. Do you not know that a little leaven leavens the whole lump (of dough)?"

Now Paul turned to the other flaw: the proud gloating of the leaders to Paul, bragging about how well the church was doing. He confronted them with the statement: 'Your boast (is) not attractive.' 'Attractive' was καλός, which was the aesthetically pleasing form of the term, 'good,' ἀγαθός. καλός can also be translated as 'beautiful,' or 'pleasing to the eye,' etc. Their gloating was not pretty.

Paul then proceeded to use a metaphor in the preparing of unleavened bread which was used for Jewish religious rituals. A tiny bit of leaven was all that was required for making 'leavened bread.' But this sin was a giant portion of sin that was intermingled with the church families. It would definitely

174

contaminate the purity of any church. Even lesser sins would corrupt the church, but this amount could have been fatal.

5:7: "Cleanse yourself from the old leaven, in order that you might be a new lump of dough, even as you are unleavened: for even Christ, our Passover, was crucified (for us)."

The order to clean up the church by dealing with this gross sin was a reminder to go through with the church service above. The service was to be seen as a 'cleansing' ritual for the church. Once that process of cleaning was completed, then the church could resume its mission. He also reminded them that Christ was crucified for sin, and there was no place in the church for a sinful activity such as this to remain. It was a disgrace to Christ who suffered so much to provide the salvation necessary for believers.

5:8: "So, let us keep the feast, not with the old leaven, nor with the leaven of evil and of immorality, but with the unleavened lumps of dough of sincerity and of truth."

'Sincerity' was εἰλικρινείας, 'purity of motive, sincerity, openness' from 'judging the purity of the sunlight,' within the word itself (Thayer). 'The pure dough of truth,' indicated that the truth cannot have any contamination from leaven. Otherwise, it will be corrupted, and will destroy the truth's effectiveness.

5:9: "I wrote to you in my epistle not to intermingle together with immoral people,"

'Wrote' was in the past tense: This was a reference to Paul's "missing" letter, written sometime before I Corinthians. This letter did not survive to modern times (Thiselton, p. 409), probably not even to the second century.

'...not to intermingle together with immoral people' 'Intermingle' was συναναμίγνυσθαι, a rare double compound word with two prepositions attached: 'with + up.' The root word, 'μίγνυμι,' meant to mix or mingle socially, as young people might do in looking for dates. This activity was forbidden by Paul in his first letter. (He will clarify the meaning in verse 10, and expand it in verse 11). 'With immoral men' was πόρνοις. The term "immoral" was related to the word used to describe the young man and his step-mother (πορνεία there, πόρνοις, here). πορνεία meant sexual immorality; πόρνοις meant a man who practiced sexual immorality. Both words were nouns: the first identified the act; the second identified the man practicing it.

5:10: **"(But) I did not mean with immoral people of this world, or with greedy people, or ravenous wolves, or idolaters, since then you would need to go out of the world."**

What Paul was saying here: Paul was now explaining that he did not expect them to avoid broad social contacts or saying hello with such people, but he seemed to be saying to avoid developing deep social relationships with them.

'...or with the greedy or the grasping or with idolaters...' Paul expanded his list to include other categories.

'...since you would be required to go completely out of the world.' Paul is now getting to the point. It would be impossible to casually meet only those people who were morally upright in just walking around the town. Paul did not expect the Christians of Corinth to withdraw from society. This is a

point that various 5th century monks seemed to overlook when they withdrew from the 'evil' society, establishing monasteries in isolated areas to avoid evil influences in the cities and towns of civilization.

5:11: **"But now I wrote to you not to intermingle with any 'so-called Christian' or who may have the nature of immorality or a greedy nature or an idolatrous nature or of a nature that practices verbal abuse or of a drunk or a of a thief: with such a person you should not even dine with."**

Note the difference in verse 10 and here: In verse 10 the Corinthians took the message to mean that they should have no dealings with "anyone" immoral. Here it is "so-called Christians" who chose that lifestyle. The "so-called Christians" who lived in these ways were doing it continually: this is the progressive present tense. The list is growing: from an immoral lifestyle to the greedy to the idolater to the verbal abuser to the drunk to the thief. These are the 'so-called Christians' with whom true Christians in Corinth should avoid having any close relationships.

Dining in the first century was an intimate social experience where relationships were forged and deepened. Public dining could have occurred in lunch counters, located across the street from the theater and other public buildings, or in temple restaurants, where the finest meat was served. Dining in private homes was also a common practice. The practice here suggested the possibility of private dining among Christians. But such a practice between a Christian and a "so-called" Christian could give the impression that the errant lifestyle of the one was tolerated or condoned by the other, and therefore 'acceptable' to the church group. The reference does not suggest the eating around the Lord's Table.

5:12: "For what business of mine is it to judge those without? Do you yourselves not judge those who are within?"

Two Questions for the Corinthians:

Question #1: *"For what business of mine is it to judge those without?"* It was not Paul's business, nor was it the business of the Corinthian Christians, nor even Christians today to judge people who are not believers. Paul was saying here: 'I am not going to spend any effort on judging the conduct of unbelievers. But I AM responsible for revealing and developing the living standards of Christians, those who are within the circle of fellowship, and make judgments on those who do not live up to those standards.' He was not recommending a certain Christian lifestyle for unbelievers.

Question #2: *"Are you yourselves judging those who are within?"* The answer to this question was NO. But it should have been YES. They should have been very discerning in promoting a Christ-like lifestyle of their fellow Christians and being careful in identifying genuine Christians from the pseudo-Christians among them. They weren't.

Who will Judge the Unbelievers and What is the Responsibility of Christians? Judging unbelievers was not the task of Christians. The main responsibility of believers of all ages was, first, to spread the Gospel message, bringing people to Christ, and, second, to help Christians grow in Christ.

5:13: "But God will judge those on the outside. (But as the Scripture says), 'Banish the evil person from yourselves.'"

'Banish the evil person from among yourselves!' Dt. 17:7; 19:19; 22:21, 24; 24:7. Deuteronomy has been the foundation of this "avoidance list." Did Paul simply copy out these words from the OT? Or were certain 'believers' in Corinth practicing these sins? Sadly, it was very likely the latter. The action required by Paul seemed to be harsh; but the sins were extremely serious and needed to be dealt with swiftly and harshly to show that the churches could not tolerate or condone these sins among their members. Of course, the point behind the harsh and rapid response was to bring the person who failed back to Christ through repentance. The churches must utilize discipline to set, and keep, those standards high, for the glory of Christ.

'Another Issue: Legal Matters' I Corinthians 6:1-11:
The Problem: Taking another Believer to a Roman Court
6:1: "Does anyone of you, having a legal matter against another, dare to bring (a Christian) to justice before the unrighteous (pagan judges) and not before the saints?"

Paul dramatically explained here the issue of bringing a lawsuit against another Christian in a Roman court of law. The matter was apparently brought as a civil complaint, rather than as a criminal complaint. The lower courts were notoriously corrupt. The higher status of one of the litigants was very often used in the decisions to benefit those corrupt judges. Also, the judges were often bribed by one side or the other. Even in the best situation, where an honest judge was found, that judge was a pagan, with a worldview totally opposed to the Christian worldview. Paul saw this practice as a dangerous precedent for Christians.

'Dare' was **τολμᾷ**, 'to do something bold,' (BDAG). The verb was the first word in the sentence for emphasis, 'How dare you' do something this audacious!'

'Legal matter' was **πράγμα**, 'a matter of contention, dispute, lawsuit,' (BDAG), although it often meant, 'any kind of matter or undertaking,' (BDAG).

'Christians are better qualified to judge than the corrupt Roman judges'
6:2: "Or, are you not aware that the saints will judge the world? And if the world is being judged by you, are you unworthy of a forum for justice, (processing) small claims?"

See Luke 22:30 (and Matthew 19:28) referring to the saints judging the 12 tribes of Israel. See also: Rev. 2:26, 27: '…to him I will give power over the nations: (v.26b), and he shall rule them with a rod of iron….' (verse 27).

This was the first statement of three: 'are you not aware,' **οἴδατε**, with the negative. It was one of the Greek words for 'know,' (see also verses 3 and 9). Paul was telling them that they should have been knowledgeable from their former training. The 'know' here expressed a transmitted knowledge that was handed down to them. The Children of God will one day be in a very special position to judge the world. Therefore, they should be far more qualified even now to settle a dispute between Christians. If real justice was the goal, let the Christians of the church arbitrate: they were far more impartial than corrupt

Roman jurists, who will be judged by God, and were not even capable to judge.

'Judging,' here was used twice. But a rare related word was also used, κριτηρὶων, 'a forum for justice, *lawcourt, tribunal*,' (BDAG), used only here by Paul, and once by James, in the NT.

A lawsuit before Roman courts would not only have been judged with partiality, but that process would have degraded the believers by airing their dirty laundry before the unbelieving world, and therefore, put a stain on Christianity in the eyes of many unbelievers.

The worldview issue was also a vital concern, as described in verse 1. A Christian point of view was critically important for Christian disputes. Paul may have recognized that a dramatic new lifestyle, developed on this earth, before the rapture, should have a totally new kind of jurisprudence. Not only should it be centered within the church, it should be fair and impartial, developed on objective evidence, and sensitive to the nature of God, His word, and based on an idealistic moral behavior handed down by Christ and the apostles. This was a far cry from the justice used in the Middle Ages when guilt was decided by throwing the accused into a lake. If he or she floated, that proved innocence. If that person sank, then he or she was guilty. Justice of the kind that Paul advocated disappeared from the human scene.

However, this incipient form of justice for believers could only be formed worldwide if Christianity succeeded in usurping the pagan system of justice, which did not happen until the age of the Emperor Constantine in 322 A.D. Even then, the results in jurisprudence declined into superstition, as education and learning gradually disappeared before and during the Dark Ages, not emerging again until science gradually overturned superstition in the 19th and 20th centuries.

6:3: "Are you not aware that we shall judge angels, and how much more (are they than) matters of everyday life?"

This was an additional area of judging responsibilities of believers. Paul used the plural, "we" here. In other words, ALL Christians had this gift, revealing a certain level of equality among Christians regarding the capability of discernment. Not only will Christians participate in judging the world, but they will also judge angels. Therefore, they should be able to handle matters of everyday life.

'Matters of everyday life' was one word in Koine Greek, βιωτικά, an adjective, but used here as a substantive, meaning 'things pertaining to daily life and living, *belonging to daily life,*' (BDAG). This word was only found 3 times in the NT, twice by Paul (6:3; 6:4), and once by Luke (21:34).

'A Major Question:'
6:4: "Therefore, if you may have a case before a court on everyday things, (Why) do you appoint these as judges who are being despised in the church?

Or, to paraphrase the question, "Why are you going to court before those judges who despise the church for trivial matters of everyday life?"

'Things of everyday life' was βιωτικά, placed first in the sentence for emphasis, stressed the trivial nature of the offenses. 'Court' was κριτήρια, 'a forum for justice, *lawcourt, tribunal,*' (BDAG). 'Appoint,' καθίζετε, 'to put in charge of something, *appoint, install, authorize.*' These pagan judges were being 'despised.' ἐξουθενημένους, was 'to show by one's attitude or manner of treatment that (a person) has no merit or worth, *disdain,*' (BDAG), probably universally, by church members as a whole.

6:5: "I say this to your shame. Is there no one, not one, among you who is wise, who is able to judge as an arbitrator between (a person and) his brother?"

Paul repeated the negative here to establish his incredulity that this statement could possibly be true: *'no one, not one?'* Paul knew of many individuals in the churches of Corinth who were mature Christians. Paul was asking them to reconsider this whole idea.

In the Graeco-Roman world, as well as the eastern regions, a 'shame culture' was very predominant. Here Paul gave them the harshest criticism he could have meted out: *'shame on you!'* 'Shame' was ἐντροπήν, 'the state of being ashamed, *shame, humiliation,*' (BDAG). Being shamed by Paul in this sense was extremely humiliating for the Christians of Corinth.

6:6: "But a brother is being judged with (another) brother, and this, before unbelievers?"

Paul repeated this allegation because he was very agitated. *'Do you really mean that one brother is going against another brother in a court of law composed of unbelievers?'* Paul could not believe what he was hearing.

6:7: "[Therefore] already it is a complete (moral) defeat for you that you have a judgment with each other. Why do you not rather suffer wrong? Why do you not rather allow yourself to be defrauded?"

'Moral defeat,' ἥττημα, 'loss, *it is a loss for you,*' (BDAG). The meaning of the verb form of the word was 'be vanquished, *defeated,*' (BDAG). 'Complete,' was ὅλως, 'a marker of highest degree on a scale of extent, *completely, wholly, everywhere,*' (BDAG). By resorting to this kind of court action, the Corinthian 'believer' who initiated it allowed Christianity to suffer an extremely painful 'moral' defeat. The faith, once delivered to the saints, was tarnished. It was a 'moral' defeat, because the court case involved the accusation of one believer against another who allegedly 'cheated' another brother, which was a moral issue.

6:8: "But you yourselves are wronging and you are defrauding, and this (is against) brothers?"

Paul was very upset at this point. He could have said, 'And you call yourself 'brothers,' 'children of God,' 'saints,'? 'How could you!' 'Where is the transformed life?' 'Where is evidence of your new birth?' 'How could you have gone this far?'

'Wronging,' ἀδικεῖτε, 'act in an unjust manner, *do wrong,*' (BDAG). Not only was the 'brother' who initiated this lawsuit 'wronging his brother,' but he was 'defrauding' him. 'Defrauding' was ἀποστηρεῖτε, 'to cause another to suffer loss by taking away through illicit means, *rob, steal, despoil, defraud,*' (BDAG). A legal accusation in that day was often believed, whether it was proved wrong later or not. An accusation taken to court could ruin the reputation of a man. This Christian brother who was accused was in serious jeopardy even if he was innocent.

'The Warnings to the Believers' I Corinthians 6:9–11:

6:9: "Or, are you not aware that the unrighteous ones are not inheriting the kingdom of God? Stop being deceived! Neither sexually immoral persons, nor idolaters, nor adulterers, nor effeminate, nor male homosexuals…"

Paul began a list here to clearly designate conduct, if proved to be a general characteristic of the person's lifestyle that would have resulted in denied entrance to the kingdom of God. Apparently some of the believers developed a false notion of morality, perhaps even the two 'brothers' who went to court. Their rationalization may have led to self-deception about sin in the Christian's life. Paul here set the record straight. 'Stop being deceived!' 'Deceived,' πλανᾶσθε, here in the passive form, indicating that they allowed an activity to happen, and, once it did, the passive form indicated a power came over them that led to their deception. The verb πλανᾶσθε meant 'to proceed without a sense of proper direction, *go astray, be misled, to deceive oneself,*' (BDAG).

6:10: "…nor thieves, nor greedy persons, nor drunkards, not verbally abusive people, not robbers, will inherit the kingdom of God."

Microanalysis: Negative Vocabulary
The Word-List:
Verse 9

'Sexually Immoral People'	πόρνοι	one who practices sexual immorality, fornicator, (BDAG)
'Idolaters'	εἰδωλολάτραι	image worshipper, idolater, (BDAG).
'Adulterers'	μοιχοὶ	one who was unfaithful to a spouse, adulterer, (BDAG)
'Effeminate'	μαλακός	pertaining to being passive in a same-sex relationship, effeminate, (BDAG)
'Male Homosexuals'	ἀρσενοκοίτης	a male who engages in sexual activity with a person of his own sex, a pederast, (BDAG). *'Pederasty' was the sexual practice of a male having sex with a young teenage boy.*

Verse 10

'Thieves'	κλέπται	thieves, (BDAG)
'Greedy Persons'	πλεονέκτης	one who desires to have more than is due, a greedy person, (BDAG)
'Drunkards'	μέθυσοι	drunkard, (BDAG)
'Verbally Abusive People'	λοίδοροι	reviler, abusive person, (BDAG)
'Robbers'	ἅρπαγες	robber, (BDAG)

Text Resumption: I Corinthians Chapter 6:
6:11: "And some of you used to be one or more of these: but you were washed, but you were declared righteous by means of the name of the Lord Jesus Christ and by the Spirit of our God."

Paul here admitted that some of the Corinthian Christians practiced one or more of these vices in a habitual manner. These practices were now, since their conversion, to be stopped. Their 'conversion' was described as 'being washed' and being 'declared righteous,' both passive verbs, indicating that God was now working in their lives in the matter of 'cleansing' and the 'declaration of righteousness.' The 'how' was also described: 'by applying the name of the Lord Jesus,' and 'applying the Holy Spirit' to their lives. The ἐν is likely the dative of agency, 'by means of,' not the dative of sphere, 'by means of the Lord Jesus and the Holy Spirit.'

'Washed,' ἀπελούσασθε, 'wash something away from oneself, wash oneself,' (BDAG). The prefix, ἀπο- modifies the cleansing to refer to 'something' being washed away: 'sin.' From God's point of view, 'sin' had been washed away at conversion; therefore, that person should no longer engage in the sins that marked his or her life prior to conversion.

'Declared righteous,' ἐδικαιώθητε, 'to cause someone to be released from personal or institutional claims that are no longer to be considered pertinent or valid, make free,' (BDAG). God made a sinner judiciously free from the effect of sin at the point of conversion. The power of Christ, acting through the Holy Spirit, initiated and maintained that freedom.

Application: Christians within the church should have had arbitrators who were gifted enough to deal with the trivial conflicts of this life. If not, then Christians should swallow their pride, take the abuse or loss, and move on. Don't ask for arbitration before unbelieving judges who could be partial or corrupt, or even unaware of the beauty and purity of the Christian life. Don't give the Christian life a sordid reputation by revealing the dirty laundry that sometimes happens among weak, feeble, and poorly developed believers.

"Your Sayings and My Sayings"
I Corinthians 6:12-20

'Christian Freedom: Lawful Versus Beneficial' Verse 12:
6:12: [You say:] "All things are lawful" [But I say:] "All things are not beneficial" [You say:] "All things are lawful" "[But I say:] I myself will not be made a slave at the hands of anything."

Many scholars think that Paul was quoting sayings which were prevailing in Corinth. These maxims were feeble attempts by the Corinthians Christians to rationalize their immoral living. The Corinthians may have claimed that they were free to use prostitutes from time to time, as was tolerated in first century Graeco-Roman society, as long as it was done in a secret place, and not in a brothel. Paul countered that even if 'your statement was true, not all things are to your advantage.' In 12b he advocated really free Christian living, which will not result in an addiction that was more akin to slavery.

'Lawful' ἔξεστιν, meant 'to be authorized for the doing of something, *it is right, is authorized, is proper*,' (BDAG). The 'keeping of the law' was no longer required of Christians, resulting in 'all things' being lawful. However, just because believers were 'free' from the law, did not mean that they were to live as lawless individuals, as some Jewish critics of Christianity were charging in that day.

But Paul was saying here that 'not all things were beneficial' to the believer. 'Beneficial' was συμφέρει, 'to be advantageous, help, confer a benefit, be profitable/useful,' (BDAG). Both verbs were in the present progressive tense, indicating a continual action.

Paul did not bring up here the issue that Christians lived by the 'law of Christ,' made effective by the indwelling power of the Holy Spirit. However, it was implied. 'All things that the Christian wanted to do' was indeed 'lawful,' because the Holy Spirit guided the Christian along that road. The 'want' of the believer was altered so that the inclination and the power to do 'all things' was switched on. Now that the believer had the assistance of the Holy Spirit in making decisions, he or she could discern between what was 'injurious' and what was 'beneficial,' that is, what had an advantage for the believer and what didn't.

Therefore, the Corinthians misinterpreted the word, 'all things.' To the mature believer, 'all things' represent 'all the things at the disposal of the believer available to please God.' They took it to mean, 'all the *sinful* things of the old man' they could still participate in and enjoy. Paul made the point that those things were not what drove Paul, and they did not fit his definition of 'all things.'

'The Transitory Nature of the Body?' Verse 13:

6:13: [You say:] "Foods are for the stomach and the stomach is for the foods, but God will destroy this (stomach) and these (foods). But [I say] the body (is) not for sexual immorality, but for the Lord, and the Lord (is) for the body:"

What were the Corinthians saying? The food that they consumed and the body that consumed that food were "of the earth," and therefore corruptible (destroyed in the eating) and consequently unimportant. They concluded then that both food appetites and sexual appetites (with a prostitute) were also insignificant because they were not connected to the soul, which was immortal and was where spiritual experiences were developed and refined by the Holy Spirit. This was a feeble attempt to compartmentalize and separate the bodily appetites from spiritual experiences, and, therefore, justify their sin.

But Paul countered that the body was part and parcel of the spiritual experience. It was 'for the Lord,' a dative of purpose: the new body of the Christian was energized by the Holy Spirit, and that body was to be dedicated to the Lord. That was the purpose of that new body. It was not the purpose of that new body, coupled with the Holy Spirit who dwelled there, to be connected in any way with sexual immorality. That was a gross misinterpretation of the Christian's body.

The Christian's new body was, therefore, not a transitory, earthly thing that was decaying and worthless, but was a sacred part of the soul, and must never be associated with immorality of any kind.

'The Permanence of the Body' Verse 14:
6:14: "But God also raised the Lord and He will raise us through His power."

The body was not destined for the permanence of the grave: it was destined to be raised from the dead. The body did have value, and it will play a major role both now and in the future. That body which the Christians at Corinth were treating with such contempt will be raised from the grave by the power of God Himself. The body therefore was holy, and not to be treated as a 'dirty, earthly thing, full of earthly cravings.'

'The Corinthians Lacked Critical Knowledge' (vss 15-19) *"Are you not aware?"*
Paul's questions: vss. 15, 16, 19.

Body Membership in a Royal Society Verse 15:
6:15: "Are you not aware that your bodies are members of Christ? Shall I then, having taken the members of Christ make those members of immorality? God forbid!"

Paul used a question here to cause them to remember Paul's teachings when he was with them. **'Are you not aware?'** This question was repeated in verse 16 and 19 with great effect. 'Aware' was **οἴδατε**, as a 'knowledge passed down from one person to another.' Their memories were selective and flawed, while trying desperately to find rationalization for their sins.

'Members' were 'bodily members,' **μέλη**, 'part of the human body, *member, part, limb*,' (BDAG). All the body parts of a believer belonged to the Lord. He had ownership over them. Since they belong to God, how could believers use those Godly parts in acts of immorality? Their logic was deeply flawed.

'The Effects of Contamination' Verses 16, 17:

6:16: "Or, are you not aware that the man having joined together with a prostitute is one body? For it says (in Scripture) the two (are made) into one flesh,
6:17: and the man who is joined together with the Lord is one spirit."

Here Paul connected the immoral act of prostitution with marriage, and used Scripture (Gen. 2:24, LXX) to support the idea. This sin was very serious and violated the sacredness of sexual intercourse in marriage. He also compared the marriage idea with the union of the Lord with the believer which involved the body.

'Joined together' in both verses was the present participle, **κολλώμενος**, 'join oneself to, cling to, associate with,' (BDAG), a unity, either with a prostitute (verse 16), or with Christ (verse 17). Both participles represented a continual action of joining (present progressive tenses).

'A Command and Another Maxim' Verse 18:

6:18: "Flee sexual immorality. [You say] Every sin a man may commit is outside the body: but [I say] the one who is sexually immoral is sinning against his own body."

'Flee sexual immorality' as Joseph ran away from Potiphar's wife (Gen 39). It did not say "keep away from."

Verse 18b (**'every sin a man may commit is outside the body'**) was likely a popular Corinthian maxim at the time, although a large variety of arguments have surfaced as to its specific meaning (Thisleton, p.471-2). Some have maintained that it gives free license for prostitution; others conclude that it applied to mistresses. Whatever the details of the sin described, the meaning is clear: since every sin committed was outside the body, then the activities of the body should have been permitted to occur, whatever they may have been, because the body was exempt from sin.

The argument seemed to be suggesting the body was not part of the soul and was morally exempt ("outside the body") from sin's effects. Therefore, even if a Christian "sinned" by having sex with a prostitute, that sin was in a separate category, very much like a "little white lie" was in a separate category of lying: a "trivial" sin, which did not affect the soul. Paul countered that the person who was sexually immoral was actually 'sinning' against his own body, and this kind of sin was actually much more serious than the Corinthians understood it to be.

'Reminder from 3:16 and 17' Verse 19:

6:19: "Are you not aware that your body is the Temple of the Holy Spirit which is in you, which you have from God, and you are not yourselves?"

The bodies of believers, therefore, were sacred and holy. Paul here described several characteristics of a believer's body. First, that body was a temple of God. The Jewish temple was being replaced by God himself. That temple had lost its purpose of existence after Christ came. In less than two decades from this writing, by AD 70, the Jewish Temple with all the sacrificial systems would be destroyed forever. The function of that temple was to signal the presence of God, where sacrifices of animals would look forward to the final sacrifice of Christ. The 'new temple' selected by God, was within each believer. As a place of God, the believer's body was sacred: all of it!

Another new characteristic of the believer's body was that it was the dwelling place of the Holy Spirit. That 'temple' was taken over by the Holy Spirit at conversion. 'Of the Holy Spirit' was a genitive of possession. That body now belonged to God, the Holy Spirit. It was His property.

Therefore, the transfer of the ownership title of that 'new temple' was handed over to the Holy Spirit by God the Father at the point of conversion, resulting in a magnificent gift from God to every believer. The 'gift' was the Holy Spirit, '…which you have from God.' Thus, 'your body, being a sacred enclosure, was not yours to freely indulge in sin.'

'The Slavery Issue Restated' Verse 20:

6:20: "For you were purchased off the auction block in the slavery market with a price: therefore glorify God with your bodies."

'Purchased' was ἠγοράσθητε, 'to secure the rights to someone by paying a price, buy, acquire as property,' (BDAG). The purchase was made in the human slave-market of the agora (civic center), where the structure was possibly located. The verb ἀγοράζω, the 'purchase' of the slave, ('agorazo') revealed that this place was where human traffic was bought and sold.

The use here was a metaphor, indicated that the purchase was a one-time event (aorist tense), that the bidder competed against another high bidder (Satan), and that the price paid was very high. As in a real slave market, the bidder was the active person (note the passive verb, ἠγοράσθητε), not the slave. Therefore, because 'you' were rescued by Christ in a bidding war in the market, 'glorify God with your bodies.'

NOTE: The believers were still slaves: not of sin, because they now had a new owner. But they now were to live as the 'new owner' required. The new owner wanted them to use their bodies to glorify Him. The paraphrase of Paul could read, "Do it! You cannot possibly pay Him back for what He did for you in the spiritual slave market."

'The Questions that the Corinthians Had'

I Corinthians 7:1-7:

Question Number 1: "In view of the soon coming of the Lord, is it better to marry or stay single?"

Remaining Celibate? Verse 1:

7:1: "Now concerning the things you wrote about, (one of which is this: Is it) good for a man not to touch a woman?"

Paul now referred to questions that the Corinthians had written to him about. The first question seemed to center around the idea of celibacy. Verse 1b could be read: **"Is it good for a man to remain celibate?"** 'Touch,' ἅπτεσθαι, probably referred to marriage: 'to touch intimately, have *sexual contact*,' (BDAG).

Did the question reveal the position of the Corinthians? Or, did it refer to Paul's own position that they were wondering about?

The first time in church history that these words were actually considered to be Paul's own position was by Methodius when he wrote his commentary sometime between AD 260 and 311 (Thiselton, p. 497). Most modern commentators accept verse 1b as a Corinthian view held by some ascetics in

Corinth. Those ascetics took the position that celibacy offered a higher state of spirituality than marriage did. Paul will refute that position in 7:7.

One argument favored the view that 1b was the Corinthian position (not Paul's) and was from Genesis 2:18b: "It is not <u>good</u> that man should be alone…." Verse 1b was opposite Genesis 2:18b. Paul probably would not take a position that was contrary to the Genesis account.

Verse 1b could also be translated as a question, as it was translated above: "(Is it) good for a man not to touch a woman?" This was quite possible since there were no question marks in the Greek of that day. Only the context would indicate the possibility of a question, which was a distinct possibility here, and would further confirm that verse 1b was <u>not</u> Paul's idea.

On the other hand, Paul did leave out the quotation marks in 1b. There was a Greek word that expressed quotation marks: the word ὅτι (pronounced 'hoti' with a short 'o'). This word expressed either a direct quotation or an indirect quotation. The direct quotation would have been quotation marks in our English translation; the indirect quotation would be the insertion of the word 'that,' reading: "Now concerning the things you wrote about, that (it is) good for a man not to touch a woman." Either would have made the position quite clear that it belonged to the Corinthians. But does its absence prove that the viewpoint was Paul's? The absence of the term (ὅτι) did create confusion, but Paul quite often left out words, just as he left out the main verb in 1b: ('It is' or 'Is it').

Therefore verse 1b was most likely a position that some Corinthians held, and others asked for Paul's clarification, possibly from the 'factions' within the churches.

Is marriage here a concession to human nature? "Get married!" Verse 2:
7:2: "On the contrary, because of various expressions of sexual immorality, let each man have his own wife and let each woman have her own husband."

Paul supported the institution of marriage in this verse. Perhaps he was thinking of Genesis 2:18b here. Paul also brought up the idea here of immorality, which could have applied to either partner, male or female. He applied the two imperatives, ἐχέτω ('have') for both sexes.

The noun, "πορνείας" was plural, indicating the possibility of various kinds of sexual immorality, not just fornication. The concession was about the vulnerability of some Christians in Corinth: but did it have a wider application? Possibly, for Paul took great pains in language to describe each partner as equal in verses 2, 3, and 4. Women were not mere property. They were full partners.

'Physical obligation among married partners' Verses 3-5:

7:3: "Let the man give (that which is) his obligation to (his) wife and likewise (let) the woman give (that which is) her obligation to (her) husband."

Paul also went into detail about marriage obligations because of further questions the Corinthians seemed to have asked in their letter. The tone suggested that Paul viewed physical relations as positive. 'Obligation,' was ὀφειλήν, 'that which one ought to do, a duty,' (BDAG), here referring to the obligation to provide physical intimacy in marriage.

'There is a reason for this obligation' Verse 4:

7:4: "The wife does not have authority over her own body, but the husband does, and likewise the husband does not have authority over his own body, but the wife does."

They have obligations to each other. The 'self' was submerged in the Christian marriage. This instruction was followed by a negative command: see verse 5:

7:5: "Stop denying (physical relations with) one another, except for a (specific amount of) time in order that you may spend time in prayer and then you may come back together again lest Satan may tempt you beyond your self-control."

Of course, this was an ideal model and applied only to Christian couples.

'Which ideas were Paul's opinions?' Verse 6:

7:6: "But this I say for the purpose of a concession, not for the purpose of a command."

The emphatic demonstrative pronoun, "this," must be examined carefully. The reader must examine closely that which Paul was referring.

One view attached the antecedent to what went on before: for example, It could also just mean verse 2, concerning marriage versus celibacy. If it was applied to verses 2 through 5, it would mean that he was expressing an opinion about celibacy and intimacy in marriage. It could also apply to verse

5b about refraining (or not) from intimacy. (This was favored by Thiselton, and likely the correct view).

It could also look forward to verse 7a where Paul put forward his opinion that he would like to see everyone as he was: celibate. But if the 'this' referred to verse 7a, it was not a command from the Lord, only Paul's opinion.

This entire section (verses 2-6) applied to men as well as women: both were equals in marriage which suggested a selfless process, each acting in consideration of the other. This was not a Roman view, nor even a Jewish view. But this view certainly made Christianity appealing to wealthy Roman women later in the first century who were living under a powerful male dominance, and was a factor for them becoming Christians. They had a freedom and liberty in Christ that that never knew before.

Was Marriage Equal to Celibacy? Verse 7:

7:7 "Certainly I wish that all men to be even as I myself (am). But each person has his own gift from God, one this way, and another that way."

It was a gift from God for some to be married; it was also a gift from God that some are celibate. These were equal gifts; and they were from God. One choice was not spiritually superior to the other. Paul was tolerant of each person's desire and need to be married or not to be married. Both were gifts from God, equal in importance.

Previously Married, Divorce and Mixed Marriages
I Corinthians 7:8-16:

The "*Used-to-be-Married*" (divorced before conversion? and Widows)
'Stay Single or Remarry?' Verses 8-9:

7:8: "But I say to the unmarried and to the widows, it is good for them if they may remain as I am."

Paul made a recommendation to those who have married, but now are not, due to divorce or the death of a partner. Paul stated his advice here: "I say…." Note that verse 7 stated his 'wish,' clearly an opinion. Verse 8 also opened with 'I say.' This was not a statement of command. Compare with verse 10, which was a command.

The "unmarried:" Although this word (ἀγάμοις) can at times mean "single," it also meant 'formerly married, now unmarried,' (BDAG). See verse

11 where the word referred to a divorced woman. The context here addressed those men or women who were single due either to the death of a partner, or divorce. Paul was assuming that they were older and beyond the temptations that the younger ones faced. Note: the average life span for a woman was about 50 years of age, although there were many exceptions.

His advice to them: 'Stay as even I (am).' This statement has been construed to mean that Paul was at one time married, and his wife either died or she left him by divorce. This claim was flawed. The main argument was that later rabbi leaders strongly advised young rabbis to marry. However, there was no evidence that this position was in effect in the first century. The obvious meaning was strong: "Stay single, as I am."

'The Exception' Verse 9:
7:9: "But if they do not have self-control, let them (re-)marry, for it is better to (re-)marry than to burn (with passion)."

Notice the attitude about remarriage: it was proper for this group, but it should not be taken lightly. 'Self-control:' he was not using a disparaging term here, or relegating them to a lower class. Remember verse 7, where he mentioned the two equal classes of Christians, the marrying kind and the celibate. The passionate ones were the marrying kind and they had that gift from God. Paul's advice to them: 'Go ahead and remarry. It's ok.' Passion was not easily controlled and Paul recognized that fact. 'Burn' was not used to describe the Hell fires. Paul never used that reference. However, 'burning with passion' was a common phrase, especially in secular literature of the first century. 'Self-control' was ἐγκρατεύονται, 'to keep one's emotions, impulses, or desires under control, self-controlled, disciplined,' (BDAG). Paul, though a single man, understood human nature quite well. He realized that some believers didn't have the strict discipline that he had. There was an option for them in that case.

'A Command from the Lord about Divorce and Paul's Opinions' Verses 10-16:
Paul's opinions were interrupted in verse 10:
7:10: "But to those who have married I command, not I but the Lord, a woman is not to divorce (her) husband."

What Paul was about to say on divorce was NOT his opinion. There were exceptions: see the sections below. This was the first half of the command. The husband's command was in 11b, after the parenthesis. Notice that the woman's command was first. This has led to the speculation that there were some Christian women in Corinth who were leaving their husbands because of their newly found freedom in Christianity, or because they were becoming prophetesses. There was no basis for these ideas, however. Nevertheless, it was unusual that so much emphasis was placed on the woman's actions. Women in Corinth were free to initiate divorce proceedings according to Roman law and earlier Greek law, but probably not Jewish law.

"…not I but the Lord…." could be interpreted that Paul was quoting from the sayings of the Lord; or that Paul had revelations from the Lord about marriage. See Matt. 5:31-32 and Mark 19:9.

When comparing the words for the woman leaving (χωρισθῆναι) and the man's leaving (ἀφιέναι), the first (in this verse) could mean 'separating from,' (but here it suggests 'divorce,' BDAG), while the second means, 'divorce.'

'The Parenthesis' Verse 11a:
7:11a: "But if she may divorce, let her remain single or be reconciled to her husband."

Notice that there was no such exception (divorce) for the husband (except infidelity of the wife mentioned by the Lord in Matt. 5:32).

'The Command for the Husband' Verse 11b:
7:11b: "…and the husband is not to divorce his wife."

(Exceptions are noted below)

'The Issue of Mixed Marriages' Verses 12-16:
7:12: "But as to the rest I say, not the Lord: if any brother has an unbelieving wife and she consents to live with him, let him not divorce her."

"But as to the rest I say, not the Lord…." The rest were Paul's opinions, not the Lord's commands. The mixed marriage, as long as it occurred before conversion (implied), was sanctioned. The idea here was to keep the family together if at all possible.

7:13: (Mixed marriage for the wife): "If a certain wife may have an unbelieving husband, and he consents to live with her let her not divorce him."

What applied to the husband, also applied to the wife; again, there was equality.

'Reasons for keeping the marriage together' Verse 14:

7:14: "For the unbelieving husband is set apart to God (literally, 'made holy') by the (believing) wife and the unbelieving wife is set apart to God by the (believing) brother: otherwise it follows that your children would not be cleansed, but now they are set apart to God."

The influence of the believer on the unbelieving partner was assumed by Paul to be profound. The children were also to be considered as reasons not to divorce. They lived in a home where at least one parent was present to set boundaries and influence the children about Christianity through teaching and modeling.

'Divorce in a mixed marriage' Verse 15:

7:15: "But if the unbeliever leaves, let (him or her) leave: the brother or the sister should not be enslaved in such situations: certainly God has called us (to live) in peace."

Paul did not mention abusive situations. See verse 16 for most situations:

7:16: "For what do you know wife, if you will (participate in) saving him? And what do you know, husband, if you will (participate in) saving your wife?"

This was a great unknown; but the believing spouse should think positive and continually pray.

'Topical study of 8-21' **The questions that the Corinthians may have had (with answers from the text):**

I Corinthians 7:8-21:

Question Number one: "But what about people who are single and widows? Should they marry, or the case of widows, remarry?" The ideal situation for divorced single people and widows: *stay single.*

7:8: "But I say to the unmarried and widows, (it is) good for them that they may remain as I myself am."

If verse 7a was Paul's opinion, then perhaps that same opinion was expressed here.

'The other option' (7:9): "But if they cannot exercise self-control (over sexual urges), then it is better to marry rather than to burn (with passion)."

The idea of marriage for this motive was a concession to the varying degrees of sexual desires in normal people. Paul was not setting up two classes of Christians: one who was more spiritual, and another who was not because of the lack of self-control.

Question Number two: "What about divorce in general, or over matters of faith?" 7:10: **"But to those having been married, I plead, not I, but the Lord, (let) not the wife divorce (her) Husband,"** 7:11: **"...and if they may divorce, let her remain unmarried or be reconciled with her husband –and (also) the husband is not to leave (divorce his) wife."**

Divorce over matters of faith: 7:12: **"And regarding the rest (of the question) I say, not the Lord: if any man has an unbelieving wife, and she consents to live with him, let him not leave her."**

Notice this statement was Paul's opinion. Also notice 7:13: **"...and if a believing wife has an unbelieving husband and this man consents to live with her, let (her) not leave her husband."**

WHY? (See verse 14):
7:14: **"For the unbelieving husband is sanctified (in a certain sense) by the (believing) wife and the unbelieving wife is sanctified (also in a certain way) by the (believing) husband: consequently your children are purified, and now (they are) set apart for God."**

Question Number three: What happens if the unbelieving spouse leaves?
7:15: **"But if the unbeliever departs (and divorces), then let that person go. A brother or a sister should not live in slavery in such situations: God called you (to live) in peace."**
7:16: **"For what do you know wife, if your husband shall be saved? Or what do you know husband, if your wife shall be saved?"**

Verse 16 seems to have related to the problem when an unbelieving spouse leaves and files for divorce: Reconciliation might bring about salvation for the unbelieving spouse; perhaps, in time, they could be reconciled.

Question Number four: "What about a Christian's station in life? Does that change at conversion?" The general answer was found in 7:17: **"But as the Lord apportioned to each person, as God has called each one, let him (or her) walk. And so I ordain in all the churches."** Whatever the station in life was when the person was converted, stay in that place. Here one must realize that

Paul was speaking to believers who lived in a highly structured society, from the rich and mighty to slaves. Paul would not want the slaves, or even married women to get the idea that they could revolt and run away from their masters (or husbands). The societal structures that were in place were to be honored by new converts. Only in Christianity were there only two classes of people: believers and unbelievers. Within the unbelieving culture, there were many classes of people, and Paul was ordering them to honor those classifications, and not revolt against them.

What about Circumcision? 7:18: "Was anyone circumcised when (he) was called? Let him not remove (or hide) his circumcision. Was anyone called in uncircumcision? Let him not become circumcised." 7:19: "Circumcision is nothing, and uncircumcision is nothing, but (what is something) is keeping the commandments of God." 7:20: "Let each one (remain) in the calling in which he was called."

What about Slavery? 7:21: "Were you a slave when you were called? Do not let that bother you. But if you were able to become free, make use (of your freedom)." Paul did suggest that if the slave could be freed from slavery, then he or she should do it. That person could be used by the Lord in either case. But Paul thought it would be more desirable for the person to be free. New opportunities might be opened for a more expansive service for Christ.

Return to the Exegetical Study of 7:17-24:
I Corinthians 7:17-24

'What Paul Was Teaching in the Churches:
Accept the Station of Life' I Corinthians 7:17-19:
7:17: "Except, as the Lord assigned (a station in life) for each person, as God has called each one, so let him/her walk. And so I am ordering in all the churches."

This was an example of **Linguistic Architecture** in the structure: an 'assignment' was built on the foundation of the 'call of God.' **'Except….'** This was a marker for a slight change of topic, but with the same theme ('living your Christian life').

Parallel construction #1: The first of two 'as' clauses: The first: **"…as the Lord (Jesus) assigned (a station in life)…."** The Lord Jesus assigned a station of life to each individual most often before he or she was saved. 'Assigned' was ἐμέρισεν, 'to make an allotment, *to distribute, assign, apportion,*' (BDAG). The direct object was missing, supplied by implication. "…as God has called…." ['as…called:' I Cor. 1:9, 1:24; 7:15: the call of God]. God the Father was also involved in the salvation aspect of conversion: God was 'calling.' These clauses suggested that while two actions were going on, either by the Lord or God the Father, then it was the believer's responsibility to accept that situation in life at the time of the 'call.' God the Father and the Lord Jesus were very active in the life of each believer: not only in his or her eternal future in heaven, but also in the station of life at conversion, the **'here and now'** aspects on this earth. Paul was here softening the revolutionary aspect of Christianity. He was not for breaking down social mores that were very much in place in the Roman, Greek, and Hebrew cultures. 'Live within them' was Paul's recommendation.

Parallel construction #2: Two 'so clauses:' "So walk…." Because God the Father and the Lord Jesus were fully involved in believer's life, so walk in whatever station he/she might be in at conversion. "So I am ordering in all the churches:" 'Because your situation in Corinth was not unique, I am ordering the other churches to follow suit.'

Parallel construction #3: Key words: **"Each one"** (ἑκάστῳ) and (ἕκαστον): Both are in the emphatic position because of the position in the sentence (being the first word for each clause). The idea of these words stresses **the individuality of each person**: conversion affects the individual; it was not a group experience. The first *each one* was the indirect object of the verb, 'assigned,' indicating a dative of advantage. 'For the benefit of **Each Person** as the Lord assigned….' Jesus assigned this station in life. The second *each one* was also emphatic: God the Father called **'each'** believer.

Verb number 1: 'Assigned' was ἐμέρισεν, The Lord Jesus took a personal interest in each believer in order to assign a station in life to him or her. Since the Lord assigned it, the believer should not rebel against it, even if it involved being confined to a lower 'human status.' The verb was a simple past tense (aorist), indicating that the action occurred in the past, before the believer was born. But, at the same time, there was no indication that the believer must stay in that position, similar to a rigid 'caste' system in some modern cultures. If an opportunity presented itself to alter that 'station,' then the believer was free to do so. If one couldn't change that 'station,' then the believer must make the most of it.

Verb number 2: God 'has called.' 'Called,' **κέκληκεν**, from **καλέω**, 'choose for the receipt of a special benefit or experience, *call*,' (BDAG). Here the perfect tense verb was intensive, and indicated the '*continual*' call for conversion. God the Father has 'called' the person to salvation, often repeatedly, and continually, a past act with continuing significance.

Theological note: 'called' meant the call that God the Father activated at conversion, not a vocational call. Paul was mandating all believers in the churches about this; it was not confined only to the Corinthians.

7:18: "Has anyone been called having been circumcised? Let him not try to hide the marks of circumcision; has anyone been called having been uncircumcised? Let him not become circumcised."

7:19: "Circumcision is nothing, but keeping the (moral, ethical, and relational) commandments of God (is everything)."

The 'calling (or conversion)' here replaced the OT circumcision. That 'calling' marked the identity of the believer. 'Were you circumcised? Accept it, and don't try to try to hide it, or change it through surgery. 'Are you not circumcised? Accept that situation as from God and don't become circumcised.' The current value of circumcision was ***zero***. It had no value. In the centuries leading to the appearance of Christ it was a 'sign of identity,' replaced now by conversion, and now including women. Imagine Paul, a Hebrew of the Hebrews, saying that circumcision was nothing. Christian Jews in Corinth must have bristled at the thought of being equal to the Gentiles. This was, indeed, a revolutionary concept. What was it that believers must do? They must follow the commandments of God, as administered through the activity of the Holy Spirit, in keeping with their identity as 'called ones.' Some at least, in the churches of Corinth, were not following God's commanments.

Remaining in the place where God has called believers: (three categories: slaves, freed slaves and free people):

7:20: *(Staying within the boundaries)*: **"Let each believer remain in the life (calling) in which he/she was called."**

Paraphrased: 'Since the Lord Jesus was active in selecting your place in life (when God called you), do not rebel against it.' 'Remain' was **μενέτω**, a present tense imperative: 'continually remain,' with the one exception for slaves in verse 21b.

7:21: "Were you a slave (when) you were called? It does not matter. But if you indeed have the opportunity to become a freed person, take advantage of that opportunity."

7:22: "For the slave who is called in the Lord is the freed-person of the Lord; likewise, are you called (as) a freed-person? (You are actually) a slave of Christ."

7:23: "You were bought with a (high) price; do not (voluntarily) become slaves of men." [Some free people voluntarily became slaves to better their economic situation.]

'When you were called, were you born into slavery?' 'Don't let it worry you' (verse 21). 'However, if you have the power to be free, take that opportunity,' although there were conflicting views of this phrase (Thiselton, pp. 554-558). After all, if people were born into slavery, they knew how to please their master. They had an advantage over others who did not have that experience. For those who were slaves when called: it is an uphill climb, but the slave must learn to do his or her duties, and consider the work done as unto Christ. Thereby the 'slave' can become a 'slave of Christ.'

7:24: A New Relationship and Status: "Let each one of you, brothers and sisters, remain in the situation in which you were called, only now you do it with God the Father by your side."

'Were you a slave when you were called by the Lord?' Here was the change: 'you are now a freed slave of Christ. Stay comfortable in that position.' However: 'You do it now with the added advantage: you are to stay in that position nestled right beside God the Father. You may still be a slave: but you are now God's slave and you have Him to lean on during rough moments.'

Advice to the Unmarried
I Corinthians 7:25-35

'The Knowledgeable bit of Advice for the Unmarried' I Corinthians 7:25-28:
7:25: "But concerning those who are unmarried I do not have a commandment from the Lord, but I am giving some advice as one receiving mercy by the Lord to be trustworthy."

"...advice...." was γνώμην (from γινώσκω), 'a viewpoint or way of thinking about a matter, opinion, judgment, way of thinking,' (BDAG). The 'unmarried' (παρθένων, 'virgins') were Christian young people who became adults, ready for marriage. Paul admitted that the Lord's commands were mute on this topic. Nevertheless, Paul believed that his comments on this subject were wise and trustworthy, but they were not given as an authoritative order.

'This is good' I Corinthians 7:26:

7:26: "Therefore I consider this (reasonable opinion) to be well-chosen on account of the present distress, that it is well for a man to be so."

Although Paul mentions that his 'advice' was 'reasonable,' and 'well-chosen,' (from καλόν, the aesthetically pleasing word, often translated as 'good'), he did not explain the 'present distress,' ἀνάγκην, which was a 'state of distress or trouble, *distress, calamity, pressure*,' BDAG). Was it a famine, or an expected increase in persecution, or some other natural disaster, or the Lord's imminent return? Or could it even have been the 'present distress,' from a young man experiencing puberty.

'Well' (καλόν) was used twice, the second time, reaffirming his view of celibacy in verse 25. Compare the same word in 7:1, where it was used as a 'wise' practice not to touch a woman.

'The Advice' I Corinthians 7:27:

7:27: "Have you been bound (to be engaged) to a woman? Do not seek a release (from that engagement). Have you been broken from an engagement? Do not seek (another) woman."

(Note: this translation accepts the view that Paul was referring to the breakup of a couple who were engaged to be married, rather than a man or woman seeking to divorce the spouse. However, the disputed verse has not yet fully been settled. See Thiselton, pp. 576-577.

Advice #1: "Have you been bound (to be engaged) to a woman?" We do not have the reason for this action, except the comment above. This may refer to the point after conversion: don't break off from the woman you find yourself engaged to at that moment. It could also refer to rebelling against an arranged marriage. 'Broken' or 'release' (λύσιν and λέλυσαι: noun and verb form) in the text meant to 'break off' or 'destroy.'

Advice #2: "broken engagement from a woman? Do not be seeking another woman." Again, there was no reason. Perhaps Paul was suggesting that young men should not be always looking for the perfect woman; or, if he broke off the relationship with the woman that his parents selected, he should not be looking himself for a replacement.

'Marriage in this situation: a Sin or Not?' I Corinthians 7:28:

7:28: "But even if you may marry: you do not sin, and if the virgin may marry, she did not sin: but such ones will have trouble in the flesh, and I myself am trying to spare you."

Let's say the young people do get married: they have not sinned. But what about a situation that was against the parent's wishes? There was a disadvantage that came with marriage: There will be 'trouble in the flesh.' Paul was trying to spare them of that trouble.

The argument to prepare Christians for their resurrected life: The "as nots" I Corinthians Chapter 7 Verses 29-31

The Reason: "Compressed Time" verse 29:

7:29: "But I say this, brothers and sisters, the time is compressed: from now on, that even the ones having wives should be as (those) not having (wives)."

(Compare with Mark 12:25: esp. the simile.)

Time was **καιρός**, not 'χρόνος.' It was now 'compressed' after the crucifixion, perhaps reduced because Christians expected the coming of Christ to be very soon. **Καιρός** was time as an event; **χρόνος** was time unfolding within allotted times periods, days, weeks, months, etc.

The first 'as not:' Husbands 'as not' having wives: the men should not be distracted from Christ by this world order, even by having wives. It was vital to recall that the destiny of every believing soul will be heaven, where there will be no marrying or giving in marriage. Each believer must grow in Christ as an individual, as well as in a corporate sense of a marriage.

'Weeping, Rejoicing and Shopping' verse 30:

7:30: "And those who weep as not weeping and those who rejoice, as not rejoicing and those who buy as not possessing."

There will be no weeping nor shopping: but believers will rejoice in HIM.

'Using the World' verse 31:

7:31: "And those who take advantage of the world, as not taking full advantage of (it): (the reason:) for the present form of this world is passing away."

The resurrected life will differ dramatically from the present earthly life.

'Practical Reasons Supporting Celibacy' verses 32-35:

7:32: "But I want you to be anxiety free. The unmarried man is concerned for the things of the Lord, how he may please the Lord:"

Word Study: "Anxiety free" was ἀμερίμνους, meaning 'without a care in the world.'

7:33: "...but the man who is married cares for the things of the world, how he may please his wife,"

"Cares" was μεριμνά, 'cares' or one who is 'overly concerned about something.'

7:34: "...and he has concerns (about her). And the unmarried woman and the virgin cares about the things of the Lord, in order that she may be holy, both in her body and spirit: but the woman who is married cares for the things of the world, how she may please her husband."

"...has concerns...." was μεμέρισται, perfect intensive tense of the same word (μεριμνά). The intensive perfect indicated a continual action of caring, to the point that he was overly concerned on a continual basis. The meaning of the word reflected the habitual anxiety, 'has been overly concerned or worried.'

7:35: "But I am saying this for your very own benefit, not in order that I may throw a noose (around) your (neck), but with a view to what (is) proper and well-suited for undistracted devotion to the Lord."

NOTE: the word 'caring' occurred six times in verses 32 to 35. 'Pleasing' the spouse occurred three times. 'Caring' for the spouse was a natural emotion expressed in marriage. Attempts to please the spouse may, however, in some cases, interfere with a believer's devotion to the Lord. Believers should not allow that to happen.

"...benefit...." was σύμφορον, meaning 'beneficial, advantageous, profitable,' (BDAG).

"...throw upon...." was ἐπιβάλω, was to 'throw over.' The image was taken from the hunt for a wild animal, throwing a halter, a βρόχον, around its neck in order to capture it, and perhaps sell it on the open market,' (BDAG).

"...proper...." was εὐσχημον, 'pertaining to being appropriate for display, proper, presentable, and in this context, good order,' (BDAG).

"...devotion...." was εὐπάρεδρον, meant, 'pertaining to be in constant attendance, constantly in service,' or, in this context, devoted' (BDAG), or literally, 'taking a good position beside the Lord.'

"...**without distraction**...." was an alpha privative, ἀπερισπάστως, α + περισπάω, ('to be over-occupied,' Thayer), but with the 'α' it meant, 'without distraction,' (BDAG).

Celibacy Conclusion
I Corinthians 7:36-40:

Summary Statement Regarding Celibacy
'The Man Who Qualifies for Marriage' I Corinthians 7:36:

7:36: "**But if a certain man thinks he behaves improperly toward his fiancé, if he may be overly stimulated, and he considers this to be right, let the man do what he wants, he does not sin, let them marry.**"

This situation dealt with the conditions for marriage. Several conditions were to be met for this man (apparently after he was converted). First, he was overly attracted, ἀσχημονεῖν, a compound verb, ἀ + σχῆμα, 'not' + 'according to a pattern or form,' thus, 'to act contrary to the standard, *behave disgracefully, dishonorably, indecently*,' and more specifically with reference to this verse, 'if anyone thinks he is behaving dishonorably toward his fiancé,' (BDAG). The young man thought this action may have been sinful. If he didn't marry her, it could have been sinful. Second, if he was sexually 'overly stimulated,' ὑπέρακμος, as applied to a man, 'with strong passions,' (BDAG), with the preposition, ὑπέρ, meaning, 'over the top,' with respect to his hormonal balance. According to Paul, these were definite signs that the young man should marry his fiancé.

The young man also thought this attraction seemed right to him, and he became obligated, or bound, ὀφείλει, (to marry), adding to his confusion. Paul suggested that this was the grounds for marriage. He was the marrying kind of person.

'The Man who qualifies for Celibacy' I Corinthians 7:37:

7:37: "**But the man who has stood steadfast in his heart, not having sexual distress, but who has authority over his own will, and this he has judged in his own heart to keep himself a virgin, he will do well.**"

Paul now contrasted the candidate for marriage with a potential candidate for celibacy. This person had continually stood ἕστηκεν, 'to stand firm in belief, *stand firm*,' (BDAG), with respect to celibacy. This perfect tense verb was intensive, indicating that it was a 'continual action' of his attitude. The quality of the standing was reinforced by the addition of ἑδραῖος, 'pertaining to being firmly or solidly in place, *firm, steadfast,*' (BDAG). This person was not swayed by excessive hormonal urges: 'not having: ἀνάγκην, 'necessity or constraint as inherent in the nature of things, *necessity, pressure,*' (BDAG). Nor did he feel the pressure of nature, and he was solid as a rock in his judgment, κέκρικεν, another perfect intensive verb: 'to come to a conclusion after a cognitive process, *reach a decision, decide, propose, intend,*' (BDAG), a decision that 'continues over time' to remain single. This 'judgment' was made at the level of his heart, not his emotion. Paul concluded, when this decision had been reached, 'he will do well.'

'Paul's Conclusion on this Matter' I Corinthians 7:38:

7:38: "And as a result, the man who marries his own fiancé will do beautifully, and the man who remains (single) will do better."

Paul concluded this matter without criticizing either position as one being more 'spiritual' than the other. He did admit that, according to his own opinion, speaking from experience, celibacy was a better choice, not based on any 'spiritual' reason, but for the added practical obligations of nurturing and caring for a family. 'Beautifully' was the adverb, καλῶς, 'pertaining to being in accord with a standard, rightly, correctly,' (BDAG). 'Better' was κρεῖσσον, 'pertaining to having a relative advantage in value, better,' (BDAG). However, a Christian man in a beautiful marriage might come to the same conclusion.

'The Limits of Marriage' I Corinthians 7:39:

7:39: "A woman has been obligated (to her husband) as long as her husband may live. But if he may die, she is free to marry with whom she wishes, only in the Lord."

Paul now turned to the wife, and her obligations to her husband. Those obligations continued as long as her husband lived. Upon death, however, her marriage contract was no longer valid, and she was then free to remarry whomever she wished, but with the only limitation, 'she should remarry another Christian.'

'Paul's Final Thoughts on this subject' I Corinthians 7:40:

7:40: "But she is happier if she remain thus (namely, single) according to my thoughtful opinion: and I think I have the Spirit of God (on this subject)."

In the final remarks about the wife who lost her husband in death, he recommended that she remain single. 'My thoughtful opinion,' γνώμην, was just that; it was not a command. From the point of view of witnessing similar situations, he made this recommendation. When he said, '**I think I have the Spirit of God (on this subject),**' he was saying that the Holy Spirit agreed with his analysis and conclusion. But in the final analysis, the woman was free to remarry if she was so inclined. Unsaid here was that the remarriage should take place after a certain amount of time grieving.

REVIEW of Chapter Seven:

1. Celibacy or marriage? Both are ok. Celibacy was preferred.
2. Husbands and wives had physical obligations to their spouses, broken only for a short time for periods of devotion.
3. For the "used-to-be-married people," Paul suggested that they remain single, (verse 8), but it was ok for them to remarry if they so chose (v. 9)
4. Divorce: It was not ok. An exception occurred when a partner was unfaithful, as mentioned in the Gospels by Christ, although Paul failed to mention this exception.
5. Mixed marriages (one partner was not a believer) were generally to continue, if the unbelieving spouse wished to remain.
6. Accept your lot in life if you cannot change your situation related to circumcision or slavery.
7. Widows, widowers, or divorced men or women were suggested to remain single, although remarriage was ok for them.
8. Young men who had raging hormones were considered normal, but were strongly suggested as candidates for marriage. Those who marry, or weep, or rejoice, or buy, should all realize that these were transitory experiences, and Christians should be detached from the world.
9. Paul wanted believers free of worldly cares, to be serving the Lord without distractions.
10. Wives were to be bound to their husbands as long as those husbands lived. After the death of the husband or wife, the remaining spouse was free to remarry, as long as the new partner was a believer.

What Was Left Out?

1. "Human sexuality for the Christian only exists for procreation." That concept was actually replaced by a joint sexual obligation of the husband

and the wife to each other (verses 3 and 4). Sexuality for the sake of bearing children was noticeably absent here. In fact, the opposite was implied in a healthy marriage.

2. Children were left out of the topic in this section. Whole families were occasionally mentioned by Paul as being converted, but on the issue of children being converted, Paul was quite silent. He centered on the concepts of individual adults (perhaps young adults, as implied with Timothy and his grandmother Lois) coming to know Christ, and growing in a Christ-centered family. Christianity for Paul was centered upon the capability of people to grasp subtle meanings. He would leave out the issues when children could grasp these issues and become converted, and for others who nurture children (parents, grandparents, relatives, and friends) to explain and participate in their spiritual development and nurturing.

3. Paul left out the idea that divorce was permissible when a spouse was unfaithful. Paul's omission of the subject should not be construed as contradicting Christ's teaching on the subject.

4. Paul left out the psychological need for a normal time of grieving for a woman who lost her husband (or vice versa) in death, before remarriage.

Closing Note

This first volume concludes with I Corinthians, Chapter 7. The decision to divide the study was made to ensure clarity and accessibility.

The journey does not end here. In Part Two, the study resumes with the remaining chapters of I Corinthians and continues through Paul's other letters, offering the same careful attention to meaning, translation, and spiritual insight.

We encourage you to carry forward into Part Two, where the exploration of Paul's writings continues with renewed depth and devotion.